Reverberations of Revolution

Edinburgh Critical Studies in Atlantic Literatures and Cultures
Series Editors: Laura Doyle, Colleen Glenney Boggs and Maria Cristina Fumagalli

Available titles
Sensational Internationalism: The Paris Commune and the Remapping of American Memory in the Long Nineteenth Century
J. Michelle Coghlan

American Travel Literature, Gendered Aesthetics, and the Italian Tour, 1824–1862
Brigitte Bailey

American Snobs: Transatlantic Novelists, Liberal Culture and the Genteel Tradition
Emily Coit

Scottish Colonial Literature: Writing the Atlantic, 1603–1707
Kirsten Sandrock

Yankee Yarns: Storytelling and the Invention of the National Body in Nineteenth-Century American Culture
Stefanie Schäfer

Reverberations of Revolution: Transnational Perspectives, 1750–1850
Edited by Elizabeth Amann and Michael Boyden

Forthcoming titles
Emily Dickinson and Her British Contemporaries: Victorian Poetry in Nineteenth-Century America
Páraic Finnerty

Following the Middle Passage: Currents in Literature Since 1945
Carl Plasa

The Atlantic Dilemma: Reform or Revolution Across the Long Nineteenth Century
Kelvin Black

Visit the series website at: www.edinburghuniversitypress.com/series/ECSALC

Reverberations of Revolution

Transnational Perspectives, 1770–1850

Edited by Elizabeth Amann and
Michael Boyden

Edinburgh University Press is one of the leading university presses in the UK. We publish academic books and journals in our selected subject areas across the humanities and social sciences, combining cutting-edge scholarship with high editorial and production values to produce academic works of lasting importance. For more information visit our website: edinburghuniversitypress.com

© editorial matter and organisation Elizabeth Amann and Michael Boyden, 2021, 2023
© the chapters their several authors, 2021, 2023

Edinburgh University Press Ltd
The Tun – Holyrood Road
12 (2f) Jackson's Entry
Edinburgh EH8 8PJ

First published in hardback by Edinburgh University Press 2021

Typeset in 11/13 Adobe Sabon by
IDSUK (DataConnection) Ltd

A CIP record for this book is available from the British Library

ISBN 978 1 4744 8158 8 (hardback)
ISBN 978 1 4744 8159 5 (paperback)
ISBN 978 1 4744 8160 1 (webready PDF)
ISBN 978 1 4744 8161 8 (epub)

The right of Elizabeth Amann and Michael Boyden to be identified as the editor of this work has been asserted in accordance with the Copyright, Designs and Patents Act 1988, and the Copyright and Related Rights Regulations 2003 (SI No. 2498).

Contents

Series Editors' Preface		vii
Acknowledgments		viii
Notes on Contributors		ix
Introduction		1
Elizabeth Amann and Michael Boyden		
1	Pugachev Goes Global: The Revolutionary Potential of Translation	13
	Malte Griesse	
2	"The Tranquil March of the Revolution": German and German-American Reverberations of Mary Wollstonecraft's Writings	36
	Alessa Johns	
3	Translation as Conceptual Reverberation: "Revolution" in Wales 1688–1937	56
	Marion Löffler	
4	Revolution in Colonial Translation: From Saint-Domingue to Haiti	77
	Jeremy D. Popkin	
5	Enlightenment Tropes in French Popular Theater on the Haitian Revolution in the 1790s	93
	Anja Bandau	
6	Reverberations of the Haitian Revolution: Media, Narratives and Political Debates, 1791–1863	115
	Florian Kappeler	

7 Ribbons of Revolution: Tricolor Cockades Across
   the Atlantic   134
   Ashli White

8 The Noble Turk: Estanislao De Cosca Vayo's *Grecia,
   ó la doncella de Missolonghi* (1830) and the Spanish
   Response to the Greek War of Independence   150
   Elizabeth Amann

Coda: Frederick Douglass and the Wild Songs of Revolution   167
   Michael Boyden

Notes   182
Index   195

Series Editors' Preface

Modern global culture makes it clear that literary study can no longer operate on nation-based or exceptionalist models. In practice, American literatures have always been understood and defined in relation to the literatures of Europe and Asia. The books in this series work within a broad comparative framework to question place-based identities and monocular visions, in historical contexts from the earliest European settlements to contemporary affairs, and across all literary genres. They explore the multiple ways in which ideas, texts, objects and bodies travel across spatial and temporal borders, generating powerful forms of contrast and affinity. The Edinburgh Critical Studies in Atlantic Literatures and Cultures series fosters new paradigms of exchange, circulation and transformation for Atlantic literary studies, expanding the critical and theoretical work of this rapidly developing field.

Acknowledgments

This book took shape under the auspices of the U4 consortium, which facilitates scholarly collaboration among Ghent University, the University of Göttingen, the University of Groningen and Uppsala University. The consortium provided the infrastructure for a research network entitled "Reverberations of Revolution." Within this framework, we organized a series of symposia at each of the four institutions on various facets of revolutionary transmission: *Sovereignty and Revolution in Comparative Perspective* (hosted by Michael Boyden at Uppsala University, September 2014); *Technologies of Print and Power in the Age of Revolution* (organized by Wil Verhoeven at the University of Groningen, September 2015); *Translation and Transformation in the Age of Revolution* (organized by Barbara Schaff and Florian Kappeler at the University of Göttingen, June 2016); and *The Power of Things: Revolutionary Icons, Objects, and Images Across Borders* (organized by Elizabeth Amann and Sarah Adams at Ghent University, September 2016).

Most of the texts that eventually made it into this book started out as presentations during these symposia, and we benefited greatly from stimulating conversations with all of the participants. We are indebted to Laura Doyle, Colleen Boggs and Maria Cristina, the editors of the Edinburgh series Critical Studies in Atlantic Literatures and Cultures, for encouraging us to write this book and for their useful feedback on various drafts of the manuscript. We also would like to thank the external experts who reviewed the manuscript. Thanks are also due to Ersev Ersoy and Michelle Houston at Edinburgh University Press for guiding the manuscript to publication. Tim McGovern proofread the manuscript before submission, and Tim Clark, our copy-editor at Edinburgh University Press, corrected the final version. James Dale worked on the proofs, and Emma Caddy compiled the index. Part of the book's production costs were defrayed by a grant from the Petra and Karl Erik Hedborg Foundation.

Notes on Contributors

Elizabeth Amann is Professor of Literary Studies at Ghent University, Belgium. She is the author of *Importing Madame Bovary: The Politics of Adultery* (2006) and *Dandyism in the Age of Revolution: The Art of the Cut* (2015), as well as many articles on nineteenth-century literature and culture. She has also edited two collective volumes: *La mitificación del pasado español: reescrituras de figuras y leyendas en la literatura del siglo XIX* (2018) and *Con el franquismo en el retrovisor: las representaciones culturales de la Dictadura en la Democracia (1975–2018)* (2020).

Anja Bandau has been Professor of Hispanic Literatures and Cultures at the Institute of Romance Languages and Literatures at Leibniz Universität Hannover and at its Centre for Atlantic and Global Studies (CAGS) since 2011. Her research focuses on the transatlantic circulation of knowledge, literatures and cultures in Spanish and French in the Americas and the Caribbean, Mexican-American literature and criticism and trans-border literature, narrations of the Haitian revolution (1791–1859), diasporic literatures and poetics, and transnational and postcolonial literary and cultural studies. Her publications include *Reshaping Glocal Dynamics of the Caribbean* (2018), *El Caribe y sus Diásporas. Circulación de Saberes y Prácticas Culturales* (2011) and *Les Mondes coloniaux à Paris au xviiie siècle. Enchevêtrement et circulation des savoirs* (2010). Together with Jeremy Popkin, she edited Jean-Paul Pillet's 1806 manuscript on the Haitian Revolution, *Mon Odyssée: L'Epopée d'un colon de Saint-Domingue* (2015). Her most recent publication is the essay "Afrodescendant Literatures in the Americas" in *The Routledge Handbook to the Culture and Media of the Americas* (2020).

Michael Boyden is a chair professor of English at Radboud University Nijmegen in the Netherlands. He is the author of *Predicting the Past: The Paradoxes of American Literary History* (2009). He has edited several collected volumes, including *Tales of Transit: Narrative Migrant Spaces in Transatlantic Perspective* (with Hans Krabbendam and Liselotte Vandenbussche, 2013), a special issue of the *Journal of World Literature* on translingualism (with Eugenia Kelbert, 2018), and a special issue of *Early American Literature* on the "new" natural history (2019). He is currently working on a second monograph with the working title *Climate and Sensibility in the American Tropics*.

Malte Griesse received his PhD from the *École des hautes études en sciences sociales* (EHESS) in Paris for a study on the evolution of personal ties under Stalin and the impact of (informal) communication on the formation of opinion. He led a research project on "Early modern revolts as communicative events" at Konstanz University, where he defended his habilitation thesis on the crisis of the seventeenth century in the light of the media revolution in Europe. His current research project is on subaltern autobiographical practices in the eighteenth and nineteenth centuries and studies how different forms of mobility are reflected in such writings. He has taught European history from the early modern period to the present at the Universities of Paris VIII, Bielefeld, Konstanz and the Humboldt-University, Berlin, and is currently teaching at the Ludwig-Maximilians-University in Munich.

Alessa Johns is Professor Emerita of English at the University of California, Davis. She has published *Bluestocking Feminism and British-German Cultural Transfer, 1750–1837* (2014), *Women's Utopias of the Eighteenth Century* (2003), and has edited *Dreadful Visitations: Confronting Natural Catastrophe in the Age of Enlightenment* (1999) and *Reflections on Sentiment: Essays in Honor of George Starr* (2016). Recent articles have appeared on Mary Wollstonecraft, Anna Jameson, and sisters of Frederick the Great, and she is co-editing, with Katrin Berndt, the *Handbook of the British Novel in the Long Eighteenth Century*, to be published by De Gruyter.

Florian Kappeler is a postdoctoral researcher at the Department of German Studies at Georg-August-University Göttingen. He received his PhD from Humboldt-University, Berlin, and worked at the Competence Center *History of Knowledge* (ETH and University of Zurich). Currently he is finishing a monograph on the German reception of the Haitian Revolution. His most recent publications are "The Chronotope of Revolution: 'Volcanic' Narrations of the Haitian Revolution" (in *Karib – Nordic Journal for Caribbean Studies*, 2018) and "Revolution der Verwandtschaft. Beziehungsweisen in Heinrich von Kleists Die Verlobung in St. Domingo" (in *Gender. Zeitschrift für Geschlecht, Kultur und Gesellschaft*, 2019).

Marion Löffler gained her PhD at Humboldt-University, Berlin, and worked at the University of Wales Centre for Advanced Welsh and Celtic Studies, Aberystwyth, as Senior Research Fellow until 2017. Currently a Reader in Welsh History at Cardiff University, she teaches eighteenth- and nineteenth-century Welsh history and regularly appears on Welsh radio and television. She is Assistant Editor of the Dictionary of Welsh Biography. Her research focuses on the cultural, political and religious entanglements of non-hegemonic Wales with Europe, Empire and the world, and especially on the transfer of ideas across linguistic, geographical and political borders. Among her main works are *The Literary and Historical Legacy of Iolo Morganwg, 1826–1926* (2007), *Welsh Responses to the French Revolution: Press and Public Discourse, 1793–1802* (2012) and *Political Pamphlets and Sermons from Wales, 1790–1806* (2014). She is currently working on a cultural biography of the Welsh historian and social reformer Thomas Stephens of Merthyr Tydfil.

Jeremy D. Popkin is the William T. Bryan Chair Professor of History at the University of Kentucky. He has published extensively on the French and Haitian Revolutions. His most recent book is *A New World Begins: The History of the French Revolution* (2019). A new edition of his *Concise History of the Haitian Revolution* will appear in 2021.

Ashli White is associate professor of history at the University of Miami. She is the author of *Encountering Revolution: Haiti and the Making of the Early Republic* (2010), and the associate curator and co-author of the catalogue for *Antillean Visions: Maps and the Making of the Caribbean* (Lowe Art Museum, February–May 2018), an exhibition that charted over 500 years of mapping the region. Her current book project, *Revolutionary Things* (under contract with Yale University Press), examines the Atlantic circulation of objects associated with the American, French and Haitian revolutions.

Introduction

Elizabeth Amann and Michael Boyden

As Ronald Paulson has observed, revolution poses a unique challenge to writers and artists: that of representing something "believe[d] to be unprecedented – hitherto unknown and unexperienced" (1983: 1). This challenge becomes even greater when the events have not been experienced firsthand, when they take place somewhere else and are observed only in mediated ways (through letters, the press, etc.). A revolution seen "from afar" can seem very different from one experienced "up close" and can lead to very different forms of artistic and literary expression.

Quite often, moreover, the view "from afar" is no less, and possibly even more, crucial for determining the revolutionary import of events than the one from "up close." Hannah Arendt has argued that what constitutes a true revolution is that it results in the creation of a new social order "where the liberation from oppression aims at least at the constitution of freedom" (2006: 35). This can be determined only with hindsight or distance. In other words, whether an event constitutes a genuine revolution resulting in the "foundation of freedom" (33), or merely a rebellion aimed at "liberation" from oppression, depends not so much on the intentions of the actors directly involved as on what becomes apparent after the dust has settled and the way its significance is interpreted by other observers. The revolutionariness of an event, that is, derives from the extent to which it "resonates" or "reverberates" outward and across time. A revolution thus becomes revolutionary when it changes the meaning of what has gone before and starts functioning as a model for other political struggles, which, by taking inspiration or deriving their legitimacy from that event, bestow upon it a special status.

The goal of this collection is to explore how writers, artists and intellectuals responded to and represented revolutions taking place in other parts of the world or in earlier times, and how discussions of these revolutions impacted domestic political discourse and debate. In so doing, it seeks to question received assumptions about what constitutes a revolutionary event. Longstanding debates regarding the differences between revolutions and "mere" uprisings or revolts, between "successful" and "failed" revolutions, or between "social" and "political" revolutions, of course have their value in the study of history. But they usually start from the earlier event and then study its after-effects. In this study, we take an opposite approach, starting from the "receiving end" and examining how it reflects on its catalyst.

By showing how political uprisings often reverberated far beyond the borders of the states directly affected, this study also aims to broaden research on revolutionary cultures, which continue to be approached in a predominantly regional or national framework, one that often overlooks how ideas and discourses travel and collide and are transformed in the process. What is traditionally referred to as the Age of Revolutions – the period between roughly 1770 and 1850 when the European old regimes collapsed and new systems of government emerged founded on ideals of freedom and representative government – can be studied as a sort of echo chamber in which ideas and doctrines were amplified, manipulated and rewritten. Such processes of reverberation cannot be captured in studies focusing exclusively on one nation. Rather, they call for a transnational, comparative approach.

While revolutions are commonly presented as new beginnings, moments when the clock is set back to zero and the whole political system is reconceptualized, it might be more appropriate to consider them as iterative events that reverberate in multiple directions. In its literal meaning, the word "reverberation" refers to the repeated reflection of waves, light, heat or sounds from surfaces. We believe this is a fruitful way to rethink the meaning of revolution. By "reverberations of revolution," we mean not simply the echoing of ideas, discourses and things but also the ways in which these bounce and reflect off of those of other periods and places. Revolutionary thought and culture often radiate out to other places, which in turn refract or redirect them. Revolutions, moreover, can also reverberate across time. As we have argued, one of the distinguishing features of revolutions is that they inspire other political events, that their impact spreads into the future. But, in spite of the truism that revolutions always go forward, their impact can also extend backward in time, as when their novelty reframes or alters the interpretation of previous events leading up to them.

Studies that have explored the revolutionary period from a transatlantic or global perspective have drawn on a variety of metaphors, such as the network, the wave or the series. Though illuminating, each of these metaphors has its limitations. The currently popular metaphor of the network or web is helpful in highlighting what Bruno Latour calls "traceable associations" among revolutionary actors or mediators that might otherwise have gone unnoticed (2005: 108). But they are essentially synchronic in nature, pointing to groups of people who interact at a specific time. As Sarah Knott argues, the metaphor of the network, while useful in pointing to "coterminous connections," ultimately "does not address temporality" (2016: 32). How do we make sense of connections that are not simultaneous or that are visible only in hindsight? The metaphor of the wave, used most prominently by Eric Hobsbawm, can be said to display a temporal dimension that the network and web lack, but it is no less problematic as it suggests that revolutionary movements and ideas have a built-in directionality. Although waves may of course change their course with the tides and currents, the metaphor is limiting because it suggests a linear, or even teleological development. In this respect, the metaphor of the series, which Claire Pettitt has used to discuss the revolutions of 1848, seems to us more productive. While the wave metaphor still suggests a cyclical pattern, series are often unforeseeable: as Pettitt notes, they can be "messy," spluttering, capricious and changeable (2020: 7).

Our notion of "reverberations" has affinities with Pettitt's seriality. It evokes multiple impulses or points of origin and, in so doing, suggests the erratic ways in which they intersect. It allows for the study not only of direct forms of transmission but also of the indirect, mediated, inadvertent and even contradictory resonances of an event. Reverberations, moreover, can be diachronic: ideas, discourses and objects can resound long after their creation and often do so in ways that their creators never intended. Overall, we prefer the concept of "reverberation" to that of seriality because it does not necessarily suggest that revolutionary events are bound to technological innovations. As our case studies will show, revolutions might reverberate from unlikely socio-historical contexts with lack of access to modern communication technologies or laboring under heavy censorship. We also prefer "reverberations" to competing concepts such as "transculturation" or "counterpower," as they are commonly used in migration history, postcolonial studies and related fields.[1] Such concepts were designed to challenge diffusionist models of revolution (which see revolutions as radiating out from the center toward the peripheries) that can still be found in studies such as Hobsbawm's. But, often, such competing concepts simply invert the direction of the diffusion, focusing on the way the periphery influences the center. The plural "reverberations," in contrast, captures the multidirectionality of revolutionary influence. In our view, the concept has an openness and malleability that makes it a preferable heuristic tool for the comparative study of revolutions. Reverberations might be used to promote an emancipatory agenda, but they might equally be mobilized by the counter-revolution. Just as the neurosciences study the brain in terms of feedforward and feedback signaling, we might approach revolutions as a continual process of perceptual "tuning" in time and space rather than as a linear causal chain. By focusing on reverberations, thus, this collection examines how the ideas, images, texts and material culture of revolution are transformed, distorted and appropriated in new contexts.

We might further clarify our approach by borrowing two analytical categories from the field of Translation Studies, namely source and target. While source-oriented approaches to translation are largely concerned with questions of equivalence between the original and the translation, target-oriented approaches do not subordinate the translation to its source but rather focus on how it functions within a given target culture. Along these lines, one might argue that the scholarship of comparative revolution tends to take either a source-oriented or a target-oriented approach. Source-oriented studies aim to trace the origins and spread of revolutions. They identify direct and indirect causes (social, political or infrastructural changes) as well as causal connections among such events across space and time. Target-oriented studies, in contrast, are less concerned with how and why revolutions take place than with the way they reverberate and propagate in contexts at a remove from their place or time of origin.

The classic comparative studies of revolution written in the twentieth century were source-oriented. R. R. Palmer's two-volume *The Age of Democratic Revolution* (1959–64) argues that the major Western revolutions of the period from 1760 to 1800 were all based on a similar set of democratic political ideals, the desire to overturn the privileges of a hereditary aristocracy and to move toward greater equality and social mobility. Eric Hobsbawm's *The Age of Revolution, 1789–1848* (1962) identifies as the catalyst of the nineteenth-century uprisings the emergence of industrial capitalism in England and the ideology of the French Revolution. Finally, Theda Skocpol's *States and Social Revolutions* (1979) shifts the emphasis away from individual actions and beliefs and toward changes in social structures which prompted revolutionary movements. Although these studies offer compelling insights into the causes of revolution, critics have taken issue with their teleological narratives and their primary focus on Western civilization and particularly the North Atlantic.

Recent scholarship on comparative revolutions has moved away from such metanarratives and has addressed these criticisms by adopting a more global and pluralist lens. Salient examples of this new approach are *The Age of Revolutions in Global Context* (ed. Armitage and Subrahmanyam 2010), *The French Revolution in Global Perspective* (ed. Desan, Hunt and Nelson 2013), *Scripting Revolution: A Historical Approach to the Comparative Study of Revolutions* (ed. Baker and Edelstein 2015) and Janet Polasky's *Revolutions without Borders* (2015). But although these studies broaden the scope of comparative revolution studies, they generally address the same source-oriented questions as earlier scholarship, probing the "roots" of revolutions and the causal connections among uprisings in different places.

Another body of scholarship focuses not on the production but on the reception of revolutionary ideas and discourses. A classic example of this target-oriented approach is Ronald Paulson's 1983 study *Representations of Revolution*, which examines how the French Revolution figures in the works of British and Spanish artists and writers. Other, more recent examples of this approach include historical-political studies such as Timothy Mason Roberts's *Distant Revolutions: 1848 and the Challenge to American Exceptionalism* (2009), Mischa Honeck's *We Are the Revolutionists: German-Speaking Immigrants and American Abolitionists after 1848* (2011), and Wil Verhoeven's *Americomania and the French Revolution Debate in Britain, 1789–1802* (2013). This target-oriented approach has also been adopted in cultural and literary studies in books such as Lawrence Reynolds's *European Revolutions and the American Literary Renaissance* (1988), Doris Garraway's collection *Tree of Liberty: Cultural Legacies of the Haitian Revolution in the Atlantic World* (2008), and Dennis Berthold's *American Risorgimento: Herman Melville and the Cultural Politics of Italy* (2009). Unlike source-oriented studies, which are often sweeping in scope, however, target-oriented scholarship tends to be geographically or temporally limited, dealing with the impact of revolutionary movements on a particular national, ethnic or literary group.

While our collection has most affinities with the target-oriented approaches outlined above, it seeks to move beyond this local focus by examining the reverberations of revolutionary ideas, concepts, images and objects in places and contexts that have often been overlooked. The essays assembled here adopt a flexible center-periphery model drawn from polysystem theory, which examines the role of translations and similar forms of cultural transfer in shaping societies and cultures (Even-Zohar 2000). Without therefore wanting to reify the terms center and periphery, we believe such an approach might be of help in conceptualizing the complexity of revolutionary reverberations. The case studies in this volume examine reverberations from centers to peripheries (e.g. from France to Wales), from peripheries to centers (e.g. from the Cossack backwaters to France and Germany), and even from peripheries to peripheries (e.g. from Greece to Spain). The study also examines transfers to and from colonial contexts (from France to Haiti and from Haiti to France or Germany), which are particularly complex, as revolutionary ideas and culture were interpreted in different ways by groups with conflicting interests: settlers, slaves, freed slaves, indigenous peoples, abolitionists and metropolitan authorities.

Haiti occupies a special space in this volume as it was at once a recipient and emitter of reverberations. The slaves who revolted in 1791 were adapting the ideals of the Enlightenment and the French Revolution to their colonial reality and in the process revealed the conflicts and contradictions implicit in these values. As Laurent Dubois points out, "the 1789 Declaration of the Rights of Man and Citizen defended both the natural right to freedom and the right to private property: in the Caribbean, where much of the propertyowners' wealth was invested in human beings, the contest between the two sets of rights raised profound questions about the nature and meaning of rights" (2004: 3). As the Haitians grappled with these ideas and sought to put them into practice, they forged new interpretations, which would reverberate not only in other colonies but also in the metropolis itself. As David P. Geggus and others have shown, the revolution, though a "small-scale affair" (2001: ix) involving just 600,000 people, had wide-ranging repercussions in Europe and the Americas. Of course, for a long time, the Haitian Revolution was "silenced" in Western historiography on the Age of Revolutions, as Michel-Rolph Trouillot's seminal work on this topic illustrated (Trouillot 1995). But as Florian Kappeler shows in this volume, the events in Haiti did in fact reverberate even during a period when imperial powers were trying hard to erase it from their official histories.

The case studies assembled here all seek to draw attention to what happens to revolutions as they cross both spatial and temporal borders. In the process, we draw attention to the crucial role of mediators who are often overlooked – booksellers, printers, translators, readers and censors – and consider not only the reception of ideas and texts but also the reverberations of the material culture of revolution. Finally, we examine the contorted and sometimes circular paths of these reverberations. The study, however, is by no means comprehensive. A number of other revolutions and uprisings – for example, the Irish Rebellion of 1798 – might be studied through a similar lens. But it is our hope that the cases examined in these chapters will serve as a useful point of comparison and contrast for future studies of those events.

The volume begins with the reverberations of what was probably the most serious revolutionary event in eighteenth-century Europe before the French Revolution: the so-called Pugachev Rebellion of 1773–75. This Cossack "uprising" was led by Emel'ian Pugachev, who posed as Peter III, the tsar who had been ousted and assassinated in 1762. After the rebellion was suppressed, Catherine the Great, Peter III's widow and successor, attempted to silence all discussion of the events in Russia. She was unable, however, to control their reverberations abroad. Malte Griesse's chapter analyzes two accounts of the uprising by foreign writers. The first is a 1775 biography of Pugachev in French (allegedly a translation of a Russian original) that represents the rebel as a cosmopolitan figure and Enlightenment reformer. The work serves both to critique despotism in France and to challenge Catherine II's monopoly on Enlightenment discourse in Russia. The second text, which seems a reaction to the first, is an anonymous German account of the revolt, which depicts Pugachev as an illiterate brute. Griesse analyzes the contexts in which these works were published and traces how these representations were "retranslated" into Russian when the taboo began to be relaxed.

The Pugachev "Rebellion" was not a revolution in the modern sense, because it was unsuccessful and its aim was the restoration of an old regime rather than the creation of a new one grounded in rights discourse. This does not mean, however, that it did not reverberate. In fact, its full significance becomes clear only if one studies the event in a comparative context. A similar pattern of silence at home and reverberation abroad characterizes the reception of the work of Mary Wollstonecraft, whose reputation suffered in Britain after the revelation of her out-of-wedlock affairs but whose revolutionary ideas about women and education continued to resonate abroad. Alessa Johns's chapter considers the reception of Wollstonecraft's work in Germany. Several of her books were translated into German by Friedrich Christian Weissenborn, a teacher at the *Erziehungsanstalt*, an innovative philanthropical school in Schnepfenthal founded by the pastor Christian Gotthilf Salzmann, whose *Moralisches Elementarbuch* (1783) Wollstonecraft had translated into English in 1790. In his introduction and footnotes to Weissenborn's 1793–94 translation of *A Vindication of the Rights of Woman* (1792), Salzmann attempts to tone down some of Wollstonecraft's more radical feminist ideas and anti-aristocratic sentiments. In both his translations and his own writings, however, Weissenborn supports Wollstonecraft's views about women's roles, though he emphasizes her gradualist vision of social change. Johns concludes by considering the reception of the work by the German-American Forty-Eighter Mathilde Franziska Anneke, who embraces Wollstonecraft's more radical feminist ideas. Johns's essay on the reverberations of Wollstonecraft's revolutionary feminism in the German states and America reveals, thus, the unlikely trajectories that a narrowly national approach to her work might overlook.

Marion Löffler's chapter continues this exploration of translation but turns the focus to Wales, a peripheral region in which the news of foreign uprisings was largely mediated by English discourse. Drawing on Reinhart Koselleck's conceptual history, Löffler traces the various words coined to convey the concept of revolution in Welsh in reaction to various moments of upheaval from the Glorious Revolution of 1688 to the American War of Independence and the French Revolution. Whereas at first writers opted for the positive *adymchweliad* (which had religious connotations suggesting a return to God) or the more neutral *cyfnewidiad llywodraeth* (a change of government), from 1797 on they began to use the more negative *chwyldro*, which evoked a dizzying circular movement. *Chwyldro* would go on to become the standard Welsh concept for revolution. As Löffler shows, this semantic shift reflected a growing concern about the direction of the uprising following the attempted French invasion of Britain through Wales. Löffler's study, thus, illustrates the reverberations of revolution not only across space but also across time as later revolutionary movements appropriate and transform the vocabulary of earlier ones.

The concepts of revolution were also difficult to translate in the New World, as Jeremy Popkin shows in his study of the appropriation of French discourses and concepts in the Haitian Revolution. His chapter opens with the decision in 1793 by two representatives of the French Republic in Saint-Domingue to translate the 1685 *Code Noir* into Creole. Although this document, which reinforced the institution of slavery, was clearly at odds with the representatives' revolutionary principles, it did guarantee certain rights and protections for the slaves. Paradoxically then, the translation of this document introduced for the first time the concept of "rights" into a society based on slavery. Popkin points to the many difficulties of translating ideas such as "liberty," "rights" and "equality" into a colonial context, in which the slaves had very different political notions and the revolutionaries' actions often contradicted their ideological principles.

Where Popkin considers the appropriation of French political discourse on Saint-Domingue, Anja Bandau's chapter focuses on the French reception of Haitian events, exploring two plays about the uprising, which were staged in Directory France: Pigault-Lebrun's *Le blanc et le noir* (1795) and Béraud and Rosny's *Adonis ou le bon nègre* (1798). Although the works belong to different genres – bourgeois drama and melodrama – and adopt different strategies, both seek to quell the violence of the uprising, drawing on Enlightenment discourse, staging improbable scenes of forgiveness and using sentimental tropes and the family romance to reconcile black and white characters. The events in Haiti, Bandau argues, are seen through the lens of the post-Terror period, which sought to avoid at all costs the bloody excesses of the recent past. In this study, the reverberations come full circle: the Haitian revolt, inspired by the French Revolution, now resonates in the metropolis.

Florian Kappeler's contribution continues this reflection on European reactions to the Haitian Revolution but returns our focus to the German-speaking world. After the defeat of Napoleon's army in 1803, discussion of the events in Haiti were heavily censored in France. In German-speaking countries, however, the events were debated in historico-political journals and later in historical monographs. As Kappeler argues, German writers focused primarily on three issues: racial equality, the potential economic impact of the abolition of slavery, and the question of whether the events in Haiti were simply an imitation of the French Revolution or an independent phenomenon. Although writers disagreed about these issues, the debates called into question the ideologies of racism, slavery and Eurocentrism in significant ways. Popkin's, Bandau's and Kappeler's chapters offer indirect approaches to the Haitian Revolution that bring out perspectives that remain largely invisible in a history of the events from "up close."

With Ashli White's chapter, we turn from the reverberations of words and ideas to those of objects. One of the most important emblems of the French Revolution was the tricolor cockade, comparable in significance to the Garibaldi shirt in Italy, or the Hecker hat in the German states. Small, cheap and portable, the French accessory quickly spread from the Old to the New World, where it almost immediately generated conflict. In the United States, disputes over tricolor or black cockades led to riots, and in Saint-Domingue, the emblem became associated with the abolition of slavery. Tracing the travels of two men who departed from Philadelphia in the 1790s – a Quaker bookseller who travelled to Montpellier and an indentured servant from the Indian subcontinent who escaped to Saint-Domingue – White draws attention to the ambiguity and instability of the cockade, which took on different meanings in different contexts. The icon could be a military emblem, a gesture of conformity, a sign of political conviction, or a depoliticized adornment, depending on the situation and the perspective of the observer.

The final essay by Elizabeth Amann shifts the focus from the 1790s to the wave of uprisings that swept across Southern Europe in the early 1820s and considers the representation of the Greek War of Independence in a romantic novel published in Spain in 1830: Estanislao de Cosca Vayo's two-volume *Grecia, ó la doncella de Missolonghi*. Although Spain had also experienced a liberal revolution in 1820, an absolutist regime had been reestablished in 1823 through French intervention, and discussion of the events in Greece was heavily censored. Cosca Vayo's work seems to be the only original novel written in Spanish on the subject. It is also unusual in that, unlike most European Philhellenic texts in which a white European man saves a Greek heroine from a sexually predatory Ottoman, its plot centers around a love story between a Greek woman and a Turkish man. Amann argues that this plot and Cosca Vayo's vision of the uprising in general are colored by his view of Spain's history of domination by a Muslim other.

The coda of the volume, written by Michael Boyden, brings us to the most famous example of reverberations of revolution: the insurrections of 1848. Examining the writings of Frederick Douglass, Boyden traces how the former slave's political vision developed as he observed and came into contact with other revolutionary projects and events such as the fight for Irish liberation and the revolutions of 1848, which echoed the antislavery struggle in the United States. Boyden's coda also points to future directions for research underscoring the importance of embodied practices in disseminating revolutionary ideas as, for example, in the reenactments performed in the "die-in" protests that have spread across the world in the wake of the murder of George Floyd.

As is clear from this overview, revolutionary ideas, discourses and objects reverberate in multiform and multidirectional ways. Not only do they radiate outward from source to target country but in some cases foreign reverberations also rebound back to the initial site of the revolution, influencing domestic politics. The objects that reverberate, moreover, take different forms: not only narratives and ideas but also words and things. Finally, through the process of reverberation, they transform in extremely varied ways: word use changes (*chwyldro* instead of *adymchweliad*), conflicts are resolved in idealizing ways (Pigault-Lebrun), and the historical experiences of one country are filtered through those of another (for instance, the Greek revolution seen through the lens of Spanish history). Sometimes, the extreme violence of revolutionary upheaval leads people to accept violent defense as the only way out, while in other cases it impels them to tone down revolutionary ideas in order to avoid more bloodshed. From our perspective, counter-revolutionary responses are no less relevant than the movements they are designed to contain, since they allow us to grasp why certain events become historical reference points while others are forgotten. It is our hope that in studying such reverberations – multiform, chaotic and often unexpected – the contributions of this volume will yield a fuller understanding of the complex and far-ranging impact of the Age of Revolutions.

Bibliography

Arendt, Hannah (2006), *On Revolution*, intro. Jonathan Schell, New York: Penguin.
Armitage, David and Sanjay Subrahmanyam (2010), *The Age of Revolutions in Global Context, C. 1760–1840*, Basingstoke: Palgrave Macmillan.
Baker, Keith Michael and Dan Edelstein (2015), *Scripting Revolution: A Historical Approach to the Comparative Study of Revolutions*, Stanford: Stanford University Press.
Berthold, Dennis (2009), *American Risorgimento: Herman Melville and the Cultural Politics of Italy*, Columbus: Ohio State University Press.
Desan, Suzanne, Lynn Hunt and William Max Nelson (2013), *The French Revolution in Global Perspective*, Ithaca: Cornell University Press.
Dubois, Laurent (2004), *A Colony of Citizens: Revolution and Slave Emancipation in the French Caribbean, 1787–1804*, Chapel Hill: University of North Carolina Press.

Even-Zohar, Itamar (2000), "The Position of Translated Literature within the Literary Polysystem," in Lawrence Venuti, ed., *The Translation Studies Reader*, London: Routledge, pp. 192–7.
Garraway, Doris Lorraine (2008), *Tree of Liberty: Cultural Legacies of the Haitian Revolution in the Atlantic World*, Charlottesville: University of Virginia Press.
Geggus, David P., ed. (2001), *The Impact of the Haitian Revolution in the Atlantic World*, Columbia: University of South Caroline Press.
Gilroy, Paul (1993), *The Black Atlantic: Modernity and Double Consciousness*, Cambridge, MA: Harvard University Press.
Hobsbawm, E. J. (1996), *The Age of Revolution 1789–1848*, New York: Vintage Books.
Honeck, Mischa (2011), *We Are the Revolutionists: German-Speaking Immigrants and American Abolitionists after 1848*, Athens: University of Georgia Press.
Knott, Sarah (2016), "Narrating the Age of Revolution," *The William and Mary Quarterly*, 73:1, pp. 3–38.
Koselleck, Reinhart (2004), *Futures Past: On the Semantics of Historical Time*, trans. Keith Tribe, New York: Columbia University Press.
Latour, Bruno (2005), *Reassembling the Social: An Introduction to Actor-Network-Theory*, Oxford: Oxford University Press.
Negri, Antonio (1999), *Insurgencies: Constituent Power and the Modern State*, trans. Maurizia Boscagli, Minneapolis: University of Minnesota Press.
Palmer, R. R. and David Armitage (2014), *The Age of the Democratic Revolution: A Political History of Europe and America, 1760–1800*, Princeton: Princeton University Press.
Paulson, Ronald (1983), *Representations of Revolution, 1789–1820*, New Haven: Yale University Press.
Pettitt, Clare (2020), *Serial Forms*. Oxford: Oxford University Press.
Polasky, Janet L. (2015), *Revolutions without Borders: The Call to Liberty in the Atlantic World*, New Haven: Yale University Press.
Pratt, Mary Louise (2008), *Imperial Eyes: Travel Writing and Transculturation*, New York: Routledge.
Reynolds, Larry J. (1988), *European Revolutions and the American Literary Renaissance*, New Haven: Yale University Press.
Roberts, Timothy Mason (2009), *Distant Revolutions: 1848 and the Challenge to American Exceptionalism*, Charlottesville: University of Virginia Press.
Skocpol, Theda (2015), *States and Social Revolutions: A Comparative Analysis of France, Russia, and China*, Cambridge: Cambridge University Press.
Trouillot, Michel-Rolph (1995), *Silencing the Past: Power and the Production of History*, Boston: Beacon Press.
Verhoeven, W. M. (2013), *Americomania and the French Revolution Debate in Britain, 1789–1802*, Cambridge: Cambridge University Press.

Chapter 1

Pugachev Goes Global: The Revolutionary Potential of Translation

Malte Griesse

The Pugachev uprising was probably the most significant revolt in eighteenth-century Europe before the outbreak of the French Revolution.[1] Emel'ian Pugachev, the main leader of the rebellion, drawing on a long and popular tradition of royal imposture in Russia (*samozvanstvo*), presented himself in 1773 as Peter III, Catherine II's predecessor and husband. Peter III had been in power only for a few months in 1762. He was ousted by a coup d'état orchestrated by his wife and soon died under suspicious circumstances. In the popular imagination, his reforms were interpreted as a prelude to the abolition of serfdom, and against this background Catherine's accession to the throne was seen as a counterstroke led by the highest nobility. Pugachev, a restless Don Cossack who became leader of the Yaik-Cossacks as the kernel of the rebellion, not only played on widespread discontent with the government's encroachments on traditional Cossack privileges and rights, but also took advantage of popular rumors according to which Peter III, the alleged reform- and liberator-tsar, had escaped the assassination attempt.[2] The years leading up to Pugachev had seen other pretenders impersonating Peter III, but none of them had been able to provoke an actual revolt (Myl'nikov 1994; Chaudon 1776: 383–6).

Pugachev's movement attained an enormous scope and would temporarily take over huge parts of Southern Russia. Unsurprisingly, the movement attracted much international interest, especially because Russia had become an important player in European politics. This had not yet been the case during the large-scale Cossack revolts of the seventeenth century (the Time of Troubles and the Razin rebellion). Furthermore, the Pugachev uprising unfolded in the wake of the Confederation of Bar and the ensuing civil war between pro- and anti-Russian forces in Poland, as well as in the shadow of the Russo-Turkish war (1768–74), both important events in European politics. Naturally, the weakening of the Russian government by a revolt was profitable to its Ottoman adversary – but also to the French government, which, under the guise of friendly relations, was trying to bridle the growing hegemony of Russia (Черкасов 1998).

Foreign correspondents in Russia reported as much as they could about the uprising, through both public and arcane channels, mainly newspapers and journals on the one hand, and diplomatic accounts on the other. But Russian media policy had changed since the preceding century and since the Razin rebellion of 1670–71, which, despite Russia's relative isolation from Europe at the time, had already provoked a European "media hype" (Welke 1976).[3]

Firstly, the government and most of the foreign observers were now in Petersburg, further away from the action than they had been during the Razin Rebellion. Secondly, the Russian government had developed means of curtailing the flow of information: Letters from regions near the uprising were intercepted, censored and held back if necessary. Retrieving information became extremely difficult (Alexander 1969: 9–10). The French ambassador Durand Distroff wrote: "[The government] tries to keep secret, as much as possible, its official letters sent to Kazan, and those that arrive from there. Concerning the private letters from these regions, it is very rare that they escape the care that is taken to suppress them."[4] And the envoy of the Republic of Dubrovnik noted that "nobody is allowed to speak about the rebellion" – according to him this also had an impact on the authorities themselves, who "still do not know the details" (Alexander 1969: 117).

Then Pugachev started to circulate manifestos and summoned the population to swear allegiance to him. He offered differentiated incentives to different social strata, including the abolishment of serfdom for the peasants. Now Catherine was forced to react and started to launch counter-manifestos (Plambeck 1982).

Immediately after the suppression of the revolt and Pugachev's public execution, though, she issued a decree of pardon that stipulated eternal oblivion (*damnatio memoriae*).[5] Henceforth it was prohibited to commemorate the events or even to mention Pugachev's name. The river Yaik was renamed Ural, and the Yaik Cossacks, who had formed the core of the rebellion (and had not been killed), were renamed "Ural Cossacks." Those who violated the taboo faced harsh punishments (Alexander 1973: 197–201).

What impact did this explicit policy of *damnatio memoriae* have on representations of the uprising? Who wrote and published about the events after the act of oblivion, and in what terms? How was the image of the rebel leader shaped by international reverberations and concomitant acts of translation and retranslation?

Limits of the Taboo Policy

Among historians of Russia it is generally agreed that a half century would pass before the first Russian historian was allowed to work on the uprising. It was none other than Alexander Pushkin who was first granted (limited) access to government archives (Блок 1949). Drawing on his archival work as well as ethnographic field work in which he collected oral accounts, verses and songs, Pushkin wrote his *History of the Pugachev Rebellion* (1834) – and subsequently his famous *The Captain's Daughter* (1836), a fictional reworking of the subject (Александр С. Пушкин 1834; Александр Сергеевич Пушкин 1836).

Nevertheless, two other anonymous Russian publications on Pugachev eluded the censors by accident and appeared in a Muscovite press in 1809, that is, twenty-five years before Pushkin. Both accounts are drawn from the French "biography" of Pugachev, called *Le Faux Pierre III* (The False Peter III), published (allegedly in London) as early as 1775, shortly after the act of oblivion issued by Catherine II (Anon. 1809a; 1809b). These translations from the French cost the censor his job as well as his position as professor at Moscow University (Степанов 1991).

This means that during the first fifty years after the rebellion its image was shaped exclusively abroad – outside the reach of the Russian government. At least this is how it seems. But what impact did Catherine's policy have on foreign representations of the revolt? Her government could not prevent numerous accounts of the events from being published. Nevertheless, practically all of them were published anonymously or under a pseudonym, which suggests that even abroad it was considered a delicate matter to write about Pugachev.

The most important and influential works, on which I will try to shed new light here, are the French "biography" of 1775, whose Russian translation passed censorship in Moscow by accident, and a detailed German account of the uprising published in 1784.

The "biography" *Le Faux Pierre III* (F. S. G. W. D. B. 1775) was immediately translated into German (F. S. G. W. D. B. 1776) and then constantly recycled and plagiarized in subsequent accounts throughout Europe (Chaudon 1776: 387–403; Schiller 1799: 232–301; Anon. 1804: 264–74). By and large, it has been ignored by historians, who dismiss it as unreliable.[6] Indeed, large parts of the biography, in particular those covering Pugachev's life before the uprising, seem to be largely fictive. But this did not prevent the work from becoming enormously popular and shaping to a considerable extent the image of the uprising, especially against the background of the concerned authorities' persistent silence.

The other influential account, in German, is entitled *Reliable News of the Insurgent Emeljan Pugachev and the Rebellion he Instigated* [my translation, MG] (Anon. 1784). It was published in Anton Friedrich Büsching's *Magazine of Political Geography* in 1784, eight or nine years after the events, and subsequently it too was used as a template for a series of accounts abroad[7] – its narrative ultimately made its way into Pushkin's *History of the Pugachev Rebellion*. The book is not a biography; it focuses almost exclusively on the uprising. The depiction of the events corresponds largely to what historians would later find in archival documents. In the late 1940s, Soviet historian Georgij Blok attributed authorship to the famous German geographer Gerhard Friedrich Müller, a close friend of Büsching's. Müller, born German, was naturalized in Russia and became a high-ranking member of the Academy of Sciences in Petersburg. He was also director of the archives of foreign affairs in Moscow, where the secret documents relating to the uprising were stored. Blok's assumption, which has been subsequently adopted by other historians, is that Müller (ab)used his position to study the archival material secretly and to write an account of the uprising that he would later hand over to his friend in Germany for publication (Блок 1949: 92–5).[8] Perfectly aware of the delicacy of the matter, Müller would have purged from his personal archive all notes relating to the rebellion[9] and then instructed Büsching not to publish the account before his death, in order to protect both his reputation and family. As a matter of course, his authorship should also be kept secret under all circumstances. In the face of the Russian government's taboo policy, the hypothesis seems highly convincing.

Still, I have to cast serious doubts on this narrative. I do not question Müller's authorship; he was indeed the only person with access to the documents and was therefore able to compose such an accurate account of the uprising and the military operations of the repressive forces. But such a risky defiance of the government's policy of *damnatio memoriae* is extremely unlikely. As far as we know, Müller was always loyal to Catherine II, who had protected his scientific work. This was a sharp contrast to the reign of Empress Elizabeth, during which he faced numerous intrigues at the Academy of Sciences and was repeatedly demoted. Especially since his nomination to the position of director of the Moscow archive in 1766, he enjoyed the highest esteem and was even honored with the newly founded Order of Saint Vladimir shortly before his death in 1783. In the early 1770s, moreover, he suffered from poor health and had several strokes. He increasingly struggled to complete assignments and required the aid of a competent assistant, who supported him in his writing. It is therefore highly improbable that he ventured on such a risky undertaking on his own.[10]

In contrast to Blok and other historians, my hypothesis is that Catherine II herself entrusted her archivist and historiographer with the study of the archival material and the composition of a comprehensive account of the Pugachev uprising. She must have sworn him to utmost secrecy. Undoubtedly the account was from the very beginning commissioned and designed for publication abroad, where there was heightened interest in the events and where it would counter *Le Faux Pierre III* (1775), whose popularity was becoming more and more offensive to Catherine's government (we will see why).

The French Biography of Pugachev

We therefore need to have a closer look at this popular French "biography" of the rebel leader, even though – or precisely because – it has been neglected by historians for its unreliability. In fact, its reliability was already questioned by contemporaries. *L'Esprit des journaux*, an important literary journal of the time, wrote in 1776:

> This work would be juicy, curious and much sought-after [in fact it was], if we were able to convince ourselves that it was the real story of this adventurer, who has only recently made such a hullabaloo – who strove for the throne only to end on the scaffold. But unfortunately, the work we are talking about is full of falseness that does not give the reader any reasons for illusory conceptions. It is announced as a translation from the Russian, but we don't know if the novel has ever appeared there, in its entirety or in parts. Most likely it has never appeared in this Empire, since nobody would have dared to

publish a biography of the rebel Pugachev that constantly praises his qualities, whereas his depicted deeds degrade him fundamentally. . . . The author has decorated the main events with all that his fantasy has given to him.[11]

Indeed, the biography is presented as a translation from the Russian, but, in reality, seems to be a pseudotranslation and the French version to be the original.[12] Without specifying his precise role or position, the alleged Russian author claims to have been close to Pugachev and therefore to have intimate knowledge about the rebel leader's life. The supposed Russian original makes it possible to introduce "the translator" as a second voice apart from the author/narrator, who renders Pugachev's thought in surprising detail. In both preface and footnotes "the translator" enters into dialogue with the "author." On several occasions, he muses about the reliability of certain episodes, especially where Pugachev's intimate conversations and reasoning are concerned. Occasionally he also comments on the moral implications of depicted deeds. This continuous controversy between "translator" and "author" anticipates subsequent reviews such as the one quoted from *L'Esprit des journaux* that would question the Russian authorship of the book and denounce it as a work of fiction.

Only about a fourth of the French biography is devoted to the actual rebellion. The longest part portrays Pugachev's earlier career. As an inverted *Bildungsroman*, it shows the hero's development from virtue to vice, from extraordinary gifts and ambition to the most horrible crime against the state and Catherine's enlightened government (that is, in the actual uprising).

After leaving his native Cossack village on the Don, the story goes, Pugachev joins a multi-national bandit gang in the steppe. There he befriends the ingenious Frenchman Boispré, who becomes his mentor. Pugachev is torn between his personal ambition and his nobler impulse to do great deeds for the common good. Boispré continually draws him toward ambition, irrespective of morals. Together they leave the country. Always assisted by Boispré, who gets him out of tight spots, Pugachev wanders through Europe (Poland, Prussia, Austria, Italy, France, England, the Balkans, the Ottoman Empire), mostly as a con man. He impersonates a Venetian nobleman and breaks several women's hearts. But he also serves as a high-ranking officer in the Seven Years' War, and later in the Prussian, Austrian and Russian armies, where he is honored for his heroic deeds. Throughout his wanderings, his declared aim is to observe closely and to study all the peoples of Europe, their orders and forms of government. He is thus depicted as a cosmopolitan representative of the Enlightenment, who rapidly learns languages and whose *peregrinatio* is, at root, aimed at the noble goal of figuring out the best possible constitution for his own country and people:

> Our hero wanted to get to know human nature, to learn about the customs and manners of all the peoples. Politics, war, commerce, the different branches of public administration, all this was part of the plan he had formed for himself; and enlightened by his friend Boispré he hoped to travel as a *philosophe* and to benefit from everything including human errors and even follies. It would be difficult to say precisely to which point he extended his progress in such a difficult object of study. The unfortunate attempt that he would make, drawing on the lessons of his travels and the principles his friend inspired in him, is not a very favorable proof of his philosophy. Maybe if he had succeeded in his culpable purpose, we would have seen him make up for all his crimes by all the virtues that characterize the great monarchs. Augustus the triumvir was a monster of cruelty: Augustus the Emperor won the admiration of the whole universe. (F. S. G. W. D. B. 1775: 191–2)[13]

The ambivalence of the passage is quite characteristic of the whole book. The "translator" often criticizes the "author" for presenting Pugachev in too positive a light, but in some of his footnotes he echoes this view, especially when he muses about crime as the (almost necessary) foundation of Empires and compares Pugachev to Romulus.

Apart from these barely veiled eulogies of Pugachev's potential to be the enlightened founder of a great Empire, another blow the "biography" strikes against Catherine's government is Pugachev's alleged support for the Polish confederates of Bar and his vehement defense of Polish constitutionalism and liberty against Catherine's attempts to interfere in Poland. In fact, according to *Le Faux Pierre III*, after all his enlightened studies of the peoples and political orders of Europe, the Polish elective monarchy becomes Pugachev's favorite, because "a government that has not come to power through a free and unanimous vote of the people is unjust and will be hated." It was Catherine's government that had jeopardized the Polish people's will by massive military intervention during the Polish elections of 1764. Turning to Boispré, Pugachev reasons:

> If I had been crowned by violence and ruse [like Stanisław II August of Poland] and my unjust ascension to the throne had caused strife among my subjects, I would lay down scepter and crown into the

subjects' hands and speak to them: "My beloved brethren, I have been lured to the idea that once in power I would be able to make you all happy; but experience has shown that I was wrong. I should have known that only all of you could give me the right to accede to the throne. I have thus usurped this right and therefore I give it back to you, happy to be your equal and to obey him whom you honor with your choice, and that you would believe more worthy than I to command men rightly zealous of their liberty." – Don't you think, my dear Boispré, that if the Count Poniatowski [that is, Stanisław II August] had spoken to the Polish people in this way, they wouldn't have rallied to him in order to reaffirm his kingdom?

[Then the author/narrator comments:] When Jemeljan expressed himself with such fervor, he certainly did not anticipate that he was himself not far from overthrowing the throne of a Sovereign, his legitimate Sovereign, who had been placed there by the unanimous will of all her peoples. (F. S. G. W. D. B. 1775: 205–6)[14]

For a contemporary audience, well aware of the coup d'état that had brought Catherine to power, it would have been hard to miss the irony of her being called a "legitimate Sovereign" chosen "by all her peoples."[15] To be sure, the biography leaves no doubt about Pugachev's imposture and about the illegal, rebellious character of his movement. But it becomes clear that, in the power struggle with Catherine II, both adversaries are usurpers in dynastic terms and have to derive legitimacy from other sources. Building on the idealized Polish example while ignoring the fact that political rights in the Rzeczpospolita pertained exclusively to the nobility, Pugachev here invokes, on the one hand, popular sovereignty, associated with the idea of elective monarchy (the right to accede to the throne should be given by all), and, on the other hand, public felicity (the duty of the monarch as *primus inter pares* "to make you all happy," as he puts it). Both refer to a common good and can be seen as complementary, if consent derives from happiness. The problem is that in order to "make one's subjects happy" (and thereby gain their consent), one has to be a governor or monarch already. Pugachev's reasoning here falls into the same consequentialism as the narrator's reflections on Augustus and the translator's reference to Romulus. With such a consequentialist ethics, a rebellion can be justified a posteriori if it turns out to be successful and to "make the subjects happier." No doubt, even though the impostor had managed to rally masses of people in support of his "recovery" of the throne and for some time it seemed that he would in fact succeed, his insurgent movement was finally crushed, and he was handed over to the authorities. The struggle between the two usurpers was won by Catherine II. For the reader, however, the question remained if or to what extent her reign made the people happier.

To be sure, the biography was written in French and addressed in the first place to a European audience outside Russia. Therefore, we have to distinguish between the aims of the book and the effect it had on the Russian government. In France it was common practice, at least since Montesquieu's *Persian Letters*, to circumvent censorship and denounce tyranny or arbitrary and illegitimate rule *at home* by writing about despotism *abroad*, preferably oriental despotism. Like Persia and the Ottoman Empire, Russia was a suitable projection screen, because in the tradition it was seen as a barbarian or backward country.[16] Moreover, the barely veiled enmity between the two governments made it hard to break diplomatic china and therefore it was particularly innocuous to write about the events in Russia that had aroused so much attention during the previous eighteen months. From this angle, the "biography," with its ambiguous denunciations of despotic rule and its reflections on (the desirability of) popular sovereignty, was in the first place aimed at a French audience that had just witnessed a whole series of hunger revolts and their repression by government troops (the so-called Flour War, April–May 1775) (Bouton 1993; Thompson and Ikni 1988). *Le Faux Pierre III*, thus, served as a proxy discourse and has to be seen as part of the intellectual prelude to the French Revolution.

But even if Catherine understood the Aesopian subtext "between the lines," whose target was the French government, she could hardly ignore the lines themselves. And the "biography" was much more than a violation of her *damnatio memoriae* policy. Since she knew perfectly well that her dynastic legitimacy was questionable after her coup d'état, she tried from the very beginning to compensate by monopolizing Enlightenment discourse. She presented herself as following in the steps of her virtual ancestor Peter the Great[17] and as the only possible civilizer of the backward country. For this purpose, she invested considerable effort in besmirching the image of the real Peter III, her predecessor and former husband, and in having him represented as an infantile drunkard, an irascible and pitiless tormentor, and at the same time a more or less ignorant fool, who did not care at all for the country he was supposed to govern (Catherine II, Empress of Russia 2005).

And now, in the French "biography," the Cossack impostor was presented as a cosmopolitan Enlightener, who had allegedly studied all European political orders and constitutions before returning to his native country and challenging her government in the name of her ousted husband and predecessor, who was thereby implicitly rehabilitated as another Enlightenment tsar. This was a major blow against the legitimacy of her rule, which she had so arduously built!

Creating a Counter-Narrative

What could she do? Her hands were tied. It would have been ridiculous to demand a prohibition of the biography from the French government.[18] *Le Faux Pierre III* (allegedly) had not even been published in France, and since diplomatic relations were strained she had no leverage. At the same time, she had learned from previous experience that prohibitive government interference in the book trade tended to render the targeted works more popular rather than deflecting readers' interest. Abroad, her policy of *damnatio memoriae* had clearly failed. The only means of intervention that remained to her was to step into the ring of European public debate. But to do so in her own name would only draw even more attention to the affair. Therefore, she had to feign ignorance of the matter and to act via proxies.

What she could do was to secretly commission critical reviews of *Le Faux Pierre III*. And it is very likely that the review quoted above from *L'Esprit des journaux* was one of them. The main goal was to denounce the "biography" as a piece of fiction that had little to do with the actual events. Unsurprisingly, however, the results of this strategy were limited. Not only because the "biography" already contained reflections on the borders between fact and fiction, but also because no coherent factual report was available that might have replaced its defective account.

This seems to be the reason why Catherine finally decided to give up her *damnatio memoriae* policy, not in Russia itself but with regard to the foreign public. She needed a serious counter-narrative and entrusted it to the most competent member of her circle: G. F. Müller. The main task of the account, apart from being serious and "factual," was to destroy the cosmopolitan image of Pugachev as a well-educated Enlightener with a realistic vision for reforming and (further) civilizing the country. This image of Pugachev was extremely harmful to Catherine II since it put them on a par. Therefore, the image of Pugachev had to be reduced to ignorance and barbarianism, and his insurgent movement had to be "autochthonalized." And this is exactly what Müller's account does. Pugachev is painted as an ignorant rapist and brute, who acts out of pure lust for murder, and his insurgent movement is characterized by senseless brutality. It is conceded that he had some natural organizing ability; otherwise he would not have been capable leading such a huge movement. But Müller's Pugachev lacks all political perspective (Anon. 1784: 10–13).

Müller combined this account with a negative assessment of the actual Peter III and his short reign in 1762. In particular, he tried to prevent any impression of enlightened tolerance. He rightly stresses the crucial role of the Old Believers (who rejected the reforms of the Orthodox Church passed by Patriarch Nikon in the mid-seventeenth century) in support of Pugachev's impersonation of Catherine's defunct husband:

> As absurd as this idea might seem, it was extraordinarily subtle in order to make rebellious such a raw people and to mobilize Southern Russia almost in its entirety. It was believed that one of the main causes for the dethronement of this Emperor [that is, the real Peter III] was that he planned to carry out numerous changes in the clergy and in the divine service of the ruling [official] church [as opposed to the Old Believers]. *Even though this was wrong*, it made him dear and precious in the eyes of the raskolniki [Old Believers] and most of the Cossacks. (Anon. 1784: 7)

Müller definitely knew better. In fact, only five weeks after his accession to the throne in early 1762, Peter III had granted free exercise of religion and instructed the authorities not to oppress Old Believers. And shortly after her accession to the throne Catherine II had revoked these measures of religious tolerance. Why would Müller have omitted Peter's religious policy if not at Catherine's behest? Only twenty years later, at the end of 1782, Catherine revised her own church policy in favor of increased tolerance (Hauptmann 2005: 75). Most likely Müller's *Zuverlässige Nachrichten* were already written at that time and it is even conceivable that his findings regarding the religious roots of the Pugachev rebellion contributed to Catherine's turnabout.

Under no circumstances, however, could it become known that the author of the German account was "Catherine's man." This is why the utmost anonymity was necessary. At the same time, unattributed authorship was known to reduce credibility. This was one of the main arguments used against *Le Faux Pierre III*. The strategy was to use a renowned savant and editor as mediator for authentication. In his preface, A. F. Büsching stated that the text had been handed over to him by an "important savant," but he did not reveal that the author was G. F. Müller (from whom he published a signed article in the same issue of his *Magazine*). In the manner of an "anonymous peer reviewer" this savant testifies to the veracity of the account, which is attributed to a German mercenary soldier in the troops of General Michelson, who played a major role in the repression of the uprising (Anon. 1784: 2 verso). At the same time, Büsching affirms that the *Zuverlässige Nachrichten* is the very first account of the Pugachev rebellion. Since *Le Faux Pierre III* was too popular to be ignored and such an assertion would have provoked disbelief among his readers, Büsching specifies that the French book was not a biography, as it claimed, but at most a novel inspired by the events (Anon. 1784: 2-verso).

Why Was the German Account Not Published Earlier?

But why was the account published as late as 1784, almost nine years after the appearance of *Le Faux Pierre III*, against which it was directed? If Catherine could rely on Müller's loyalty, why should she wait until the old savant's death (at the end of 1783)? It is unlikely that it took Müller such a long time to work through the documents. My hypothesis is that Catherine was reluctant to subvert her own *damnatio memoriae* policy and that we have to take into account a series of factors that were closely related to the global reverberations of the brewing Age of Revolutions and which constantly aggravated rather than diminished the danger of the biography in the eyes of the Russian government:

When the *Le Faux Pierre III* came out in 1775, ideas of popular sovereignty were still, first and foremost, theoretical discourses that seemed unlikely to be put into practice. But this would rapidly change in the years that followed, especially with the American and French revolutions. In 1775, the Revolutionary War had already broken out in North America, but the Declaration of Independence was proclaimed only in 1776. George III of Great Britain repeatedly asked for Russian military assistance against the rebellious colonies, but Catherine declined all his pleas. Unofficially, she blamed Britain for the conflict. Officially, she observed strict neutrality and propagated her policy to prompt the creation of the First League of Armed Neutrality (1780–83). This initiative jeopardized the British blockade policy against what it considered as contraband (especially by French ships) and it indirectly favored the insurgent American colonists (Болховитинов 1976).

Even though the Declaration of Independence would not be published in Russia until the second half of the nineteenth century (under Alexander II), the political ideas of the American revolutionaries were leaked to the Russian political elite, especially with the publication of

Abbé Raynal's *Révolution de l'Amérique*, which was included in the 1780 edition of his famous *Histoire des deux Indes* (History of the two Indies), first published in 1770. As early as 1776, the *Saint Petersburg Gazette*, the leading Russian newspaper run by the Academy of Sciences, listed Raynal's *Histoire* among the books to be translated. But Catherine II became more and more prohibitive, so that actual translations only began to appear in print at the beginning of the nineteenth century under Alexander I. However, Russian Enlighteners under Catherine did read Raynal and in 1783/4 the prominent Enlightener N. I. Novikov published a series of articles in the *Supplement to the Moscow Gazette* that drew heavily on Raynal's *Histoire*, to the extent that historians have taken them for translations.[19] Raynal's Enlightenment philosophy is based on a Lockean theory of property as derived from free human labor (of the land), which is understood as an appropriation of nature, in the American case the taming of the wilderness. This amounted to a clear stance against slavery. Applied to Russia, the derivation of property from labor was potentially explosive, especially with regard to the institution of serfdom: Serfs were far from being able to take possession of the land by their labor. On the contrary, they were bound to the land, with the obligation to labor on it for the lord.[20] Moreover, and in this same vein, Raynal upholds the right of any society to create its own constitution, which he labels "political liberty" as distinguished from (personal) natural and civil liberty. The direct corollary of political liberty is the fundamental right to resist tyranny, a state into which all governments would devolve when they were not submitted to the permanent control of the people. Raynal (and his co-authors) were radical enough to argue that "society" – that is, the people (sometimes the "nation") – had the right to change its government independently of how the ruling authority had been installed (whether by force or by consensus), for the free decision of the ancestors was not to infringe upon the liberty of their descendants. What the oppressors called "revolt" was therefore the fundamental right of any society. He thus vehemently welcomes American independence as an act of the people's appropriation of government on the basis of popular sovereignty.[21]

The most spectacular transformation of Raynal's political ideas in the context of Catherine's Russia is to be found in Alexander Radishchev's *Journey from Petersburg to Moscow*, which was published anonymously in 1790. Radishchev transgressed Catherine's policy of taboo and blamed both the Russian nobility and the government for the Pugachev uprising, while making serfdom a cornerstone of his criticism. The book was immediately prohibited, and Radishchev identified as the author and exiled to Siberia (Radishchev 1958). But this was well after the publication of the *Zuverlässige Nachrichten*, and Catherine II rather tended to attribute Radishchev's initiative to the pernicious influence of the French Revolution.

Before that, however, the statesman and long-term advisor of Catherine II, Nikita Panin, seems to have played an ambiguous role. Panin largely shaped Russian foreign policy and may have even been responsible for the creation of the League of Armed Neutrality (favoring the American revolutionaries). At the same time, he was the tutor of Duke Paul, Catherine's son and designated successor to the throne. Already at the time of Catherine's coup d'état against her husband, in which he took an active part, Panin proposed a significant limitation to autocratic power in the form of a cabinet council of ministers, which was ultimately declined by the tsarina (Чечулин 2011). But instead of giving up his plans of reforming the Russian political system, he continued to elaborate what was later considered the first constitutional project in Russia. According to some he even spearheaded a conspiracy to put his ideas into practice. The Decembrist (a member of the group that led the Decembrist uprising of 1825) Mikhail Fonvizin asserted later that a whole series of leading politicians, militaries and clerics were involved – including his uncle, the famous playwright Denis Fonvizin, from whom he learned the details of the events, and Panin's brother Peter, who had commanded some of the forces that repressed Pugachev's troops. But one of the plotters seems to have betrayed the plan to Catherine, who managed to disarm the conspirators quietly without visible repressions. Like Raynal and the Anglo-Saxon tradition, Nikita Panin, the mastermind of the plot, had based his political philosophy on the right to private property as a *conditio sine qua non* of political freedom. In this vein, his constitutional project seems to have delineated a liberal, religiously tolerant political order. Autocratic rule, with its power to interfere arbitrarily in matters of property, should be abolished and replaced by a constitutional monarchy, whose head would be subject to the same binding law as everybody else (Н. Эйдельман 1993). American influence was certainly important, and some of Panin's ideas matched the project of the Pugachev depicted in the biography.

Panin represented a tiny enlightened elite that incubated projects of reform or revolution from high positions within the government or administration. This enlightened elite culture seemed completely detached from popular culture. Reformers and even revolutionaries in the state administration such as Panin would not embrace an insurgent initiative from below, such as that of Pugachev. Conversely, the lower strata that had supported Pugachev (as Peter III) were far from embracing the revolutionary projects of the intellectual elite, as became all too evident in the disastrous failure of the Decembrist uprising in 1825. The Pugachev of the "biography," though, had managed to bridge these two cultures: His supporters at court are represented as having pulled the wool over Catherine's eyes by trivializing both the scope and the potential of the movement. They convinced her that under her beneficial reign there were no discontented people and therefore the insurgents, a mere gang of brigands, would not be able to rally support. These flatteries would have lured Catherine to dispatch completely insufficient troops against the insurgents, which enabled them in turn to expand their power and territory considerably (F. S. G. W. D. B. 1775: 257–9).

But wasn't this alliance of the two protest cultures pure fiction? Weren't these cultures incompatible? And wasn't the Pugachev of *Le Faux Pierre III* utterly inconceivable? Why would Catherine have worried about that?

In fact, shortly before Müller's account was published by Büsching, Catherine was confronted with the elaborate case of a certain Ivan Trevogin, an adventurer and impostor, which seemed to suggest a conjunction of the two protest cultures. Trevogin came from a poor family in a small Ukrainian village. His father, a church painter, died from drunkenness in Ivan's early childhood. Trevogin received some initial education in a foundling hospital, but acquired most of his knowledge and skills (languages, sciences, etc.) as an autodidact. After working for some time in the publishing house of the Academy of Sciences in Petersburg and establishing a circle of educated friends, he founded his own Enlightenment journal, the *Parnasskie Vedomosti*, in which he sought to popularize knowledge from all disciplines. The journal was part of his larger (utopian) project of creating an "Empire of Knowledge" (*Imperiia Znanij*), a sort of democratically organized *Gelehrtenrepublik*.[22] After three issues, authored and edited exclusively by himself, he was financially ruined and had to flee his creditors (Старцев 1958; Светлов 1966). He boarded a merchant vessel to Amsterdam, sought work in the Netherlands, and after not being admitted to the University of Leyden, was hired on another vessel in Rotterdam where he passed as a Frenchman named Roland Infortune (*nomen est omen*). After a few months of seafaring, he came to France and finally turned up at the Russian embassy in Paris, where he asked permission to return to Russia, which he claimed to have left as a captive. Ambassador Bariatinskii, who, nine years earlier, had downplayed the Pugachev rebellion before his French interlocutors, lodged him in the embassy's boarding house, and reported to Petersburg that this well-read young man was extremely thirsty for knowledge and "wanted to learn by heart all the libraries of the kingdom," where he spent most of his time. When Trevogin found out that the suspicious Bariatinskii planned to send him back to Russia under escort, that is, as a prisoner, he started to impersonate an exotic prince and successor to the throne of the fantastic Golkonda on the Isle of Borneo,[23] and claimed to have survived an attempt on his life by plotters (much like Peter III in Pugachev's back-story). In the first instance, Trevogin wanted to disclaim his status as a subject of Russia in order to be treated with more respect, as he asserted later in prison. But he supported his new imposture with royal manifestos, which resembled those issued by Pugachev (as Peter III) in 1773–74, with sketches for a new town to be built, and drafts for an equitable constitution for his country, which should become an ideal kingdom. Since he needed royal credentials, he went to a jeweler and had him coin some coats of arms and medals. To pay him, Trevogin pilfered some silverware from the boarding house where he lived. He told the jeweler another story, though, namely that he was delegated by the mighty "ruler of the Cossacks, who would soon arrive in Paris with his cortege, of which he was part." When the theft was discovered, he was thrown into the Bastille, where he further elaborated his story and apparently won friends and admirers among the guards and the inquisitor.[24] Meanwhile, Bariatinskii reported the case to Petersburg, including the story Trevogin had told the jeweler. The Russian authorities were alarmed and requested that the French government extradite him. They transferred him to Petersburg, to the fortress Peter and Paul, where he was interrogated repeatedly in great detail by the Secret Expedition, the highest body of political persecution, which had previously been charged with questioning Pugachev. Finally, he was put into a *smiritel'nyi dom* (a special prison for people with "indecent" lifestyles, who were constantly kept doing manual work), where he remained for two years, before being exiled to Siberia as a soldier under special custody (Макеев 2008; Курмачева 1983: 221–34).

All this was closely followed by Catherine II. She personally took the decisions and gave the orders, which testifies to the importance she accorded to the case. She understood that Trevogin was not only fascinated by Pugachev's imposture and uprising, about which he gathered as much information as he could, but that he had also read *Le Faux Pierre III* during his stay in Europe. With his lengthy reflections on a better order, Trevogin clearly had the potential to appeal to critical intellectuals in the state administration such as Panin,[25] but at the same time he came from the bottom of society, so he might also appeal to the discontented popular masses. People like Trevogin embodied the potential to bridge the gap between the dissident milieus at the top and at the bottom, and to succeed where the real Pugachev (unlike the hero of the French "biography") had failed.

Epilogue

After the publication of *Le Faux Pierre III*, it was clear that Catherine's *damnatio memoriae* policy had failed abroad. But Trevogin's case showed the danger of the story's retranslation into the Russian context. People like Trevogin could undermine Catherine's *damnatio memoriae* within Russia – and even worse, the elaborate story of the popular Enlightener and rebel leader under the banner of the legitimate tsar might even be made true by a new impostor, be it Trevogin or somebody else.

It is likely that Müller wrote his account of the uprising earlier (as an anti-*Faux Pierre III*), but Catherine hesitated to have it published. After the translation abroad threatened to provoke retranslation at home and the large-scale revolt had been transformed into a far-reaching revolution in its international reception, the situation had become too hot, and Müller's account had to be published as quickly as possible.

Müller's work not only re-distorted Pugachev in an autochthonous context and retransformed him into an ignorant and barbarian Cossack, but also responded with dry and hard military facts to the novelistic style of the adventure story of *Le Faux Pierre III*. Therefore, the account found some echo in a small community of Germans who had somehow been involved in the repression of the uprising (Freymann 1794). But at the same time its dryness was probably the main reason why the account was unable to rival the popularity of *Le Faux Pierre III*.

Pushkin's *History of Pugachev*, published in the 1830s, still half a century later, used Müller's account as a template and was written in a similar matter-of-fact style with a main focus on military events. Despite the fame of its author, Pushkin's *History* could not outdo *Le Faux Pierre III* in terms of popularity. Pushkin himself was dissatisfied with his work (Александр С. Пушкин 1834), and presumably it was also the persistent success of the French "biography" that incited him to write his famous *Captain's Daughter* (Александр Сергеевич Пушкин 1836). This novel represented Pugachev (once again) in an autochthonous Russian context, but thanks to its outstanding literary quality it completely ousted *Le Faux Pierre III* and its cosmopolitan internationalist underpinnings from both Russian and international commemorations of the Pugachev movement.

Whereas in his *History* Pushkin had overtly attacked *Le Faux Pierre III* as fictitious, in *The Captain's Daughter* his commentary is of a more mocking nature. One of the characters, who appears on the first page of the novel, is called Boispré, a name that is rendered in Russian as "Bopre" instead of "Boapre," which the English translation correctly re-transliterates as Beaupré. The passage deserves to be quoted at length:

> by the time I was twelve years of age [...] my father] engaged a Frenchman, M. Beaupré, to be my tutor. Savelitch [the family's groom and the protagonist's Russian "governor"] was much put out upon his arrival. "Thank goodness," muttered he to himself, "the child is washed, combed, and fed. Where is the use of wasting one's money and engaging *Moussié*, just as if one's own people were not sufficient!"
>
> Beaupré had been a hairdresser in his own country, and a soldier in Prussia; he then came to Russia, *pour être Outchitel* [teacher] without quite understanding the meaning of the word. He was a good fellow, but flighty and debauched to a degree. His greatest weakness was admiration of the fair sex, and he frequently met with such rough usage in return for his advances, that he would groan for days together. He was not *inimical* (as he expressed himself) *to the bottle*, that is to say (in plain Russian) he liked an extra drop. ... He and I got on very well, and although he bound himself by his agreement to teach me *French, German, and all the sciences*, he found it more advantageous to himself to pick up from me, after a fashion, a smattering of Russian, after which lesson, each of us went his way. We lived hand in glove with each other. I did not wish for another mentor. But fate soon parted us, owing to the following circumstances:
>
> The laundress Paláshka, a fat pock-marked girl, and the one-eyed dairy-maid Akoulka, had, it appears, agreed to throw themselves at my mother's feet, and whilst accusing themselves of culpability, to complain weepingly of *Monssié*, who would take advantage of their inexperience. My mother did not treat such matters as a joke, and carried the complaint to my father. His way of settling it was summary. He immediately sent for that rascal of a Frenchman. He was informed that *Monssié* was giving me my lesson. My father came into my room. Beaupré was sleeping on my bed the sleep of innocence. I was busy. [... A map] had hung on the wall without the slightest use having been made of it, and its size, and the good quality of the paper, had long tempted me. I decided upon making a kite of it, so,

taking advantage of Beaupré being asleep, I set to work. My father walked in as I was about to attach a wisp tail to the Cape of Good Hope. Perceiving that these were my studies in geography, my father pulled my ears, then rushing at Beaupré, he awoke him roughly, and assailed him with reproach. In his confusion, Beaupré would have risen, but he could not – the unfortunate Frenchman was dead drunk. My father dragged him off the bed by the collar, pushed him outside the door, and sent him off that same day, to the inexpressible joy of Savelitch. Thus ended my education.[26]

In the fantastic "biography" the mysterious Boispré was Pugachev's Mephistophelian mentor, the *spiritus rector* of the entire rebellion and the most conspicuous symbol of its alleged international dimension and sophisticated nature. Here, as the noble protagonist's "tutor," he is presented on the other side, but his role is reduced to a bit part: he is nothing but a ridiculous skirt chaser, a dork and a drunkard. Pushkin brushes him aside on the first pages of the novel, wherein Boispré/Beaupré never shows up again.

Bibliography

Alexander, John T. (1969), *Autocratic Politics in a National Crisis: The Imperial Russian Government and Pugachev's Revolt, 1773–1775*, Russian and East European Series 38, Bloomington: Indiana University Press.

Alexander, John T. (1973), *Emperor of the Cossacks: Pugachev and the Frontier Jacquerie of 1773–1775*, Lawrence: Coronado Press.

Anon. (1776), "[Compte Rendu] Le Faux Pierre III. Ou La Vie & Les Aventures Du Rebelle Jemelian Pougatschew . . .," *L'esprit Des Journaux* IV (April), pp. 119–25.

Anon. (1784), "Zuverlässige Nachrichten von Dem Aufrührer Jemeljan Pugatschew Und Der von Demselben Angestifteten Empörung," in *Magazin Für Die Neue Historie Und Geographie*, ed. Anton Friedrich Büsching, 18, pp. 3–70, Halle: Curt.

Anon., ed. (1804), *Eccentric Biography; or, Sketches of Remarkable Characters, Ancient and Modern . . . The Whole Alphabetically Arranged; and Forming a Pleasing Delineation of the Singularity, Whim, Folly, Caprice, &c. &c. of the Human Mind. Ornamented with Eight Portraits. First American from the Second London Edition*, London: B&J Homans.

Anon. (1809a), *Анекдоты о Бунтовщике и Самозванце Емельке Пугачеве*, Москва: вольная типография Федора Любия.

Anon. (1809b), *Ложный Петр III, Или Жизнь, Характер и Злодеяния Бунтовщика, Емельки Пугачева*, Москва: В вольной типографии, Федора Любия.

[Bellermann], [Johann Joachim] (1792), *Bemerkungen Über Esthland, Liefland, Russland. Nebst Einigen Beiträgen Zur Empörungsgeschichte Pugatschews, Während Eines Achtjährigen Aufenthalts Gesamlet von Einem Augenzeugen*, Prague and Leipzig: Meissner.

Bouton, Cynthia A. (1993), *The Flour War: Gender, Class, and Community in Late Ancien Régime French Society*, University Park: Pennsylvania State University Press.

Catherine II, Empress of Russia (2005), *The Memoirs of Catherine the Great*, trans. Mark Cruse and Hilde Hoogenboom, New York: Modern Library.

Chaudon, Esprit Joseph (1776), *Les Imposteurs Démasqués: Et Les Usurpateurs Punis, Ou Histoire de Plusieurs Aventuriers Qui, Ayant Pris La Qualité d'empereur, de Roi, de Prince, d'ambassadeur, de Tribun, de Messie, de Prophete, Etc., Ont Fini Leur Vie Dans l'obscurité, Ou Par Une Mort Violente*, Paris: Chez Nyon.

Donnert, Erich (2008), "Revoltierung und Massenaufruhr in der Frühen Neuzeit. Katharina II. und der 'Marquis de Pougatschef.'" In *Europa in der frühen Neuzeit: Unbekannte Quellen. Aufsätze zu Entwicklung, Vorstufen, Grenzen und Fortwirken der Frühneuzeit in und um Europa. Inhaltsverzeichnisse der Bände 1–6. Personenregister der Bände 1–7*, ed. Erich Donnert, 7, pp. 873–94, Weimar: Böhlau.

F. S. G. W. D. B. (1775), *Le Faux Pierre III. Ou La Vie Et Les Avantures Du Rebelle Jemeljan Pugatschew. D'Après L'Original Russe de Mr. F. S. G. W. D. B. Avec le Portrait de l'Imposteur, & des notes Historiques & Politiques*, London: C. H. Seyfert, En Angel Court Westminster.

F. S. G. W. D. B. (1776), *Leben Und Abentheuer Des Berüchtigten Rebellen Jemeljan Pugatschew, Welcher Sich in Dem Südlichen Rußland Für Peter III. Ausgab. Nach Dem Russischen Original Des Herrn F.S.G.W.D.B. in Das Französische Und Aus Diesem in Das Deutsche Übersetzt*, London [i.e. Leipzig]: [Heinsius], at <https://reader.digitale-sammlungen.de//de/fs1/object/display/bsb10065983_00005.html> (last accessed October 20, 2020).

Freymann, Ferdinand von (1794), "Getreue Darstellung der Expedition wider die (damaligen) jaikischen Kosaken, wie auch hernach wider den Rebellen Pugatschow zur Berichtigung und Widerlegung einiger im Büschingschen Magazin davon vorkommenden teils unvollständigen, teils falschen Miszellaneen," *Neue nordische Miscellaneen* 7–8, pp. 355–410.

Griesse, Malte (2014), "State-Arcanum and European Public Spheres: Paradigm Shifts in Muscovite Policy toward Foreign Representations of Russian Revolts," in Malte Griesse, ed., *From Mutual Observation to Propaganda War: Premodern Revolts in Their Transnational Representations*, Histoire 56, Bielefeld: transcript, pp. 205–69.

Griesse, Malte (2016), "Von der Barbarei zur Rückständigkeit: Russland als Projektionsfläche der Aufklärung," in David Feest and Lutz Häfner, eds,

Die Zukunft der Rückständigkeit. Chancen – Formen – Mehrwert. Festschrift für Manfred Hildermeier zum 65. Geburtstag, Cologne: Böhlau, pp. 140–66.

Griesse, Malte (2017), "Pugačev-Bilder vor der Kanonisierung. Transnationale Deutungskämpfe in der Vormoderne," *Jahrbücher für Geschichte Osteuropas* 65:1, pp. 52–72.

Günzerodt, Werner (1958), "Der erste Roman über Emeljan Pugačev," *Zeitschrift für Slawistik (Berlin)* 3, pp. 711–16.

Hauptmann, Peter (2005), *Russlands Altgläubige*, Göttingen: Vandenhoeck & Ruprecht.

Hoffmann, Peter (1975), "Der Bauernkrieg Unter Der Führung Pugacevs in Der Darstellung Der Deutschsprachigen Historiographie," *Jahrbuch Für Geschichte Der Sozialistischen Länder Europas* 19:2, pp. 147–60.

Hoffmann, Peter (2005), *Gerhard Friedrich Müller (1705–1783): Historiker, Geograph, Archivar im Dienste Russland*, Frankfurt am Main: Lang.

Hoffmann, Peter and Horst Schützler (1962), "Der Pugacev-Aufstand in Zeitgenössischen Deutschen Berichten," *Jahrbuch Für Geschichte Der UdSSR* 6, pp. 337–65.

Kupsch-Losereit, Sigrid (2014), "Pseudotranslations in 18th Century France," in Karlheinz Spitzl and Klaus Kaindl, eds, *Transfiction: Research into the Realities of Translation Fiction*, Philadelphia: John Benjamins, pp. 189–202.

Longworth, Philip (1974), "The Pugachev Revolt: The Last Great Cossack-Peasant Rising," in Henry A. Landsberger, ed., *Rural Protest: Peasant Movements and Social Change*, Basingstoke: Palgrave Macmillan, pp. 194–256.

Madariaga, Isabel De (2014), *Politics and Culture in Eighteenth-Century Russia. Collected Essays by Isabel de Madariaga*, London: Routledge.

Maier, Ingrid and Winfried Schumacher (2009), "Ein Medien-Hype Im 17. Jahrhundert? Fünf Illustrierte Drucke Aus Dem Jahre 1666 Über Die Angebliche Hinrichtung von Sabbatai Zwi," *Quaerendo* 39:2, pp. 133–67.

Myl'nikov, Aleksandr S. (1994), *Die Falschen Zaren: Peter III. Und Seine Doppelgänger in Rußland Und Osteuropa*, Eutiner Forschungen 3, Eutin: Struve.

Natalizi, Marco (2011), *La Rivolta Degli Orfani: La Vicenda Del Ribelle Pugacëv*, Saggi Storia e Scienze Sociali, Roma: Donzelli.

Peters, Dorothea (1973), *Politische und gesellschaftliche Vorstellungen in der Aufstandsbewegung unter Pugacev (1773–1775)*, Forschungen zur osteuropäischen Geschichte 17, Wiesbaden: Harrassowitz.

Plambeck, Petra (1982), *Publizistik im Russland des 18. Jahrhunderts: Analyse der Aufrufe zur Zeit des Pugacev-Aufstandes, 1773–1775*, Hamburger historische Studien 10, Hamburg: Buske.

Pushkin, Aleksandr (2017), *The Captain's Daughter (Illustrated)*, trans. Ekaterina Telfer, Clap Publishing, LLC.

Radishchev, Aleksandr Nikolaevichhg (1958), *A Journey from St. Petersburg to Moscow*, Cambridge, MA: Harvard University Press.

Raynal, Guillaume-Thomas (1713–96) Auteur du texte (1780), *Histoire philosophique et politique des établissemens et du commerce des Européens dans les deux Indes. T. 4*, Geneva: Jean-Leonard Pellet, imprimeur de la Ville & de l'Academie.

Schiller, Friedrich (1799), *Schauplatz der ausgearteten Menschheit oder Nachrichten von den merkwürdigsten Lebensumständen berüchtigter Bösewichter und Betrüger.*

Thompson, Edward Palmer and Guy-Robert Ikni (1988), *La Guerre Du Blé Au XVIIIe Siècle: La Critique Populaire Contre Le Libéralisme Économique Au XVIIIe Siècle*, Librairie Du Bicentenaire de La Révolution Française, Montreuil: Editions de la Passion.

Toury, Gideon (1995), *Descriptive Translation Studies – and Beyond*, Philadelphia: John Benjamins.

Welke, Martin (1976), "Rußland in Der Deutschen Publizistik Des 17. Jahrhunderts, 1613–1689," *Forschungen Zur Osteuropäischen Geschichte* 23, pp. 105–276.

Блок, Г. (1949), *Пушкин в работе над историческими источниками*, Москва: Ленинград.

Болховитинов, Николай Николаевич (1976), *Россия и война США за независимость, 1775–1783*, Москва: Мысль.

Каменский, А. Б. (1989), "Академик Г.-Ф. Миллер и Русская Историческая Наука XVIII в," *История СССР* 1, pp. 146–54.

Курмачева, М. Д. (1983), *Крепостная интеллигенция России: вторая половина XVIII-начало XIX века*, Москва: Наука.

Лехтблау, Л. (1939), "Из Истории Просветительной Литературы в России," *Историк-Марксист* 71:1, pp. 197–202.

Макеев, Сергей (2008), "Королевич Из Голконды," *Совершенно Секретно* 234:11, at <http://www.sovsekretno.ru/articles/id/2040> (last accessed October 20, 2020).

Полное собрание законов Российской империи [Собрание 1-е. С 1649 по 12 дек. 1825 г.] (1830), Vol. 20 [С 1775 по 1780 = № 14233–15105], Санктпетербург: Типография II Отделения Собственной Его Императорскаго Величества Канцелярия, at <http://dlib.rsl.ru/viewer/01003821621#?page=2> (last accessed October 20, 2020).

Пушкин, Александр С. (1834), *История пугачевского бунта*. Санкт Петербург: Типография II Отделения Собственной Е.И.В. Канцелярии.

Пушкин, Александр Сергеевич (1836), "Капитанская дочка," *Современник* 4.

Ростовцева, Ю. А. (2014), "Утопический проект Ивана Тревогина 'Учёная область' и образовательная политика Екатерины Второй," *Педагогика и просвещение* 15:3, pp. 9–16.

Светлов, Л. Б. (1966), "Исчезнувший Журнал," *Литературная Россия* 51.

Старцев, А. И. (1940), "О западных связях Радищева," *Интернациональная литература* 7/8, pp. 256–65.

Старцев, А. И. (1958), "Иван Тревогин – Издатель 'Парнасских Ведомостей,'" *Новый Мир* 9, pp. 278–84.

Степанов, Л. А. (1991), "К истории создания 'Капитанской дочки' (Пушкин и книга 'Ложный Петр III')," *Пушкин: исследования и материалы* 14, pp. 220–34.

Трефилов, Евгений Николаевич (2015), *Пугачев. Жизнь замечательных людей*, Москва: Молодая гвардия.

Черкасов, П. П. (1998), "Людовик XV и Емельян Пугачев: французская дипломатия и восстание Пугачева. По документам дипломатических архивов Франции и России. Вып. 2," in *Россия и Франция: XVIII–XX века*, Москва: Наука, pp. 21–46.

Чечулин, Н. Д. (2011), *Проект Императорского Совета в первый год царствования Екатерины II*, Москва: Книга по требованию.

Эйдельман, Натан (1993), "Где секретная конституция Фонвизина – Панина?," in *Из потаённой истории России XVIII–XIX веков*, Москва: Высшая школа, pp. 214–26.

Эйдельман, Натан Я. (1989), *Мгновенье славы настает . . . Год 1789-й. Историческая библиотека "Петербург – Петроград – Ленинград: Хроника трёх столетий,"* Ленинград: Лениздат.

Chapter 2

"The Tranquil March of the Revolution": German and German-American Reverberations of Mary Wollstonecraft's Writings

Alessa Johns

Mary Wollstonecraft, the feminist author of *A Vindication of the Rights of Woman* (1792), was a progressive thinker advocating radical reform. Nevertheless, after witnessing the turbulent results of revolution in France, she decided that the implementation of liberationist ideas should be the gradual work of many actors over time – a deliberate conversion rather than sudden change via violent rebellion or peremptory decree:

> the pacific progress of every revolution will depend, in a very material degree, on the moderation and reciprocity of concessions made by the acting parties ... The stubborn habits of men, whom personal interest kept firm to their ground, it was morally certain would interrupt the tranquil march of the revolution. (Wollstonecraft 1794: 302)

Continental supporters furthered her ideas about the need for a "tranquil march" to confer broad benefits; they translated and promoted her work over the nineteenth century and across the Atlantic. Here I consider three of her German and German-American advocates – Georg Friedrich Christian Weissenborn, Johann Wilhelm von Archenholz and Mathilde Franziska Anneke. They insured that Wollstonecraft's message of gradual social improvement continued to be read even after her death in 1797, and even after her husband, the anarchist philosopher William Godwin, injudiciously revealed her extramarital liaisons in his *Memoirs of the Author of* A Vindication of the Rights of Woman (1798). Godwin's revelations resulted in a loss of her reputation and, among some in Britain, her credibility, but she retained her influence among German adherents who promoted Wollstonecraft's program to advance women's education and socio-political equality. When British feminists and suffragists later revived Wollstonecraft's ideas in the mid-nineteenth century, spurred in part by international social movements, they were drawing on Wollstonecraftian influences that had not simply taken cover in England but had ricocheted and rebounded from the Continent and America back to Britain, so that her rehabilitation was an international achievement as much as a native British undertaking. Wollstonecraft's career is therefore viewed most productively in an international rather than a strictly national context.

Georg Friedrich Christian Weissenborn (1764–1834): Translating and Teaching Reform

Wollstonecraft's most active German translator was Friedrich Weissenborn, an instructor at the Erziehungsanstalt, the renowned Philanthropist school at Schnepfenthal, Germany (near Gotha, in Thüringen). This institution was established in 1783 by Christian Gotthilf Salzmann, and its pedagogy was inspired by Locke's psychology and Rousseau's concept of natural education. Salzmann had trained at the first renowned Philanthropist establishment, the experimental school at Dessau headed by Johann Bernhard Basedow. Salzmann founded a press at the Erziehungsanstalt, which published widely distributed texts for children, parents and teachers that promoted progressive educational ideas.

In London, Mary Wollstonecraft translated Salzmann's best-known pedagogical work, the *Moralisches Elementarbuch* of 1783, at the suggestion of the liberal English publisher Joseph Johnson. *Elements of Morality for the Use of Children* appeared in 1790, and it made innovative German pedagogical ideas widely available to an English-speaking audience. It was extremely successful and often reprinted: it saw eleven editions brought out in Britain, Ireland and North America between 1790 and 1811.

Some of the institution's progressive impetus was fueled by masonic goals of creating active citizens and cosmopolitan leaders. Duke Ernst II of Sachsen-Gotha-Altenburg, Salzmann's patron who sponsored the school, belonged to the Freemasons and Illuminati, and was committed to furthering their ideas. Salzmann's plan coincided closely with his aims, as Christine Schaubs has pointed out: "The Schnepfenthal

Project could function as a national model for the ethical upbringing of a future, moral elite ... for achieving an orderly, cooperative life of people coming together from different faiths and nationalities and consequently as a model for the cosmopolitan education of humankind" (Schaubs 2005: 305, 306).[1] Salzmann and Weissenborn, too, belonged to the Freemasons, and the school's press and its publications were intended as a way of furthering the moral and physical development of tolerant, healthy citizens of the world.

After Wollstonecraft's translation of the *Elements of Morality* appeared, it seems that she began corresponding with Salzmann; the Erziehungsanstalt reciprocated and published Weissenborn's translations of several of her works. Indeed, Weissenborn actively promoted Wollstonecraft's feminist philosophy over the following years, not only by translating *A Vindication of the Rights of Woman* (1792) as *Rettung der Rechte des Weibes* in 1793–94, but also by rendering Wollstonecraft's *Original Stories from Real Life* (1788) as *Erzählungen für Kinder* in 1795. This was followed by a local (German) publication of Wollstonecraft's English translation of Salzmann's *Elements of Morality*, which Weissenborn used at the school as an English-language acquisition text. Then, he offered a German version of her biography (Godwin's *Memoirs of the Author of* A Vindication of the Rights of Woman, rendered as *Denkschrift auf Maria Wollstonecraft Godwin, die Vertheidigerin der Rechte des Weibes* in 1799). And finally, he composed important feminist articles and reviews, which I will discuss below.

Weissenborn's translations and supporting works furthered a feminist pedagogical politics that was revolutionary, not by virtue of advocating any violent overthrow or radical rebellion, but by calling for reform of a range of social practices, encompassing natural education, human development, gender socialization and future political legislation. It became part of what I have elsewhere called a larger reproductive utopian project that would confront substitutionist revolutionary forms in the late eighteenth and early nineteenth centuries (Johns 2003, 2010). That is, it promoted sustainable shifts in concrete social practices rather than simply and violently replacing one social blueprint with another. In this context Wollstonecraft's politics and Weissenborn's translations dovetail with what Margaret Jacob has characterized as the utopian aims of the Freemasons (Jacob 1991: 224).

Weissenborn's first translation of Wollstonecraft, the *Rettung der Rechte des Weibes* (1793–94), was advertised – as were all Schnepfenthal publications – in Salzmann's vast distribution network, and the publisher participated in the Leipzig book fair, where the text would have been introduced to a large market. Elisabeth Gibbels estimates that Salzmann could have reckoned with a readership of 1,000–2,000, judging from the common printing run of the Schnepfenthal press, and, given a multiplication factor of ten – that is, Gibbels's estimate of the extent to which the texts would have been lent to acquaintances, shared among reading circles, and borrowed from lending libraries – the number of readers might have swelled to 10,000 or even 20,000 (Gibbels 2004: 83–5).

Indeed, the German subscription list suggests that the book was ordered, sometimes twenty copies at a time, across the entire German-speaking region (including what are now parts of Denmark and Poland). Aristocrats of both sexes, academics, military and business men, ministers and their wives, booksellers and printers, even a pharmacist and a pewterer signed up for copies of the book, with two institutions and 121 people (including forty-three women) subscribing. The Schnepfenthal press's vast network was interested in the new pedagogical practices emanating from the Erziehungsanstalt, and translations of foreign texts, particularly English ones, were increasingly in demand.

Salzmann, director of the Erziehungsanstalt, added a preface and footnotes to Weissenborn's translation of *A Vindication*. His paratexts offer a clear indication of a contrast between his and Weissenborn's reception of Wollstonecraft. Salzmann felt obliged to tone down Wollstonecraft's most radical pronouncements, especially those suggesting women's careers and political representation, coeducation for boys and girls, and severe criticism of the aristocracy. For example:

> Mrs. Wollstonecraft must forgive me for contradicting her here. Every businessman realizes that he cannot fulfill the duties toward his children as he would wish; if then his wife were also to desire to participate in governing the state: what would then become of the children? Oh, a wife who fulfills the duties of a mother and raises a few good citizens, does enough for the state and also has such a variety of tasks, that she could hardly have time left over to participate in government. (Wollstonecraft 1793–4: II 214)[2]

Elisabeth Gibbels argues that it was not only Salzmann's more traditional understanding of gender roles but also concern about the possible intervention of the censors that motivated him to include a mollifying preface and this kind of mitigating paratextual material. She emphasizes that Salzmann largely admired Wollstonecraft's *Vindication*, and that the attempt to dampen its radical nature would increase its distribution, reception and acceptance. Gibbels takes her argument further in a subsequent article, where she suggests that German translators of Wollstonecraft's *Vindication* in general unconsciously became "tacit censors" by removing the roughness of Wollstonecraft's heretical text and making it "readable and acceptable ... The fluid, smooth, a-pleasure-to-read translations ... are testimonies to domesticated language use and the results of censorship made natural" (Gibbels 2009: 74–5). It would appear that the process of translation itself, with its aim of making a foreign text understandable to a German audience, thus contributed to soothing the text's inflammatory rhetoric.

Such a softening appears paradoxically to have furthered the scope of the text's subversive influence by increasing its distribution. Laura Kirkley argues that Salzmann sought to endorse a more conservative German approach, among other things, because some German principalities "were still autocratic and would not have permitted the sale or reprinting of a feminist text within their borders" (Kirkley 2009: 196). She goes on to argue that the lost Dutch translation of *A Vindication of the Rights of Woman* (*Verdediging van de Rechten der Vrouwen*, 1796) was probably translated from the German rather than directly from the English, since the evidence suggests that it echoes Salzmann's reservations. Consequently, the Dutch edition invites the conclusion that the German translation proliferated and spread beyond German borders precisely because it was not perceived as controversial or likely to be convulsive. The Danish translation, *Et forsvar for kvindernes rettigheder* (1801), also taken from the German version, was "accented with a satin binding and pink ribbon," according to Eileen Hunt Botting, which "delicately affirmed Salzmann's conservative reading of the book's compatibility with traditional gender roles" (Botting 2016: 45).

Heikki Lempa explains Salzmann's calming interventions by looking less at European socio-politics in general and more at the politics of the Schnepfenthal school itself. He suggests that Salzmann was anxious about the increasing presence and prominence of girls at the school – especially the growing number of Salzmann's own daughters – at an institution that, Lempa argues, he had conceived of to turn boys into (masculine) men. Lempa suggests that translating Wollstonecraft offered Salzmann an opportunity to draw lines.

> Salzmann did not find it difficult to accept some of Wollstonecraft's more radical proposals, such as ... the overall increase in women's intellectual and physical education. But to the political main point

of Wollstonecraft's argument, Salzmann gave the cold shoulder . . . [He] ultimately assigned them to subservience to their husbands and fathers because the man was physically stronger than the woman. (Lempa 2006: 746)

Salzmann's attempt to soften the most radical and anti-aristocratic pronouncements of the text was, on the one hand, a mark of deference to Duke Ernst, who had financed the founding of his institution, and, on the other hand, in keeping with the traditional view of gender roles prevalent in German-speaking lands. It could, however, be argued that, whatever Salzmann's motives, his mollifying footnotes ended up drawing attention to Wollstonecraft's most radical ideas. Indeed, Wollstonecraft's arguments about female education were translated in full; her suggestions for a national system of coeducation for boys and girls were allowed to stand, along with her arguments for women's employment and women's political representation. Salzmann may have inserted his footnotes calling into question the feasibility of expanding the education project into a full national system, and he overtly disagrees with Wollstonecraft's argument for allowing women to have their own political representatives. But nothing is omitted; the words are translated literally on the page. According to Emma Rauschenbusch-Clough, a study of the book's reception suggests that: "The propositions against which the English critic warned the public, seemed to the German critic mere exaggerations, which might well be overlooked, since the book contained so much that was sensible and wise" (Rauschenbusch-Clough 1898: 193).[3]

In fact, Friedrich Weissenborn's translations and especially his articles demonstrate an enthusiastic endorsement of Wollstonecraft's radical feminist philosophy. Weissenborn had come to the Schnepfenthal Erziehungsanstalt after finishing work at the universities of Jena and then Göttingen, where he studied for four years. He learned English and spent time with the Englishmen who were studying there. He then came to Schnepfenthal as tutor to the Princes of Philippsthal, was hired as an instructor at the school in 1792, and in 1796 he married Salzmann's accomplished daughter Wilhelmine, who herself taught geography to the younger pupils ("Weissenborn" *Nekrolog* 1836: 292–5).

Wollstonecraft's standing at the Erziehungsanstalt remained high, not only because of the translations, but also because her work and ideas became a part of the fabric of the institution itself. First, the English language was taught there using Wollstonecraft's *Elements of Morality* – her translation of Salzmann's *Moralisches Elementarbuch*. We know about the curriculum from the institution's newsletter, the *Nachrichten aus Schnepfenthal: für die Eltern und Freunde der dasigen Zöglinge.* This newsletter was basically a diary of the institution; it was published regularly, and was collected into yearly accounts uninterrupted from 1786 to 1903. It offered interested parties a thoroughgoing description of the pedagogical project at Schnepfenthal, with details for parents about their own children's progress. The *Nachrichten* entries, initially dated every two or three days, include, for example, summaries of the content of devotional lectures (they were not called sermons, in keeping with the school's aims of tolerance and cosmopolitanism), the names of visitors, lists of students who excelled at exercises in all fields from geography to languages to physical education, names of instrumental pieces performed by the students, and even reports about the weather and measurements of the children's physical growth. The Erziehungsanstalt enjoyed an international reputation and was attended by children of the established classes and the nobility, including, for example, sons of the aristocratic families of Schaumburg-Lippe, Battenberg, Sachsen-Weimar and Hessen-Philippsthal-Barchfeld. It also graduated such notable figures as Julius Beerbohm, a merchant who moved to England but then sent his three sons to study at the Erziehungsanstalt: Herbert, who became a renowned actor and manager; Ernst; and Julius, who gained fame for his exploration of Patagonia. There were eight members of the Brockhaus publishing family; the scholar Carl Ritter; and Goetz von Berlichingen, a descendant of the man portrayed in Goethe's drama (Lindner 2006). A sample of English instruction appears in the record for May 10, 1809: the students were tested on recitation of a memorized English passage; they read aloud, then translated from Wollstonecraft's version of the *Elements of Morality*; and they were subsequently given a German letter to translate orally into English (*Nachrichten aus Schnepfenthal*, May 10, 1809: 36).[4]

Weissenborn's most lively and heartfelt advocacy, however, appeared in his written articles and reviews. In the first issue of the *Bibliothek der pädagogischen Literatur*, edited by the famous geography and physical education instructor Johann Christoph Friedrich GutsMuths, Weissenborn contributed a long article (that extended into the second issue) titled "How the female sex has been set back up to now" ("Ueber die bisherige Zurücksetzung des weiblichen Geschlechts"). It makes Wollstonecraftian arguments about how moral progress will be hindered if half of the population is kept down; it sees humans holistically, as physical, mental and spiritual beings who need to engage the world on all levels; it views marriages as political as well as emotional unions, where partners carry out their socio-political duty and where true friendship is impossible without equality; and it suggests that, while domesticity is a social good, and both men and women must act as effective parents, this is only part of their socio-political existence: women, like men, need to be able to find happiness in the pursuit of a calling they themselves select. "All individuals must be allowed to seek their happiness where they wish, as soon as they can reason, and as soon as, because of this, they do not seek their wellbeing in something immoral." However, in nineteenth-century Germany this was not yet the case: "Women's happiness is restricted solely to domestic pleasures," he points out, and "the husband also looms as the head of domestic society, just as he does in civil society" (Weissenborn 1800: 1:1, 81–99 and 1:2, 195–210, 204, 205). So Weissenborn urges women to be strong: "Just have the courage to be strong, and you will be! Seek to become that, which you ought to be, and one will be obliged to give you what you are owed! Become familiar with your duties: and one will not be able to deny you your rights!" (209).[5] Weissenborn recognizes that this will take time; it is not the work of a single book or battle or change in government. Indeed, these times of upheaval, which are "bound up with the most terrible internal and external wars" (205), make such progress *less* likely. It will instead be the work of generations:

> if you cannot yet dare to demand these rights for yourselves, then at least seek to gain for posterity what you must still do without. Educate your daughters better than you yourselves were educated, and thereby clear the path for them to educate their own daughters even better. A future, happier and better generation will bless you for it one day; and the consciousness of having prepared something good for the future will diminish the pains of the present for you. (210)[6]

Improvement will happen gradually and reproductively: that is, by the individual, incremental effort of each mother to raise and teach her daughters, so that eventually, across nations and time, all women will enjoy greater happiness.

Angelika Bammer, studying the 1970s, and drawing on the theories of Ernst Bloch, has argued that feminist authors of that era redefined revolution: "Revolution was defined in terms of process. And the concept of utopia became concrete" (Bammer 1991: 2). I have argued, in my book on *Women's Utopias of the Eighteenth Century*, that Enlightenment women anticipated this transformation; they imagined the spread of utopian ideas and practices through a process of reproduction or replication, where families and communities would improve themselves and then expand outward through time and space, teaching social change to neighbors, new generations and societies beyond (Johns 2003: 2). Friedrich Weissenborn picks up on this idea in Wollstonecraft and sees women's rights asserted, not through the substitutional approach that came to be associated with the French Revolution, but through a revolutionary *process*, a "tranquil" revolution, that worked incrementally and that nonetheless aimed to change the world.

The example of reciprocal translations – that is, Friedrich Weissenborn as translator of Wollstonecraft's revolutionary work and Wollstonecraft as translator of Salzmann's work – reveals a transnational network of progressives interested in promoting enlightened pedagogy that, by teaching new views of gender roles and domestic authority, would instill a different approach in the new generation, which would pass it on to its own progeny and thereby spread enlightenment through time and space. A product of the 1790s, their work partook of French Revolutionary fervor, but it changed form, outlasted the violence of the period, and promoted educational reform in European countries and colonies into the nineteenth century.

Johann Wilhelm von Archenholz (1741–1812): Circulating the "Tranquil" Revolution

Like Weissenborn, Johann Wilhelm von Archenholz emphasized Wollstonecraft's ideas about the importance of gradual and steady reform – a "tranquil march of the revolution" – doing this most emphatically through a translation of long segments from Wollstonecraft's *Historical and Moral View of the French Revolution*, which he published in his well-respected journal *Minerva*. Archenholz, also a Freemason, spent six years in Britain on three trips between 1769 and 1779 and wrote an important travel book comparing England and Italy (*England und Italien*, 1785). A translation of the English portion appeared as *A Picture of England* in 1789.[7] He produced a standard history of the Seven Years' War among other prominent historical books. He also edited English-language journals in Hamburg (the *English Lyceum* and the *British Mercury* (1787–90)) that offered extracts from current British periodicals; and he published a German-language series about British history (*Annalen der brittischen* (sic) *Geschichte*, 20 vols, 1788–96, index 1800), which was advertised as a continuation of *England und Italien*, even though it was all about Britain. This periodical contained notices of many women writers and performers – for example, Frances Burney, Elizabeth Inchbald, Angelika Kauffman, Elizabeth Montagu,

Hester Lynch Piozzi, Ann Radcliffe, Anna Seward, Sarah Siddons, Charlotte Smith, Hannah Sowden, Eliza Dorothea Tuite, Priscilla Wakefield, Anne Yearsley – and it included two reviews of Mary Wollstonecraft's books.[8]

Archenholz's conflicted feelings about the French Revolution paralleled Wollstonecraft's to a good extent, and might have led him to include his translation of her history. Archenholz was initially excited about the French Revolution and moved to Paris to write about it. He frequented the German Club headed by Count von Schlabrendorf, who expressed great admiration for Wollstonecraft as a thinker and a person.[9] Archenholz was disappointed at the turn to violence and bloodshed during the Terror and had to abscond back to Germany to avoid being guillotined for his unflattering, critical publications. He settled in Hamburg and continued to edit his historical and political periodical *Minerva*. This was a liberal magazine, read by such prominent authors as Johann Wolfgang von Goethe and Friedrich Schiller, that intended to offer multi-faceted views of past and current events, with not only attention to factual presentation but also incisive analysis. The motto of *Minerva* was in English, taken from Hamlet's speech to the players emphasizing the need to hold a mirror up to nature: "To show . . . the very age and body of the time, its form and pressure" (Act III, Scene 2).

Perhaps with this in mind, Archenholz decided to offer *Minerva* readers a long excerpt from Wollstonecraft's *An Historical and Moral View of the Origin and Progress of the French Revolution; and the Effect It Has Produced in Europe* (*Minerva* 1795: 157–76).[10] (The commonly used abridged form of Wollstonecraft's title, *An Historical and Moral View of the French Revolution*, fails to convey her intention of emphasizing the impact of the revolution beyond France's borders.) Wollstonecraft's work was published by Joseph Johnson in 1794, and the German translation appeared in *Minerva* in January 1795. Archenholz introduces Wollstonecraft as an "Englishwoman well-known through her writings" and calls her the author of several novels and works on education, morals and the rights of women (*Minerva* 1795: 157).[11] Having left France before Wollstonecraft arrived, Archenholz could not have met Wollstonecraft herself; in fact, in his headnote to the translation he furthers an erroneous rumor that she was imprisoned in Paris and spared execution only because of the death of Robespierre.

However, despite his imperfect knowledge of Wollstonecraft's biography, Archenholz's grasp of her intentions for reform is sure. The passages Archenholz chooses to present ascribe the chaos following the storming of the Bastille to the moral failings of the revolutionary leaders, and, in particular, to their inability to work with others. Instead of being guided by patriotism, their vanity leads them to abandon the cause just when they should be cooperating to devise social improvements for all people, not merely to attain glory for themselves. The upshot proves disastrous for the nation. Tellingly, the parts Archenholz omits, aside from detailed summaries of events and verbatim transcriptions of National Assembly debates, are those focused on denouncements of specific aristocrats – perhaps to avoid legal repercussions or censorship – and philosophical-historical explanations about how the course of civilization will privilege "domestic felicity" over war and "the false glory of sanguinary devastation" (Wollstonecraft 1794: 308–9). This is not because Archenholz favors fighting; indeed, he includes Wollstonecraft's critique of needless wars carried on by courts that simply wish to perpetuate their power (*Minerva* 1795: 166). Instead, he appears to disagree with the philosophical approach to historiography employed by Wollstonecraft and/or to dislike her focus on the virtues of domesticity.

Archenholz's main concerns are revealed in his repeated choice of passages from Wollstonecraft supporting gradual reform and peaceful social improvement based on the increased virtue of a free people. To start off with, the title of the excerpt avoids the language of rebellion or uprising and focuses instead "On the French and their Change of Government" (*Minerva* 1795: 157).[12] He then begins the body of the translation with Wollstonecraft's declaration that "Vanity had made every Frenchman a theorist," in Book III, Chapter 3, a portion that considers the meeting of the Estates-General, and includes her long derogatory characterization of a self-important French leadership:

> selfishness being incompatible with noble, comprehensive, or laudable views, it is not wonderful, keeping in sight the national foible, that at the meeting of the states-general every deputy had his particular plan to suggest. Few of the leaders embraced the same; and acting, without coalescing, the most violent measures were sure to be the most applauded ... had they combined, and directed their views by a pure love of their country, to one point; all the disasters, which in overwhelming the empire have destroyed the repose of Europe, would not have occurred to disgrace the cause of freedom.
>
> Every great reform requires systematic management; and however lightly weak daring heads may treat the gravity of such a remark, the pacific progress of every revolution will depend, in a very material degree, on the moderation and reciprocity of concessions made by the acting parties ... It was peculiarly urgent, indeed, to form such a

coalition, to counteract the dangerous consequences of old prejudices. The stubborn habits of men, whom personal interest kept firm to their ground, it was morally certain would interrupt the tranquil march of the revolution ["den ruhigen Gang der Revolution"]. (Wollstonecraft 1794: III. 3. 299, 301–2; *Minerva* 1795: 158, 160–1)[13]

"The tranquil march of the revolution" depends on collaboration, deliberation, consensus and gradual implementation, as opposed to the pushy individual theorizations of Frenchmen suffering from vanity, "the national foible." Archenholz renders Wollstonecraft's critique in a careful, fairly literal translation (see his version in note 13) that only gently adjusts syntax but fully captures her aggravation at the French leaders' moral limitations.

As with Weissenborn's use of Wollstonecraft's arguments, Archenholz proceeds to uphold Wollstonecraft's preferred vision of a slower, piecemeal solution. His next section takes up Book IV, Chapter 1 of Wollstonecraft, where the emphasis is again on how "The revolutions of states ought to be gradual" (1794: IV. 1. 355) ("Revolutionen müssen ihrer Natur nach Stufenweise geschehn" (*Minerva* 1795: 169)):

> When the members of a state are not directed by practical knowledge, every one produces a plan of polity, till the confusion becomes general, and the nation plunges into wretchedness, pursuing the schemes of those philosophers of genius who, advancing before their age, have sketched the model of a perfect system of government. Thus it happened in France, that Hume's idea of a perfect commonwealth ... was nevertheless chosen as the model of their new government, with few exceptions, by the constituent assembly: which choice doubtless proceeded from the members not having had an opportunity to acquire a knowledge of practical liberty. Some of the members, it is true, alluded to the improvements made by the americans on the plan of the english constitution; but the great majority, despising experience, were for forming, at once, a system much more perfect. And this self-sufficiency has produced those dreadful outrages, and attacks, made by the anarchists of that country, on personal liberty, property, and whatever else society holds sacred. (Wollstonecraft 1794: 356–7; *Minerva* 1795: 169–71)

Wollstonecraft's critique targets the intellectual visions of the ideal state, the complete theorizations and blueprints that do not leave room for contingency, practical experience, or natural evolution that she sees in this instance as a hallmark of Anglo-American methods.

Interestingly, instead of being entirely bound to the current events in France, Wollstonecraft's critique draws also on the longstanding bluestocking style of utopianism I have discussed elsewhere, a tradition that expresses distaste for completed visions of a perfect society or "blueprint utopias," and instead voices preference for a gradual, peaceful and practical movement toward social happiness (Johns 2010).[14] Witnessing social upheaval firsthand in France, Wollstonecraft sees advantages in a less radical and slower, but perhaps in the long term more grounded, sustainable and successful, reform.

Archenholz completes his translation with a passage from Book V, Chapter 4, in which Wollstonecraft argues that courts and the luxury to which they were dedicated led to the development of cities, but that in a republic, as virtue takes hold of individuals, they will return to the country, leaving cities like Paris to "crumble into decay":

> In proportion as the charms of solitary reflection and agricultural recreations are felt, the people, by leaving the villages and cities, will give a new complexion to the face of the country – and we may then look for a turn of mind more solid, principles more fixed, and a conduct more consistent and virtuous (Wollstonecraft 1794: 508; *Minerva* 1795: 176).

In this vision, Wollstonecraft echoes the kind of gradual utopianization expressed by bluestocking Sarah Scott in *Millenium Hall* (1762): the luxuries, corruptions and competition of the city give way to a moral, prudent, harmonious way of life in the country which, through a virtuous style of social reproduction (i.e. the education of children by a group of enterprising bluestockings and marriage among the country folk promoted by them), colonizes the rest of the countryside (Johns 2003: 91–109).

Archenholz's translation of carefully selected passages consequently emphasizes Wollstonecraft's justification for political change: that it generates moral renewal in all classes, leading to social and environmental reform, with communities striving together to cultivate the earth, promote the wellbeing of animals and enhance the landscape. This, to Wollstonecraft, represents the "tranquil march" of a successful revolution, which unfortunately is not what is transpiring in France. Nor in Archenholz's estimation is it happening in Britain, where a previously vaunted British liberty is vanishing. Wollstonecraft's words represent, in Archenholz's view, a laudable but obsolescent British influence. In the *Annalen* published in 1794, Archenholz laments that "The British virtues, that used to shine supreme on account of their substance in the moral history of Europe, have for the most part ceased to be an object of wonder to the nations" because of the great limitations on individual freedom, the increase in luxury, and the regression of the culture in general on account of Britain's reactionary politics (*Annalen* 1794: 379).[15]

Mathilde Franziska Anneke (1817–1884): Trans-Atlantic Advocacy

Despite this, in America Mary Wollstonecraft the feminist continued to be a model of a spirited, independent thinker for German women and men into the nineteenth century, conveying in a modern idiom a longstanding ideal of British liberty. The example of Mathilde Franziska Anneke demonstrates how Wollstonecraft's message survived the Napoleonic period and came to be translated across the Atlantic in order to promote progressive views among German immigrants in the United States.

German immigrants did not all come to America to live out revolutionary goals in the early nineteenth century, but they were incited to adopt progressive viewpoints by Anneke, who herself *did* participate in the 1848 revolution, fighting alongside her husband, Fritz Anneke, and who was forced to flee to the United States. There she became associated with socialist and feminist advocates such as Susan B. Anthony, Elizabeth Cady Stanton and Lucretia Mott (Anderson 2000: 10, 25–6). As Michaela Bank has argued, Anneke's value to American reformers was "as a mediator and translator between the women's rights movement and the German-American community"; she was a "woman of two countries," whose "foreignness became the source of her power" (Bank 2012: 104–5). Anneke thus contributed to the movement by furthering the political education of fellow German-Americans in the German language, and she employed the writings of Mary Wollstonecraft along with those of other contemporary feminists to lend weight to her arguments for women's rights and abolition.

Anneke explained her career and intentions in a biographical letter to Alexander Jonas, who had written to an aged Anneke in 1877 asking her to describe her life, publications and political efforts for his planned History of the Feminist Movement among Germans in the United States. (The book, it seems, never appeared.) Her long response offers the best information we have about her feminist goals. She began as "a victim of the Prussian justice system" (*ein Opfer der preussischen Justiz*) during inequitable proceedings for divorce from her first husband (Friesen 1977: 35). She was then moved to action by "the golden book" of Theodor Gottlieb von Hippel, *On Improving the Status of Women* (*Ueber die bürgerliche Verbesserung der Weiber*, 1792), which she excerpted in the *Deutsche Frauen-Zeitung*, a German-language newspaper she founded in Milwaukee in 1852.

It was there in the *Deutsche Frauen-Zeitung* that Anneke translated Mary Wollstonecraft as well. She reports that she offered "translations from Mary Wollstonecraft, Margaret Fuller and others" (Friesen 1977: 37), giving her German readers an education in feminist argument and history. Anneke published the *Deutsche Frauen-Zeitung* for two and a half years. Unfortunately, there is only one extant issue of the paper (15 October 1852), and there are no known existing copies of the numbers that included the translation of *A Vindication of the Rights of Woman* (Anderson 2000: 69; Botting 2013: 519).

However, we do have copies of another German-American newspaper for which Anneke wrote feminist articles: the *New-Yorker Criminal-Zeitung und Belletristisches Journal*, founded by Rudolph Lexow in 1852. No scholars have yet discussed Anneke's contributions to the *Belletristisches Journal*, but they are worth considering, as her articles reveal how she communicated as a feminist – in keeping with the pattern of gradualist utopianism I have described, sounding Wollstonecraftian themes. The series of articles she wrote brings together examples of mistreated German, American and British women under the title: *Licht- und Schattenbilder aus dem Leben verschiedener Frauen* (Pictures of Light and Shadows from the Lives of Various Women).

The women Anneke portrays are the German Louise Aston, the American Ann Wheeler, the American writer Margaret Fuller, and the British poet Felicia Hemans. Louise Aston was a controversial figure whom Anneke had written about in her earlier polemic, *Woman in Conflict with Society* (*Das Weib im Konflikt mit den socialen Verhältnissen*, 1847). Aston was a divorced woman banished from Berlin because of her beliefs, and Anneke uses her example to expatiate on the injustices of gender inequality and the narrow compass of women's action and women's lives.[16]

The second article tells the story of an 1852 Milwaukee murder. Ann Wheeler was abused by John Lace, whom she then shot to death in broad daylight. The sensational trial that followed resulted in Wisconsin's first verdict of temporary insanity. Anneke, however, concludes that Wheeler was *not* insane: "it was self defense, to free herself and humankind from a brute." Anneke speaks especially to German women, invoking their assumptions about cultural differences and even playing to their national prejudices: how can we know what American women's passions are when such enormous differences exist between the sincerity and devotion of an American and a German woman? But she then uses the story to insist that, while one does not wish to justify murder, nonetheless it is understandable and "who would dare to accuse her?" Anneke thereby urges Germans to cross the cultural divide, to overcome national pride, and to take the side of the betrayed American young woman.[17]

The next two articles focus on female authors. The third, about Margaret Fuller, emphasizes Fuller's precociousness, remarkable education, authorship of *Woman in the Nineteenth Century*, and her professional life as editor of the *Dial* and reporter in Europe. Anneke is especially interested in Fuller's involvement in the 1848 revolutions in Rome, where she worked indefatigably as a nurse. She also dwells on the final scenes of the shipwreck in which Fuller, her Italian husband Count Ossoli, and their daughter drowned just before arriving back in the United States.[18] The fourth piece, in two parts, covers British poet Felicia Hemans, who was also precocious. Her husband left her, but her mother served as a crucial support in her attempt to raise her five sons. Hemans was interested in German literature, especially Schiller and Goethe; she knew many European languages, undertook translations, and appreciated and wrote about foreign cultures. Later, her dutiful son Isidor, studying in Bonn, Germany, sought a translator for his mother's poems.[19]

Anneke thus supplies remarkable biographies of four extraordinary international women who offer plenty of evidence of Anneke's Wollstonecraftian impulses. She emphasizes the plight of the female genius, the need for women's systematic education, the importance of women being able to work and to control the money they earn, the oppression they suffer due to legal and political inequality, their need for political representation, their right to emotional freedom and freedom from violence, and their fortitude in spite of their profound disadvantages.

Anneke gave speeches as well. In 1852 she undertook a seven-month lecture tour taking in Chicago, Cleveland, New York, Boston, Philadelphia, Baltimore, Cincinnati, Louisville, Dayton, Pittsburgh and elsewhere, and she was invited to speak at several national conventions as well as before a Senate Committee at the

U.S. Capitol. Her Washington D.C. speech was, unusually, delivered in English, and a Mrs. Hooker described her performance:

> Madame Anneke, the German patriot who fought with her husband and slept beside her horse in the field, carried the day over everyone else. It was fairly overwhelming to hear her English, so surcharged with feeling yet so exact in the choice of words, and the burden of it all was that the trials of the battle-field were as naught compared to this inward struggle of her soul toward liberty for woman. Her presence, gestures, oratory were simply magnificent. (Friesen 1977: 44, note 46)

Anneke's life and works thus furthered feminist and, more particularly, Wollstonecraftian goals. Not only did Anneke focus on women's lives and public achievements in her writing; she became fully engaged in the campaigns for women's suffrage and abolition; she toured and gave public lectures; she founded her feminist newspaper (where she sought to reserve women jobs as typesetters, a move that met with resistance from male workers); and, toward the end of her life, she set up and ran a girls' school. Called the "Milwaukee Töchter-Institut," it offered a solid general education: "German and English language including grammar, essay writing, literature and conversation; the French language; world and cultural history; the fields of geography, natural science and arithmetic; drawing, music, and rhetoric; and finally women's handiwork" (Piepke 2006: 118). She thus sought through education to engender change in the next generation.[20]

Conclusion

In sum, Wollstonecraft's work received sustained, serious and positive attention on the Continent and in the United States, with translations of a variety of her writings appearing remarkably soon after the original English versions became available, and reviews and renewed editions ensuring the continued circulation of her ideas through time and space. Given Wollstonecraft's regard on the Continent and in America, her British rehabilitation in the mid-nineteenth century would appear to have depended at least as much on her positive reception beyond Britain as on native British efforts (Johns 2020: 328). Indeed, the movement from Weissenborn to Archenholz to Anneke demonstrates a "tranquil march of the revolution" across Germany and across the Atlantic to America. Wollstonecraft's feminist vision easily came to accommodate cosmopolitan and masonic elements and then also encompassed early socialist content too. Wollstonecraft's message appealed to men as well as to women, to Germans and Americans as well as to British radicals, with its international, utopian, egalitarian and feminist concerns (Chernock 2010; Johns 2014: 39–87; Johns 2020). As Barbara Taylor put it:

> The *Vindication* is usually described as the founding text of modern bourgeois feminism . . . and yet the interpretation is not adequate. Both in terms of content and context, Wollstonecraft's . . . writings represented a high point of democratic radicalism in its revolutionary phase: an extended manifesto linking the emancipation of women to the social and political liberation of "the people" as a whole. (Taylor 1983: 5)

Early socialists took Wollstonecraft's ideas into account in a process of transnational "cross-fertilization" involving German, French, English, Irish, Scottish and American adherents, many of whom traveled and acted internationally in the early nineteenth century to promote progressive reforms (Botting 2013: 519; Taylor 1983: 59–70). Activists such as Flora Tristan, Jeanne Deroin, Anna Wheeler, Frances Wright, Fredrika Bremer, Anna Jameson, Margaret Fuller and others, in addition to Mathilde Franziska Anneke, all advanced Wollstonecraft's agenda in the first decades of the nineteenth century and have in fact been characterized by Bonnie S. Anderson as the "First International Women's Movement" (Anderson 2000).

Consequently, the generally positive reception of Wollstonecraft's translations on the Continent, the persistence of her ideas in European discourses on education and women's roles, as well as her lionizing in the United States – all of these made themselves felt in British intellectual and progressive circles via mediators and networks. They translated Wollstonecraft's arguments into the Victorian era to press for women's education, work opportunities, married women's separate property rights, divorce and suffrage, seeking thoroughgoing social, political and economic reform. As a result, a national British figure like Mary Wollstonecraft is actually viewed more clearly from an *international* vantage point; German translators and reviewers, as I have argued, played a significant role in promoting her message so that it would reverberate meaningfully across time and space.

Bibliography

Anderson, Bonnie S. (2000), *Joyous Greetings: The First International Women's Movement 1830–1860*, New York: Oxford University Press.

Annalen der brittischen Geschichte des Jahrs 1792 (1794), ed. Johann Wilhelm von Archenholz, Volume 9, Section 9, Carlsruhe: Schmieder.

Archenholz, Johann Wilhelm von (1789), *A Picture of England: Containing a Description of the Laws, Customs, and Manners of England*, London: Edward Jeffery.

Bammer, Angelika (1991), *Partial Visions: Feminism and Utopianism in the 1970s*, New York: Routledge.

Bank, Michaela (2012), *Women of Two Countries: German-American Women, Women's Rights, and Nativism, 1848–1890*, New York: Berghahn Books.

Botting, Eileen Hunt (2013), "Wollstonecraft in Europe, 1792–1904: A Revisionist Reception History," *History of European Ideas* 39:4, pp. 503–27.

Botting, Eileen Hunt (2016), *Wollstonecraft, Mill, and Women's Human Rights*, New Haven: Yale University Press.

Chernock, Arianne (2010), *Men and the Making of Modern British Feminism*, Stanford: Stanford University Press.

Friesen, Gerhard K. (1977), "A Letter from M. F. Anneke: A Forgotten German-American Pioneer in Women's Rights," *Journal of German-American Studies* 12:2, pp. 34–46.

Gibbels, Elisabeth (2004), *Mary Wollstonecraft zwischen Feminismus und Opportunismus: Die diskursiven Strategien in deutschen Übersetzungen von "A Vindication of the Rights of Woman,"* Tübingen: Gunter Narr Verlag.

Gibbels, Elisabeth (2009), "Translators, the Tacit Censors," in Eiléan Ní Chuilleanáin, ed., *Translation and Censorship: Patterns of Communication and Interference*, Dublin: Four Courts Press, pp. 57–75.

Jacob, Margaret (1991), *Living the Enlightenment: Freemasonry and Politics in Eighteenth-Century Europe*, New York: Oxford University Press.

Jochmann, Carl Gustav (1836), *Reliquien: Aus seinen nachgelassenen Papieren*, ed. Heinrich Zschokke, Hechingen: Ribler.

Johns, Alessa (2003), *Women's Utopias of the Eighteenth Century*, Urbana: University of Illinois Press.

Johns, Alessa (2010), "Feminism and Utopianism," in Gregory Claeys, ed., *The Cambridge Companion to Utopian Literature*, Cambridge: Cambridge University Press, pp. 174–99.

Johns, Alessa (2014), *Bluestocking Feminism and British-German Cultural Transfer, 1750–1837*, Ann Arbor: University of Michigan Press.

Johns, Alessa (2020), "Translations," in Nancy E. Johnson and Paul Keen, eds, *Mary Wollstonecraft in Context*, Cambridge: Cambridge University Press, pp. 323–31.

Kirkley, Laura (2009), "Feminism in Translation: Re-Writing the *Rights of Woman*," in Tom Toremans and Walter Verschueren, eds, *Crossing Cultures: Nineteenth-Century Anglophone Literature in the Low Countries*, Leuven: Leuven University Press, pp. 189–200.

Lempa, Heikki (2006), "Patriarchalism and Meritocracy: Evaluating Students in Late Eighteenth-Century Schnepfenthal," *Paedagogica Historica* 42:6, pp. 727–49.

Lindner, Frank (2006), *Schülerwege aus Schnepfenthal*, Bucha bei Jena: Quartus Verlag.
Maurer, Michael (1987), *Aufklärung und Anglophilie in Deutschland*, Göttingen: Vandenhoeck & Ruprecht.
Minerva (1795), ed. Johann Wilhelm von Archenholz, Volume 13, Number 1.
Nachrichten aus Schnepfenthal: für die Eltern und Freunde der dasigen Zöglinge (1786–1903), Schnepfenthal: Erziehungsanstalt.
New-Yorker Criminal-Zeitung und Belletristisches Journal (1859), Volume VII, Numbers 47, 48, 50, and Volume VIII.
Piepke, Susan L. (2006), *Mathilde Franziska Anneke (1817–1884): The Works and Life of a German-American Activist*, New York: Peter Lang.
Rauschenbusch-Clough, Emma (1898), *A Study of Mary Wollstonecraft and* The Rights of Woman, New York: Longmans, Green, and Co.
Schaubs, Christine (2005), "Ernst II. und der Einfluss der geheimen Gesellschaften auf die Gründung der Erziehungsanstalt Schnepfenthal," in Werner Greiling, Andreas Klinger and Christoph Koehler, eds, *Ernst II. von Sachsen-Gotha-Altenburg: Ein Herrscher im Zeitalter der Aufklärung*, Cologne: Böhlau, pp. 295–309.
Taylor, Barbara (1983), *Eve and the New Jerusalem: Socialism and Feminism in the Nineteenth Century*, New York: Pantheon Books.
Weissenborn, Georg Friedrich Christian (1800), "Über die bisherige Zurücksetzung des weiblichen Geschlechts," *Bibliothek der pädagogischen Literatur* 1:1, pp. 81–99, and 1:2, pp. 195–210.
"Weissenborn, Georg Friedrich Christian," *Neuer Nekrolog der Deutschen 1834* (1836), Volume 12, Part 1, Weimar: Voigt, pp. 292–5.
Wollstonecraft, Mary (1792), *A Vindication of the Rights of Woman, with Strictures on Political and Moral Subjects*, London: J. Johnson.
Wollstonecraft, Maria (1793–94), *Rettung der Rechte des Weibes*, trans. Friedrich Weissenborn, intro. and notes Christian Gotthilf Salzmann, 2 vols., Schnepfenthal: Erziehungsanstalt.
Wollstonecraft, Mary (1794), *An Historical and Moral View of the Origin and Progress of the French Revolution; and the Effect It Has Produced in Europe, Volume the First*, London: J. Johnson.

Chapter 3

Translation as Conceptual Reverberation: "Revolution" in Wales 1688–1937

Marion Löffler

"Revolution," according to Reinhart Koselleck, is a "basic concept of modernity" ("ein Grundbegriff der Moderne"), whose meanings "in their diversity and complexity, were not bundled until 1789" ("in ihrer Vielfalt und Komplexität erst 1789 gebündelt wurden") (Brunner, Conze and Koselleck 1994: 653). These declarations, which introduce over 200 pages of reflections in the eight-volume historical encyclopedia of politico-social language *Geschichtliche Grundbegriffe* published by Otto Brunner, Werner Conze and Reinhart Koselleck between 1972 and 1997, highlight not only the significance of "revolution" as a political concept, but also the central place of the French Revolution of 1789 in its history. This chapter will chart the conceptual reverberations of "revolution" in the British Isles from 1688 to the beginning of the twentieth century in the largely unexplored cultural space of Welsh, one of the politically subordinate Celtic languages spoken there. Tracking the development of "revolution" enables us to observe social and political changes and conceptual peculiarities in the British Isles; analyzing the terms created by translation to express "revolution" allows us to explore the relationship between translation and political concepts. It is hoped that this analysis, in addition to highlighting the central role of the 1789 caesura, will also contribute to our knowledge of the "lingering impact of the ground-breaking rebellion against British rule in the American colonies" in British political life (Verhoeven 2013: 3).

Conceptualizing "Revolution"

While it is impossible in a piece of this length to sketch the general development of a key concept like revolution and its expression, or to review the literature on it, a few main stages in its development may be suggested. "Revolutio" was first documented in early Christian literature referencing the removal of the stone from Christ's grave, and the transmigration of the soul. As a loan word, it first appeared in French in the twelfth century, in English in the late fourteenth, and in German in the early modern period (Bulst 1994: 670–89). As a political concept, it entered European thought via astronomy in 1543, in the form of a metaphor based on Copernicus's *De revolutionis orbium caelestium* (Koselleck 1994: 717–18; 2004: 46). Like the celestial objects repeating their never-ending circle, revolutions referred to calamitous events that befell both countries and humans and concluded with a return to the previous state of affairs. In this, the concept was close to a "bundle" of meanings inherited from early modernity, which included civil war, uprising, riot and rebellion (Koselleck 2006: 243). The repetitive element of the metaphor also chimed with the classical notion of the "circulation of constitutions" which envisaged monarchy as the natural form of rule, whose corruption led to aristocracy, oligarchy, democracy and ochlocracy, before the return of monarchy (Koselleck 2004: 45). The Cromwellian revolution and Commonwealth experiment in England, which concluded with the return of Charles II to the throne, were perceived as examples of this cycle (Koselleck 1994: 718–19; 2004: 46; 2006: 243). As the eighteenth century progressed, revolution acquired the potential to enable a quasi-religious salvation, the possibility of achieving a higher, more perfect state of existence as a result of its completion. At the same time, awareness grew that this achievement might be preceded by a phase of violence (Koselleck 2006: 243–4). Enlightenment philosophers added an interpretation of revolution as a "dynamic transformational process, an expression of the historical rhythm of the progress of the human mind" undertaken by humans themselves, and confirmed by the American Revolution of 1775 (Koselleck 2004: 43–56). From the 1780s, French political writing also defined "revolution as crisis," a looming catastrophe that would make or break European civilization in the near future (Baker 1990: 212). These apparently contradictory elements of the concept explain why the French Revolution was cautiously welcomed by leading philosophers, writers and politicians in Europe, and initially defended even after the first acts of violence against the French royal family. At the same time, political discourse established *the* 1789 revolution in France as a most important singular, man-made occurrence which fundamentally changed the social and political order (Baker 1990: 202–3; Roger 2000: 315). Since 1789, the two main uses of the concept have been to reference sudden, violent and fundamental political changes, but also long-term structural developments arising from the past and affecting the future, indicated in uses like the "industrial revolution" (Koselleck 2006: 241). While these semantics were fully developed by around 1800, "revolution" has continued to take on new connotations (Koselleck 2006: 245).

The British State, the Welsh Language and Translation

Located to the west of England on the shores of the Irish Sea, Wales was peripheral to European absolutist monarchies, battlegrounds and centers of political power. It had been united with the expanding English Tudor state by the Acts of Union of 1536 and 1542, and was incorporated into England with the Wales and Berwick Act of 1746. News of political upheavals echoed from afar here, filtered through English politics and the English language. Welsh, the Celtic language spoken by the majority of the population, had been politically subordinate since the 1536 Act of Union had declared English the official language for the whole kingdom. Not unusually for multi-ethnic states, colonization sparked translation activity to support governance and aid political unity, but translation also came to be utilized for the expression of private political opinions. Like other European cultures, Wales developed a print culture in the wake of the Welsh Bible translation of 1588 (Roberts 1997: 407–40). Reading religious texts was taught in "circulating schools" so that a relatively high percentage of the population was literate in their native language (White 1997: 235–87). Yet, until after the Napoleonic Wars, most publications in Welsh were translations from English. The introduction and expression of new political concepts was thus influenced by and depended on translation.

Translation activity in the political domain resulted from political crises which concerned Wales directly, such as the Jacobite rebellion of 1715, the American War of Independence of 1775–83 and the French Revolution of 1789 – which featured an attempted invasion of west Wales in 1797 (Davies 2013: 247–70). For the resulting political texts, a vocabulary expressing key concepts like "revolution" and "republic" was required. Considering the creation of a political vocabulary under such circumstances, concerns that translators into small languages "become the grave-diggers of their own language by accepting borrowings on a large scale" or maintain "the standards of linguistic purity at the risk of being misunderstood or not understood at all" (Cronin 1996: 66) are understandable, yet did not apply to Wales. As this chapter will show, the Welsh terms revealed conceptual commonalities deriving from a shared government and political culture, but also changing conceptual meanings.

The "Glorious Revolution" as Restoration

English may have employed the same Latin-derived term as most continental European languages to express political revolution, but the concept developed a more widely accepted positive meaning in what would be Great Britain earlier than in other European countries. From 1688, the political discourse in Great Britain (and some philosophers on the Continent) used the term "Glorious Revolution" to refer to the process which brought William of Orange to the throne and established the radically new governmental system of constitutional monarchy peacefully, and apparently by arrangement between a Protestant monarch and his nation (Koselleck 1994: 719–20). In Great Britain itself, this use was sharpened by the challenges faced by the new monarchy and its state Protestantism, most seriously through the first Jacobite rebellion when the Catholic James Stuart, son of the deposed James II of England (James VII of Scotland and Ireland), attempted to regain the Crown of Great Britain with the help of France. Most of Wales was loyal to the Protestant King George I, who had ascended to the throne in 1714, but pockets of Catholicism and Jacobite support posed a political threat serious enough for a group of Loyalist Welshmen to commission the first privately financed translation of a political text into Welsh. Radical Whig Bishop William Fleetwood (1656–1723) of Ely, who had only just left the Bishopric of St Asaph in north-east Wales, had used a thanksgiving sermon – in English – to preach the political unity of the country for Protestantism's sake and to highlight the nation's contribution to victory (Fleetwood 1716). A group of Welsh "well-wishers to the present government" ("ewyllyswyr da i'r llywodraeth bresenol") (ab Dewi 1716: title page) decided to make this sermon available to their Welsh-speaking compatriots by commissioning a translation. By so doing, they sponsored the first non-state political publication in Welsh as well as the creation of the first Welsh terms to denote "revolution" and "to make a revolution." James Davies (also Iaco ab Dewi, 1648–1722), one of the first professional translators in Wales and a keen member of a circle of Protestant poets and scribes in Carmarthenshire (Hughes 1953, 1959), was commissioned and coined a number of new terms for hitherto unexpressed political concepts, most importantly here, "revolution."

At two central points in his text, Fleetwood contrasted the "revolution" of 1688, when "the whole nation" and their monarch established the governmental system that allowed the ascent to the throne of George I in 1714, with the recent Jacobite rebellion which, for Fleetwood, was saddled with negative connotations associated with sedition, rebellion and civil war, because it had been directed against the rightful government:

> Because a **Revolution** in favour of the Protestant Religion, and of the Laws and Liberties of the Nation was so easily brought about, therefore the hot and thoughtless Heads of the Conspirators, imagined such another might be brought about, with as much Ease, if they could work the People into Discontents and Disaffection to the Government. (Fleetwood 1716: 8)

> This Nation had been frequently and strongly Allarmed with the Fears of Popery in the Reign of King Charles II . . . It join'd the Prince of Orange, **made a Revolution**, declared the People's Rights, and placed the Crown upon the Prince and Princess's Heads, with certain Limitations. (Fleetwood 1716: 14)

In the right hands, revolution was a peaceful process, controlled by an alliance of reasonable people, but in the hands of "thoughtless" Catholics, it had the potential to destroy kingdom and nation. Davies translated both passages closely:

> O blegid dwyn oddi amgylch **Adymchweliad** mor hawdd ym Mhlaid Crefydd y Protestant, Cyfreithieu a Breinieu y Genedl, am hynny fe feddyliodd Penneu eiddigeddus y Cydfradwyr y gellid dwyn un arall oddi amgylch cyn hawsed a hynny, os gallent annog y Bobl i bryderu ac angharu y llywodraeth. (ab Dewi 1716: 9)

> Y genedl yma a ddychrynwyd yn fynych ac yn fawr gan ofn Pabyddiaeth yn Nheyrnasiad Charles yr II . . . hi ynghyd a Thywysog Orange a **Ad-ddychwelodd**, ac a arddangosodd gyfiawnder y bobl; ac a osodod y goron ar benneu'r Tywysog a'r Dywysoges, dan ryw Derfynneu. (ab Dewi 1716: 16)

To express "a revolution," Davies created the noun "adymchweliad." The verb "ad-ddychwelaf," that is "to revolutionize," was coined to translate "made a Revolution." Both terms were ultimately based on the noun "chwêl," which denoted a "turn," but also a "commotion, disturbance" (GPC: "chwêl"). The prefixes "ad-" and "ym-" added elements of repetition and intensification. Significantly, both denoted a "return . . . to a previous or original condition," but also to "restore." Since the overwhelming majority of Welsh publications of the time were religious, both terms carried connotations of a return to God, a restoration of the right faith, or a redemption, thus conceptually echoing the English use of the "glorious revolution" as a restoration of Protestantism. In addition, Davies translated "the designed *Change*" (Fleetwood 1716: 9), a reference back to the 1688 revolution, as "y *Cyfnewidiad* oeddent yn eu amcanu" (ab Dewi 1716: 10). "Cyfnewidiad" simply meant a "change" or "exchange" (GPC: "cyfnewidiad"), so that "revolution" also signified a transformation of state and government which was so harmless that it could be expressed by a commonplace word.

Revolution as a "Change of Government"

All this may not have been significant in English and in England, where a number of political publications and pamphlets that used terms like "revolution" appeared every year. However, no further political pamphlets or sermons in Welsh appeared between 1717 and the outbreak of the American War of Independence in 1775. The term "cyfnewidiad llywodraeth," which had normalized revolution as a "change of government," only remained in use in translations of religious literature and became firmly linked with Protestantism. In 1774, *The Protestant Dissenters' Catechism* reminded worshippers of the significance of 1688, appending an explanatory note on the terminology to be used:

> *William* Prince of *Orange*, a Protestant of glorious and immortal memory, by the management of the Whigs, was brought into *England* to support the Protestant-cause at which *James* being intimidated, abdicated the throne, which *William* (with his amiable consort *Mary*) was invited to accept.
> N. B. This event is called the *Revolution*. (Palmer 1774: 19)

The Welsh translation, *Catecism yr Ymneilltuwyr*, simply transliterated "the revolution" as "y refolusion," but felt the need to explain this loan further, adding "*Nodwch*, Mae'r tro hwn yn cael ei alw y Refolusion, sef *cyfnewidiad* llywodraeth" (Anon. 1775a: 18), that is "*Note*, this turn is called the Revolution, namely a *change* of government." By then, Samuel Johnson's *Dictionary of the English Language* had been in the public domain for twenty years. Both author and translator of the catechism probably drew on it for their definition, since Johnson had also explained political revolution as a "Change in the state of a government or country. It is used among us *kat exochen*, for the change produced by the admission of king William and queen Mary" (Johnson 1755: 1702; Koselleck 1994: 716).

The outbreak of war between Great Britain and its most important colony America in 1775 evoked a lively response from England's pamphleteers and politicians (Conway 2000; Verhoeven 2013: 28–32). In Wales, its most visible cultural echo was the production of some popular ballads and the swift translation of two pro-American pamphlets into Welsh. In 1775, William Smith's *Sermon on the Present Situation of American Affairs* appeared as *Pregeth ar Helynt Bresennol America*. This English sermon asserted that the people of America "know their rights and will not consent to passively surrender them" and that "religion and liberty must flourish or fall together in America" (Smith 1775: iii, 21). It linked the metaphors for sudden and long-term change, and derived the American struggle for independence from the Glorious Revolution of 1688 by asking: "Did not their example, and consequent sufferings, kindle a flame that illuminated the land, and introduced that noble system of public and personal liberty, secured by the revolution?" (Smith 1775: 21). In Britain as in America, most eighteenth-century progressives preferred the political tradition of the Glorious Revolution of 1688, which had restored a balance of power between king and people peacefully, to the more radical Commonwealth republicanism, which remained tainted with the regicide of 1649 and the subsequent bloody civil war (Morton and Smith 2002: 8–10). It makes sense, then, that the anonymous Welsh translator followed the religious translations and Samuel Johnson in rendering "the revolution" as "cyfnewidiad y llywodraeth*." An explanatory footnote glossed this term as "*the Revolution" (Anon. 1775b: 16). Educational paratexts (Magnuson 1998: 5–6) in the form of footnotes or brackets, which provided English equivalents like "*Theocracy," "*Monarchy" and "*The Revolution," were increasingly used to define the new political terms. This Welsh Enlightenment habit surely enhanced the conceptual influence of English political writing in Wales, but it also highlights the meaning of the new terminology for the researcher.

The French Revolution of 1789 and Its Long-Term Effect

The American Declaration of Independence in 1776 had boosted the political movement to reform the British parliamentary system, which perceived itself as restoring the liberties and rights established during the Glorious Revolution (Conway 2000: 218–33; Verhoeven 2013: 28–32). The fact that the French Revolution coincided with its one-hundredth anniversary reinforced the view that France was now attempting to achieve what England had done a century earlier – a constitutional monarchy and balanced system of governance (Philp 2014: 119, 126). On November 4, 1789, senior representative of the reform movement Richard Price (1723–91) celebrated this in his *Discourse on the Love of our Country*, delivered at an anniversary dinner "of our deliverance at the Revolution from the dangers of popery and arbitrary power" (Price 1789: 2; Roger 2000: 5–6). References to philosophers like Milton, Locke and Montesquieu, to whose writings were owed "those revolutions in which every friend of mankind is now exulting" (Price 1789: 14), highlighted the long-term philosophical underscoring of 1789. The "INEQUALITY OF OUR REPRESENTATION" as the "most important instance of the imperfect state in which the Revolution left our constitution" (Price 1789: 39) in 1689 was cited as the fault which, he hoped, the French Revolution would help remedy. His rousing final remarks united all three revolutions in one glorious event:

> I have lived to see THIRTY MILLIONS of people, indignant and resolute, spurning at slavery and demanding liberty with an irresistible voice; their king led in triumph, and an arbitrary monarch surrendering himself to his subjects. – After sharing in the benefits of one Revolution, I have been spared to be a witness to two other Revolutions, both glorious. (Price 1789: 49)

Price's publication and his assertions set the tone for the reception of 1789 in progressive circles, but it also inaugurated a bitter argument over the place of this and any revolution in history, the existence of any "natural rights" and the proper seat of political power. The public discussion was opened with Edmund Burke's rejoinder, *Reflections on the Revolution in France*, and played out in what has been called the "French Revolution debate" (Claeys 1995, 2007; Plummer Crafton 1997; Verhoeven 2013).

Though Price was of Welsh descent, he did not participate in the Welsh-language debate. Nevertheless, the democratization of the existing English political discourse brought about by the public contestation of key political concepts was echoed in Wales by the emergence of a parallel public discourse in Welsh and English. Between 1715 and 1789, only five non-governmental political texts had appeared in Welsh. During the long decade following 1789, Welsh intellectuals democratized their discourse, publishing at least twenty-five political pamphlets and 720 pages of politico-religious writing in radical magazines in the Welsh language (Löffler 2012). Altogether, over 120 political pamphlets and posters in Welsh and English appeared between 1789 and 1805 (Löffler 2014).

"Revolution," which had first found a home in the Welsh language in 1716 as "adymchweliad" – a Glorious Revolution which had restored the Protestant ascendancy while enabling a constitutional monarchy – and then as "cyfnewidiad llywodraeth," i.e. a "change of government" which had led to political and religious liberty in America in 1783, now became the carrier of political and Millenarian religious hopes of liberation and salvation à la Price.

The bilingual debate about the French Revolution in Wales opened with *A Charge Delivered to the Clergy of Llandaff, June 1791* by the Bishop of Llandaff Richard Watson (1737–1816) and its translation. A progressive Churchman, Watson cautiously welcomed some of the changes in France while avoiding mentioning revolution in the title of his pamphlet. The translator, in contrast, by altering the title to *Meddyliau yr Esgob Watson am y Cyfnewidiad Diweddar yn Llywodraeth Ffraingc*, that is "The Considerations of Bishop Watson on the Recent Revolution in France" (Anon. 1793a), highlighted the concept. Watson himself had opened his *Charge* by indicating the fundamentally new character of this revolution, which "exceeded all comparison" (Koselleck 2004: 50):

> A Revolution, as to the mode of its Accomplishment, unparalleled in the Annals of the World, has taken place; or, to speak more properly, is now taking place in the Civil and Religious Constitution of one of the greatest Kingdoms in Europe. I deliver no opinion of censure or approbation on the supporters or opposers of this Revolution. (Watson 1792: 1)

The Welsh translator rendered this first sentence quite literally as: "cyfnewidiad, o ran y modd y dygawd oddiamgylch, heb ei gyffelyb yn hanesion y byd, sydd wedi cymmeryd lle" (Anon. 1793a: 1), that is, "a revolution, as to the mode it was brought about without its like in the histories of the world, has taken place." This pamphlet set the tone until almost the end of the century, because here, a Bishop of the Anglican Church, a representative of the state, publicly referred to "this revolution" as "y cyfnewidiad hwn," thus endowing the French Revolution with all the positive connotations carried by "cyfnewidiad" since 1716. Drawing on Price and vindicated by Watson, the Welsh radicals who dominated the political discourse celebrated the French Revolution as the historical apex of Protestant privileges and liberties by using "cyfnewidiad."

Morgan John Rhys (1760–1804), a Baptist minister who had travelled to France in the wake of the revolution to convert the third estate to Protestantism (Constantine 2013: 75–7), founded the first Welsh political journal, Y *Cylch-grawn Cynmraeg*, in 1793. "Cyfnewidiad" was favored by him in news bulletins on the revolution and the wars on the Continent as well as in translations of speeches delivered before the House of Commons. Reporting on a speech by William Petty-Fitzmaurice, Earl Wycombe, for instance, the journal stated:

> Fe derfynodd gan ddymuno i lai o wawd-iaith a dirmyg gael ei arferyd gan foneddigion yn erbyn cenedl Ffraingc, er eu bod wedi cael eu gyrru i bellafoedd, yr oedd **y cyfnewidiad** yn y wlad honno wedi cael effaith hynod ar amgylchiadau dynol, a ni wyddwyd yn iawn beth fyddai'r canlyniadau o hono yn y byd. (Rhys 1794: 270)

> (He ended by wishing that less sarcasm and derision was used by noblemen against the French nation, though they have been driven to extremes, the **revolution** in that country had had a remarkable effect on human conditions, and it was not known yet, what its consequences in the world would be.)

Rhys's anti-war and anti-Catholic pamphlet *Cyngor Gamaliel* (Gamaliel's Counsel) opened with "The revolution" and its promise of salvation:

> Mae'r *****cyfnewidiad** ac a ddigwyddodd yn ddiweddar yn *Ffraingc* wedi creu cynnwrf mawr trwy holl Ewrop. Wrth weled 25 Miliwn ar yr un waith yn ysgwyd ymaith haiarnedd iau caethiwed a chyhoeddi eu hunain yn bobl ruddion, fe synnodd llawer. (Löffler 2014: 91)

> The *****revolution** which happened recently in *France* has created a great commotion throughout Europe. At the sight of 25 Million people at once shaking off the iron yoke of slavery and pronouncing themselves free people, many were astonished. (Löffler 2014: 100)

"*Cyfnewidiad" was again footnoted with "*revolution." Unitarians Thomas Evans (1764–1833) and David Davies (d. 1807), the editors of two further radical periodicals published between 1794 and 1796, also favored "cyfnewidiad." Within weeks of its appearance in the English *Chester Chronicle*, Davies had translated the series "A Brief Sketch of the French Revolution" as "Achosion o'r Cyfnewidiad yn Ffrainc," that is "The Causes of the French Revolution," for his periodical *Y Geirgrawn*. Both texts demonstrate the understanding of the revolution as related to its American predecessor, but in Welsh the choice of the term "cyfnewidiad" (Davies 1796: 23) highlighted this particular connection:

> The part which the King of France took in the American contest, was attested with consequences unfortunate to himself. He assisted the Americans to obtain their independence, which eventually operated to the destruction of his own. The officers and soldiers that were sent to fight for America, and saw that memorable Revolution completed, returned home with new ideas of freedom which they liberally discussed amongst their countrymen. (Anon. 1795: 4)

Until 1797, "y cyfnewidiad" was the dominant term for public references to the French Revolution. The reason for this preference, which conceptualized 1789 as a continuation of 1688 and 1775, was that most political texts were produced by radicals whose beliefs derived from Liberals like John Wilkes, Charles James Fox and Richard Price. Welsh Loyalists were reluctant to translate or compose educational political tracts until necessity forced their hand, because any non-religious reading material they produced was focused on educating those whose purpose in life was unquestioning obedience. It speaks to the strength of the term and concept that when publications condemning the revolution began to appear, "cyfnewidiad" was utilized at first. The Methodist John Owen (1757–1829), who initiated the Welsh Loyalist counter-attack in 1797, called his pamphlet *Golygiadau ar Achosion ag Effeithiau'r Cyfnewidiad yn Ffrainc* (The Meaning and Effects of the Revolution in France) (Owen 1797).

"Revolution" Contested

By 1797, the British government had passed a range of legislation designed to oppress radical politics, from the suspension of Habeas Corpus in 1793 to the Treasonable Practices Act of 1795 and the steep taxes levied on printed matter from 1797, which ended most of the new political discourse. At the same time, the French Revolution appeared to turn toward the circular course of its predecessors. The democratically elected Republican Convention had given way to a less democratic Directory in 1795, and to rulership by a single individual in 1799, when Napoleon Bonaparte conducted the coup d'état which made him First Consul. The radical discourse favoring the French Revolution had continued longer in Welsh than in English, because it was difficult to police seditious publications which were so geographically and linguistically distant from the metropolitan center, but it too was drawing to a close. Its protagonists had either emigrated to America like Morgan John Rhys, been bullied into silence like David Davies, or were facing prison sentences for treasonable practices, like Thomas Evans (Löffler 2012: 26–35; Verhoeven 2013: 7–8). The attempted French invasion of Britain via south-west Wales had raised anti-French fears to almost hysterical levels (Löffler 2012: 16–18) and increased the output of cheap Loyalist pamphlets and posters. It was at this point that Welsh Loyalists began to contest *this* revolution by introducing a terminology designed to sever the link with the positive religious and political connotations of 1688 and 1776.

One way of achieving the break was the blurring of conceptual boundaries to re-combine related political concepts into negative bundles. In 1792, Hannah More's influential populist dialogue *Village Politics* had condemned French concepts of "liberty," "Rights of Man" and "revolution" in a pamphlet which combined racism, religious intolerance and political conservatism: "We follow the French? Why I'd sooner go to the Negers to get learning, or to the Turks to get religion, than to the French for freedom and happiness" (More 1792: 5). This pamphlet was only translated when the specter of a French invasion overrode Loyalist desires to restrict Welsh publications to religious texts. Even then, the translator Edward Barnes deleted the original's central passage on "The Revolution" (More 1792: 9), while combining "revolution" and "reform" as undesirable societal changes in the term "diwygiad," i.e. "political reform" in the remainder of the text (More 1792: 4–5; Barnes 1796: 4–5). But increasingly, Loyalists drew on the earlier concept of a full circle of calamitous events to express their view of revolution. The translator of *One Penny worth of Truth*, a tract in the series *Liberty and Property Preserved against Republicans and Levellers*, referred to the French "revolutionaries" as "cylchdro-wyr" (Owen 1798), i.e. men who committed a full turn.

A related term which would become the standard expression for the metahistorical concept of "revolution" appeared in a translation of the pamphlet *Reform or Ruin. Take Your Choice!* by John Bowdler (1746–1823) in 1798. The reform suggested in the title was a return to the values of the Anglican Church in all aspects of life. In lurid detail, the British population was warned against the revolutionary promise of salvation: "It was said the French revolution would make the French nation free and happy. But it has now gone on for seven or eight years, and produced confusion, oppression, cruelty, poverty, all sorts of mischief and wickedness, and no good whatever" (Bowdler 1797: 7).

This text was so important that it was translated twice, in north and in south Wales, both versions appearing in 1798. The northern translator Walter Davies (1761–1849), a Loyalist intellectual who had, however, frequented the same circles as the radical authors of the early 1790s, chose "cyfnewidiad" to translate revolution (Davies 1798: 8). The second translator, William Evans of Carmarthen, coined a new term, "Chwyldro y Ffrangcod (*French Revolution*)," clarifying its meaning in the usual way by adding the English equivalent (Evans 1798: 8). "Chwyldro" signified a circular motion like "cylchdro," but with an almost dizzying quality. Both elements of the compound, "chwŷl and "tro," denoted turning in a circle; their combination intensified meaning and motion (GPC: chwyldro; chwŷl; tro). In addition, "chwŷl" also signified "revenge, retaliation," and was often confused with "chwil," which denoted "reeling, staggering, frisky, wild," as well as "intense, extreme" (GPC: chwil[3]). All these highly undesirable qualities and states of existence were packed together in "chwyldro," a one-word warning against the awful consequences of overturning traditional society, breaking with the past and turning away from established religion. Yet, "chwyldro" (and its derivation "chwyldroad") became the Welsh standard term to denote revolution in its main metaphorical meanings. Unwittingly, the Loyalist translator had highlighted the significance, novelty and uniqueness of *this* revolution at the very end of the revolutionary period. He had done so in a text that appealed to Welsh readers because it was focused on religious values. The translation was published in Carmarthen, then the main center of publishing in Wales, and part of south Wales, a region whose population and lines of communication were growing fast as a result of the developing copper, iron and coal industries there. During the first decades of the nineteenth century, this population explosion facilitated the development of a religious and political radicalism that not only expressed itself in publications and the rise of an almost hermetically sealed radical Nonconformist culture, but also in serious riots and revolts which challenged the authority of the British state.

Settling Concept and Terminology

Koselleck refers to the period between 1750 and 1870 as the "threshold time" ("Sattelzeit") (Koselleck 2004: xiv–xv; Ball 1988: 9), during which abstract political concepts developed, stabilizing in meaning and expression, and the social base of their use expanded. In this process, the proliferation and democratization of the publishing and communication industries, and increasing pressure for the standardization of the languages used in them, certainly played a role. Evans's translation of *Reform or Ruin* had appeared in Carmarthen, and it was there in the same year, 1798, that William Richards (1749–1818), a Baptist minister and energetic religious and political pamphleteer, published his *Geiriadur Saesneg a Chymraeg*, an English and Welsh Dictionary. This "agreeable Companion for the Welsh Youth of both Sexes, and for Welsh readers in general" (Richards 1798: title page) defined Welsh revolutionary concepts and made them widely available. It had the support of over 120 subscribers, some of them signing up for twenty-five copies. Among them were bookbinders, millers, students, surgeons, ministers, rope makers and postmasters. Radical authors and ministers, such as Thomas Evans and David Davies, subscribed, the latter ordering several copies for use in his school. It was sold cheaply in Welsh market towns as well as in the English border towns of Chester, Oswestry and Shrewsbury, and in Bristol and London. By the 1870s, the dictionary had gone through at least ten reprints and new editions, in Wales itself as well as in Liverpool, London and Utica, U.S.A. This was a main reference work for the Welsh in Britain as well as for the American expatriate community.

Richards listed twelve words to signify the physical, astronomical and astrological concepts of "revolution," but singled out "The French Revolution" as a sub-entry, giving as Welsh equivalents a choice of "atchwyl Ffraingc" and "chwyldro y Ffrangcod" (Richards 1798: 306). In 1808, "chwyldroad" was used by influential fellow Baptist Titus Lewis (1773–1811) in his *Llyfr Rhyfeddodau neu Amlygiadau o Waredigaethau Rhyfeddol Duw i'w Weision* (The Book of Marvels or Manifestations of God's Amazing Deliverance of his Servants) to describe the "history of England down to the Revolution" of 1688 as "Hanes Lloegr i lawr i'r Chwyldroad (*Revolution*)" (Lewis 1808: 52).

Lewis had added "-ad," a suffix indicating completion of an action, but also the abstract character of a noun (*GPC*: -iad¹, -ad²), which corroborates Koselleck's reasoning on the development of concepts into collective singulars during these decades (Koselleck 2004: 36). The context reconnected the term with the Glorious Revolution, while the suffix helped generalize it. By 1839, Richard's dictionary gave only "*The French Revolution*, y Chwyldroad Ffrengig."

Welsh publishing experienced a "golden age" between the Napoleonic Wars and the end of the nineteenth century (Jones 2000), as a result of which the course of the concept and its expressions is more difficult to chart in the increased volume of material. However, digitally available databases, such as Welsh Newspapers Online, allow us to observe that the main metaphorical meaning of the concept was settled, while it acquired additional connotations. Revolution was defined as a singular event in *Encyclopaedia Cambrensis Gwyddoniadur Cymreig*, a ten-volume national reference work published between 1854 and 1879, with a second edition appearing in 1881. Here, in a work proclaiming itself to be "the most important national publication in the Welsh language" ("y gwaith cenedlaethol pwysicaf yn yr iaith Gymraeg") (Gee 1891: title page), its conceptual meaning was also metahistoricized by gaining general coinage. The French Revolution became the angle point from which revolution reverberated in temporal, geographical and semiotic directions. The heading "Chwyldroad Ffrengig, Y," that is "French Revolution, The," was followed by a definition which explained: "Wrth 'chwyldroad' y meddylir cyfnewidiad llwyr a chyflym yng nghyfansoddiad gwlad, pa un bynag a fydd wedi ei ddwyn i ben trwy foddion cyfreithlawn, ynte anghyfreithlawn" (By "revolution" is meant a complete and swift change in the constitution of a country, whether that be accomplished through lawful or unlawful means) (Gee 1891: CHWY).

Utilizing the older "cyfnewidiad" to explain "chwyldroad," the entry foregrounded the events of 1789, but proceeded to summarize the 1830 and 1848 revolutions in France, and the Paris Commune of 1871. It concluded with "a list of the main revolutions of the world" that went back to 47 AD, when "the Roman Empire was founded on the ruins of the republic by Julius Caesar." Including England's revolutions of 1649 and 1688, and "North America 1775," it was also the first to mention the opposite, "counter-revolution," i.e. "gwrth-chwyldroad," in describing the reversion of Holland from the Batavian Republic to a monarchy in 1813 (Gee 1891: CHWY).

From the 1860s until the 1910s, both "chwyldro" and "chwyldroad" not only described the national and class uprisings and revolutions in Italy, Hungary, Greece and Russia, but also began to signify longer-term and peaceful changes and developments. The democratization of British politics through successive Reform Acts from 1832 was cautiously described as "a revolution, however, which is carried out, most probably, without any riot or bloodshed" ("chwyldroad, pa fodd bynnag, a ddygir ynmlaen, yn ôl pob tebyg, heb na therfysg na thywallt gwaed") (*Baner ac Amserau Cymru*, July 3, 1867). At the same time, the concept was transferred to a variety of subject areas and registers. In 1887, Welsh Liberal MP Thomas Edward Ellis (1859–99) spoke of the effects of the "huge economic revolution" ("chwyldro masnachol aruthrol") on Welsh agriculture (*Y Goleuad*, February 12, 1885). By the beginning of the twentieth century, it was possible to describe changes introduced in a traditional local prize competition ironically as a "chwyldro" (*Yr Herald Cymraeg*, November 27, 1906). William John Gruffydd (1881–1954), one of the most influential intellectuals of twentieth-century Wales, completed the process of conceptualizing revolution by referring to the nineteenth century in a sentence which included both "cyfnewidiad" and "chwyldro" and described sudden qualitative changes in combination with processes: "Daeth llawer o gyfnewidiadau arloesol gyda'r chwyldro diwydiannol" (Gruffydd 1937: 48), that is, "many ground-breaking changes came with the industrial revolution." The increasing application of the concept in a range of popular publications, by a variety of social groups and outside the political domain, confirms Koselleck's view that such concepts became democratized during the long nineteenth century (Koselleck 1994: 252).

Conclusion

Charting the course of a concept as central to modern politics as "revolution" in a chapter is easier in languages with an early political discourse so limited that an almost complete survey of public uses may be attempted, at least until the onset of mass publication in the nineteenth century. Such languages, however, tend to be non-state, their political texts often derived from or at least influenced by political writing and thought in the larger political cultures in which they are embedded. This poses challenges but also offers the opportunity for insights into the workings of political and cultural hegemony. By following the conceptual reverberations of "revolution" in Wales from 1688 to 1937, I hope to have demonstrated that the creativity of Welsh translators and creators of political texts reveal conceptual changes in the general British discourse by coining new terms for new meanings. The creation and use of the first Welsh terms, "adymchweliad" and "cyfnewidiad (llywodraeth)," and the use of the latter until the late 1790s, reveal the conceptual dominance of the Glorious Revolution of 1688 and the after-glow of the American Revolution of 1775 in the British discourse, which led to the interpretation of the French Revolution of 1789 as heir to both, and as the apex of a century of Protestant state politics. The Loyalist creation of the term "chwyldro(ad)" clarified British Loyalist attempts to sever the French Revolution from this positive content in the second half of the 1790s. Ironically, it was the use of this term in a radical dictionary that ensured its stabilization toward the end of the threshold period, as the concept's two main metaphorical meanings settled and became democratized. This line of development, laid bare by translation, corroborates Koselleck's findings on the development of the political and philosophical terminology of German, and to a degree French, but also highlights the slightly different development of the concept in the Anglo-American public sphere, which stemmed from the Glorious Revolution of 1688. The Welsh example also demonstrates that the reverberations of political concepts and their expression in small, colonized or non-state languages beyond the traditional European core nations may be attempted successfully, and that new insights may be gained from thus extending the geographical scope of conceptual history.

Bibliography

ab Dewi, Iaco (1716), *Pregeth a Bregethwyd yng Nghapel Ty-Ely yn Holbourn yn Llundein Ar Ddydd Merchur ym Mehefin y 7, 1716. Sef Dydd y Diolchgarwch Cyhoeddus Am Fendith Duw ar Gynghorion ac Arfeu ei Fawrhydi yn Llonyddu y Gwrthryfel Annaturiol diweddar*, Mwythig: Siôn Rhydderch.

Anon. (1717), *Pregeth a Bregethwyd yng Nghapel Ty-Ely yn Holbourn yn Llundein Ar Ddydd Iau Mehefin 7, 1716. Sef Dydd o Gyhoedd Ddiolchgarwch am Râd a bendith Dduw ar Gynghorion ac Arfau'r Brenin, yn gostegu'r diweddar Wrthryfel Annaturiol. Gan y gwir Barchedig Dâd yn Nuw William Arglwydd Esgob Ely. A gyfjeithwyd or chweched Argraphiad yn Saesonaeg gan un o ffyddlon Ddeiliaid Brenhin George*, Mwythig: John Rhydderch.

Anon. (1775a), *Catecism yr Ymneillduwyr Protestanaidd . . .*, Caerfyrddin: Ross.

Anon. (1775b), *Pregeth ar Helynt Bresennol America A Bregethwyd yn Christ-Church ar Mehefin 23, 1775*, Brysto: William Pine.
Anon. (1793a), *Meddyliau yr Esgob Watson am y Cyfnewidiad Diweddar yn Llywodraeth Ffraingc, Rhydd-did Crefyddol, a Hawl yr Ymneillduwyr*, Caerfyrddin: J. Ross.
Anon. (1793b), *Liberty and Property Preserved against Republicans and Levellers. A Collection of Tracts. Number I*, London: J. Sewell.
Anon. (1795), *Chester Chronicle*, 13 November.
Baker, Keith Michael (1990), *Inventing the French Revolution: Essays on French Political Culture in the Eighteenth Century*, Cambridge: Cambridge University Press.
Ball, Terence (1988), *Transforming Political Discourse: Political Theory and Critical Conceptual Theory*, Oxford: Basil Blackwell.
Ball, Terence, James Farr and Russell L. Hanson, eds (1995 (1989)), *Political Innovation and Conceptual Change*, Cambridge: Cambridge University Press.
Barnes, Edward (1796), *Rheolau Llywodraeth yn y Llan, yn Annerch at Holl Grefftwyr, Gweinidogion, a Gweithwyr ym Mhrydain Fawr*, Croeoswallt: W. Edwards.
Bowdler, John (1797), *Reform or Ruin. Take your Choice! In which the Conduct of the King, the Parliament, the Ministry, the Opposition, the Nobility and Gentry, the Bishops and Clergy, &c., &c., are considered and that Reform pointed out which alone can save the Country*, London: J. Hatchard.
Brunner, Otto, Werner Conze and Reinhart Koselleck, eds (1994), *Geschichtliche Grundbegriffe. Historisches Lexikon zur politisch-sozialen Sprache in Deutschland. Band 5 Pro–Soz*, Stuttgart: Klett-Cotta.
Bulst, Neithart (1994), "Mittelalter," in Otto Brunner, Werner Conze and Reinhart Koselleck, eds, *Geschichtliche Grundbegriffe. Historisches Lexikon zur politisch-sozialen Sprache in Deutschland. Band 5 Pro–Soz*, Stuttgart: Klett-Cotta, pp. 670–89.
Claeys, Gregory (1995), *Political Writings of the 1790s*, 7 vols, London: Pickering.
Claeys, Gregory (2007), *The French Revolution Debate: The Origins of Modern Politics*, Basingstoke: Macmillan.
Constantine, Mary-Ann (2013), "The Welsh in Revolutionary Paris," in Mary-Ann Constantine and Dafydd Johnston, eds, *"Footsteps of Liberty and Revolt": Essays on Wales and the French Revolution*, Cardiff: University of Wales Press, pp. 69–92.
Conway, Stephen (2000), *The British Isles and the War of American Independence*, Oxford: Oxford University Press.
Cronin, Michael (1996), *Translating Ireland: Translation, Languages, Cultures*, Cork: Cork University Press.
Davies, David (1796), "Crynodeb o'r Achosion o'r Cyfnewidiad yn Ffrainc," *Y Geirgrawn* 1:1, pp. 23–5.

Davies, Hywel (2013), "Terror, Treason and Tourism: The French in Pembrokeshire 1797," in Mary-Ann Constantine and Dafydd Johnston, eds, *"Footsteps of Liberty and Revolt": Essays on Wales and the French Revolution*, Cardiff: University of Wales Press, pp. 247–70.

Evans, William (1798), *Diwygiad neu Ddistryw: Cymmerwch eich Dewis! Yn yr Hwn yr ystyrir Ymddygiad y Brenin, Y Senedd, y Swyddogion, Y Gwrthwynebwyr, Y Pendefigion a'r Boneddigion, Yr Esgobion a'r Offeriaid &c. &c.*, Caerfyrddin: Ioan Evans.

Fleetwood, William (1716), *A Sermon Preach'd at Ely-House Chapel in Holbourn, On Thursday June 7, 1716. Being the Day of Publick Thanksgiving, For the Blessing of God upon His Majesty's Counsels and Arms in Suppressing the late Unnatural Rebellion*, London: D. Midwinter.

Gee, Thomas, ed. (1891), *The Encyclopaedia Cambrensis Y Gwyddoniadur Cymreig*, Dinbych: T. Gee a'i Fab.

Geiriadur Prifysgol Cymru / A Dictionary of the Welsh Language (GPC), at <www.geiriadur.ac.uk> (last accessed October 21, 2020).

Gruffydd, William John (1937), *Owen Morgan Edwards: Cofiant*, Aberystwyth: ab Owen.

Hughes, Garfield H. (1953), *Iaco ab Dewi 1648–1722*, Caerdydd: Gwasg Prifysgol Cymru.

Hughes, Garfield H. (1959), "Davies, James (Iaco ap Dewi; 1648–1722)," in *The Dictionary of Welsh Biography*, at <http://yba.llgc.org.uk/en/> (last accessed August 8, 2017).

Johnson, Samuel (1755), *A Dictionary of the English Language*. A Digital Edition of the 1755 Classic by Samuel Johnson, ed. Brandi Besalke. Last modified: December 6, 2012, at <http://johnsonsdictionaryonline.com> (last accessed October 5, 2018).

Jones, Philip Henry (2000), "Printing and Publishing in the Welsh Language," in Geraint H. Jenkins, ed., *The Welsh Language and its Social Domains*, Cardiff: University of Wales Press, pp. 317–47.

Koselleck, Reinhart (1994), 'Revolution IV. Von der Frühen Neuzeit bis zur Französischen Revolution', in Otto Brunner, Werner Conze and Reinhart Koselleck, eds, *Geschichtliche Grundbegriffe. Historisches Lexikon zur politisch-sozialen Sprache in Deutschland. Band 5 Pro–Soz*, Stuttgart: Klett-Cotta, pp. 690–788.

Koselleck, Reinhart (2004 (1979)), "Historical Criteria of the Modern Concept of Revolution," in *Futures Past: On the Semantics of Historical Time*, trans. and intro. Keith Tribe, New York: Columbia University Press, pp. 43–57.

Koselleck, Reinhart (2006), "Revolution als Begriff und Metapher. Zur Semantik eines einst emphatischen Wortes," in *Begriffsgeschichten. Studien zur Semantik und Pragmatik der politischen und sozialen Spache*, Frankfurt am Main: Suhrkamp, pp. 219–39.

Lewis, Titus (1808), *Llyfr Rhyfeddodau neu Amlygiadau o Waredigaethau Rhyfeddol Duw i'w Weision*, Carmarthen: J. Evans.

Löffler, Marion (2012), *Welsh Responses to the French Revolution: Press and Public Discourse 1789–1802*, Cardiff: University of Wales Press.

Löffler, Marion (2014), *Political Pamphlets and Sermons from Wales 1790–1806*, Cardiff: University of Wales Press.

Magnuson, Paul (1998), *Reading Public Romanticism*, Princeton: Princeton University Press.

More, Hannah (1792), *Village Politics. Addressed to all the Mechanics, Journeymen, and Day Labourers, in Great Britain*, London: F. and C. Rivington.

Morton, Timothy and Nigel Smith (2002), "Introduction," in Timothy Morton and Nigel Smith, eds, *Radicalism in British Literary Culture, 1650–1830: From Revolution to Revolution*, Cambridge: Cambridge University Press, pp. 1–26.

Owen, John (1797), *Golygiadau ar Achosion ag Effeithiau'r Cyfnewidiad yn Ffrainc*, Machynlleth: E. Pritchard.

Owen, Trevor (1798), "Llythyr Saesneg Thomas Bwl at ei frawd John, wedi ei cyfieithu ir gymraeg yn y mis Mehefin," National Library of Wales, Canon Trevor Owen Papers, no. 326.

Palmer, S. (1774), *The Protestant Dissenters' Catechism containing 1. A Brief History of the Nonconformists; 2. The Reasons of the Dissent from the National Church*, Belfast: James Magee.

Philp, Mark (2014), "English Republicanism in the 1790s," in *Reforming Ideas in Britain: Politics and Language in the Shadow of the French Revolution, 1789–1815*, Cambridge: Cambridge University Press, pp. 102–32.

Plummer Crafton, Lisa (1997), *The French Revolution Debate in English Literature and Culture*, Westport: Connecticut.

Price, Richard (1789), *A Discourse on the Love of Our Country Delivered on Nov. 4, 1789, at the Meeting-House in the Old Jewry to the Society for Commemorating the Revolution in Great Britain . . .*, London: George Stafford for T. Cadell.

Richards, William (1798), *Geiriadur Saesneg a Chymraeg. An English and Welsh Dictionary in which the English Words and sometimes the English Phraseology are accompanied by those which Synonymise or Correspond with them in the Welsh Language . . .*, Carmarthen: J. Daniel.

Rhys, Morgan John (1794), "Areithiau y Seneddwyr," *Cylch-grawn Cynmraeg* 4, p. 270.

Roberts, Brynley F. (1997), "The Celtic Languages of Britain," in Geraint H. Jenkins, ed., *The Welsh Language before the Industrial Revolution*, Cardiff: University of Wales Press, pp. 407–40.

Roger, Phillipe (2000), "Trading Words, Waging War: The Mystified Relationship between British Radicals and French 'Revolutionnaires,'" *The Huntington Library Quarterly* 63:3, pp. 299–317.

Skinner, Quentin (1995 (1989)), "Language and Political Change," in Terence Ball, James Farr and Russell L. Hanson, eds, *Political Innovation and Conceptual Change*, Cambridge: Cambridge University Press, pp. 6–23.

Smith, William (1775), *A Sermon on the Present Situation of American Affairs*, Philadelphia: Edward and Charles Dilly.

Verhoeven, W. M. (2013), *Americomania and the French Revolution Debate in Britain, 1789–1802*, Cambridge: Cambridge University Press.

Watson, Richard (1792), *A Charge Delivered to the Clergy of Llandaff, June 1791*, London: Thomas Evans.

Welsh Newspapers Online, at <newspapers.library.wales> (last accessed October 5, 2018).

White, Eryn M. (1997), "Popular Schooling and the Welsh Language 1650–1800," in Geraint H. Jenkins, ed., *The Welsh Language before the Industrial Revolution*, Cardiff: University of Wales Press, pp. 235–87.

Chapter 4

Revolution in Colonial Translation: From Saint-Domingue to Haiti

Jeremy D. Popkin

When we think about the translation of revolutionary ideas about liberty and equality during the Age of Revolutions at the end of the eighteenth century, we must consider both the translation of documents such as the French Declaration of the Rights of Man and Citizen of 1789 into other languages, and the way in which the significance of such ideas changed as they were translated or transferred from the contexts in which they were originally articulated into new situations. Such acts of translation required translators, historical actors familiar with more than one language and one social and political context and able to act as intermediaries between them. The notion of translation raises important questions about the connections between movements for liberty and equality in different parts of the world during the revolutionary era, and the reasons for their varying outcomes. Most fundamentally, it raises the question of whether the principles of the French Revolution were truly universal, or whether their meaning was significantly changed when translators put them into other languages and applied them in different circumstances.

In both a literal and a metaphorical sense, one of the most extraordinary acts of translation carried out in the entire revolutionary era occurred in the French Caribbean slave colony of Saint-Domingue, today's Haiti, on May 5, 1793. On that date, Léger-Félicité Sonthonax and Etienne Polverel, two representatives of the metropolitan French government who had been sent from Paris to enforce new revolutionary laws, issued a remarkable proclamation. Four months after the execution of Louis XVI, these representatives of the French Republic reissued the *Code Noir*, Louis XIV's edict of 1685, which constituted the legal charter of slavery in the French Empire, along with a royal ordinance of December 1784 which had attempted to limit slaveowners' abuses of their powers. It was remarkable enough that Sonthonax and Polverel, both firm supporters of the revolutionary movement whose basic statement of principles, the Declaration of the Rights of Man and Citizen, began by announcing that "all men are born and remain free and equal in rights," should have given their official approval to a document that so flagrantly contradicted those principles. Even more remarkable, however, is the fact that they translated their proclamation into Creole, the language of Saint-Domingue's black slave population, and ordered that it be read aloud to the slaves (Popkin 2010: 142–4).

This act of translation was revolutionary in a number of ways. In the first place, it meant the creation of a written version of the Creole language. As far as is known, this was the first legal document ever printed in Creole, a lingua franca created by the enslaved blacks themselves from the various West African languages they brought with them to the Americas and the French spoken by the white population in the colony. Although most of the colonists in Saint-Domingue understood Creole, and those who were born on the island learned it in childhood from the blacks who cared for them, whites regarded it as a "jargon," a primitive form of communication suitable for a race whose mental faculties they regarded as inferior. The idea that Creole could serve as a vehicle for the expression of the law, the highest collective achievement of a political community, was a radical act that translated the language of the enslaved population into an equivalent of French, which whites regarded as the language of civilization.

Sonthonax and Polverel's proclamation of May 5, 1793 was equally radical because it brought the black population of Saint-Domingue into the community created by the revolution and translated the notion of rights into a society based on slavery and a hierarchy based on racial descent. Until Sonthonax and Polverel issued their decree, blacks, especially the "bossales" brought from Africa and who did not know French, a group that made up at least half of the island's population in the early 1790s, had not had any way to know the content of the *Code Noir*. As the colony's white slaveowners were only too aware, the *Code Noir* imposed certain restrictions on them, obliging them to provide their slaves with a minimum of food, clothing and other necessities. The *Code Noir* also specified that free people of color were to have equal rights with whites.

Major provisions of the *Code Noir*, particularly those meant to provide the slaves with some protection from their masters, had never been enforced, and defenders of slavery insisted that their application would fatally undermine the institution. The pro-slavery journalist Claude-Corentin Tanguy-Laboissière responded to the commissioners' initiative by reiterating this position:

> It has always been judged so absurd that its execution has never been attempted. It is completely contrary to the spirit of slavery that any authority should be interposed between the master and the slave. Obviously this undermines the respect and obedience that the one owes to the other. See, in this respect, what Montesquieu wrote in his great work, *The Spirit of the Laws*, on the nature and the principle of despotic government. (AN, D XXV 47, d. 453, May 17, 1793)

For the defenders of slavery in Saint-Domingue, the translation of the *Code Noir* into Creole and its transmission to the slaves was thus an unacceptable translation of the basic idea that all individuals had rights under the law into a context where this idea simply did not apply. The commissioners' action clearly signaled their intention to bring the blacks under the protection of the law and to enable them to take advantage of its provisions. Some modern scholars of slavery have argued that the essence of slavery consisted in the "social death" of the slave, who "had no social existence outside of his master" and was denied any enforceable claim to rights (Patterson 1982: 38). Sonthonax and Polverel, however, attempted to institute a situation in which the slaves of Saint-Domingue, while still obligated to work for their masters, would have had a certain minimum of guaranteed rights and protection from the government. Their pro-slavery opponents understood what was at stake. "Have you read the proclamation translated into Creole?" the white agitator Thomas Millet wrote. "There we see that the civil commissioners, after having spread a spirit of dizziness among all the colored colonists, are now doing the same among the slaves" (AN, D XXV 47, d. 453, May 28, 1793).

The proclamation of May 5, 1793 was thus a challenge to the bases of slavery as the white colonists understood them. The commissioners certainly intended it as a gesture to the black population. The preamble to the Creole version stated that they were issuing their decree to protect the blacks from mistreatment, and the commissioners added that they did not hold the slaves responsible for the violent insurrection against slavery that had begun in the northern part of Saint-Domingue in August 1791: "It is not among the Negro slaves that one needs to look to find the cause of your uprising, they are not the leaders of it . . ., it is others who misled you" (*Moniteur général*, May 26, 1793). The decree of May 5 was meant as an "improvement" of slavery, a way of making it more humane while not undermining the economic basis of the colonial plantation system. In accordance with the instructions they had been given before they left Paris in June 1792, the commissioners continued to assure both the white population and the slaveowning free people of color on the island that they were not aiming at the immediate abolition of slavery. In Port-au-Prince, Polverel's secretary Jean-Baptiste Picquenard, the editor of a journal devoted to the commissioners' party, denounced rumors spread by the whites that the French National Convention was moving toward such a step.

> It knows, better than you yourselves, that this class of men is not ready for freedom . . . It knows that the first use a slave makes of his freedom is to murder the man who kept him in chains with the irons that he has broken, and that freedom granted to *these* would be as dangerous as a dagger in the hands of a child. (*Ami de l'égalité*, May 9, 1793)

The paradoxical way in which French revolutionary officials tried to translate the revolution's principles via a translation of the laws authorizing and regulating slavery in May 1793 is a vivid illustration of the difficulties of translating the ideals of liberty and equality to the world of slavery in the Americas, and especially to France's plantation colonies in the Caribbean. Nowhere else in the Atlantic world were the contradictions and paradoxes of the effort to translate revolutionary ideals into practice so evident as in Saint-Domingue, the most valuable of all the European colonies at the time of the French Revolution. Sonthonax and Polverel's effort to reconcile the realities of slavery with the humanitarian ideals of the revolution in May 1793 through their translation of the *Code Noir* was not successful. Less than two months later, when sailors from the French navy and white colonists led by the military governor of Saint-Domingue, François-Thomas Galbaud, attacked the commissioners in a violent challenge to their racial policies, Sonthonax and Polverel issued the first of a series of proclamations offering freedom to the colony's black slaves. The most important of these proclamations were also published in Creole and brought into that language the vocabulary of the French Revolution (Popkin 2010: 260, 268–74).

Sonthonax and Polverel's translators, whose identities we do not know, faced the challenge of explaining the French revolutionary notion of "liberté" in Creole words that would be clear to their black audience. "Quand nion nation gagné liberté, si li vlé toujou libe, faut que li commencé par gagner bon conduit," announced their proclamation of July 11, 1793, freeing the wives and children of black men who had gained their freedom by enrolling in the commissioners' army. ("When a nation gains its freedom, if they want to remain free, they have to start by demonstrating good conduct" (CAOM, Col. F 3 198, Moreau de Saint-Méry papers).) They faced the challenge of explaining to the blacks that they were now citizens of a republic, and Sonthonax would soon complain that the significance of that idea did not translate well for a population whose notions of political culture were very different from those of Europeans. "The idea of a king is simple. It can be understood by the most stupid of Africans; even the most sophisticated of them cannot conceive of the idea of a republic," Sonthonax wrote to Polverel in late October 1793. "The Convention's principles are so foreign to them that several times in Le Cap they proposed to make me king *in the name of the Republic*" (AN, D XXV 44, d. 420, October 27, 1793).

The difficulties of translating the principles of the French Revolution to France's slave colonies did not begin in 1793: they were inherent in the relationship between metropolitan France and its overseas possessions. Indeed, translation, in both the literal and the figurative sense, was the stuff of daily life in colonial societies that brought together Europeans and Africans from many different "nations" who struggled to communicate in many different tongues and to bridge enormous cultural differences. In the revolutionary upheaval of the 1790s, a talent for translation even brought one man the title of "king," as Guy-Joseph Bonnet, an early Haitian leader, recounted in his memoirs. In the midst of one episode of fighting, a man of mixed race named Bélisaire, who

> had learned to speak the different idioms of all the African nations … approached each group in succession and took part in their discussions. To the Congos, he spoke Congo, to the Aradas, Arada, to the Mandingos, to the Nagos, to the Aoussas, to each their peculiar tongue. They were all astonished. They asked who this man could be; certainly, they thought, he was sent by Providence, he could only be the *Grand-Mouché*, the "Grand Monsieur." So they surrounded him with respect, and he became king. (Bonnet 1864: 15)

The concept of translation provides a fruitful way of looking at the complexities of the relationship between the metropole and the colonies throughout the revolution. Furthermore, this relationship was not just a one-way transmission of ideas from Paris to the periphery. From the start of the revolution, representatives of the colonists worked tirelessly to translate their own values into language that would speak to the metropolitan population. White colonists defended slavery and the legal superiority of whites over free people of mixed ancestry as necessities for the survival and prosperity of the country. They appropriated the revolutionaries' language for their own purposes, and they brought into French public discourse a language of overt biological racism – the claim that people of different skin colors had fixed moral as well as physical characteristics – that had been developed in the colonies by writers such as the legal expert Moreau de Saint-Méry (Garraway 2005: 260–75).

White defenders of slavery were not the only residents of the colonies who attempted to translate their concerns into revolutionary language. Members of colonial society's "third race," the free people of color, were also active intermediaries between the colonial world and that of the metropole, offering a "translation" of the colonial situation that differed strikingly from that put forward by the whites and demanding that the French revolutionary government translate its own ideals into legislation that would fundamentally alter colonial structures of power. Free men of color were able to engage directly in metropolitan debates because they were able to cross the ocean and speak and write in French. Spokesmen for this group, such as the Cap Français businessman Vincent Ogé, the plantation owner Julien Raymond and the renegade white plantation owner turned journalist Claude Milscent, played important roles in the period's debates. Raymond, an ally of the revolutionary abolitionist leader Brissot de Warville, was part of the group that chose Sonthonax and Polverel for their mission and worked out the policies they were sent to implement. Milscent, who was married to a woman of color, used his newspaper, the *Créole patriote*, to agitate for full equality for free people of color in the colonies and even to suggest the immediate abolition of slavery (Popkin 2017).

Finally, we can think of the leaders of the black movement for emancipation that historians now call the Haitian Revolution as engaging in their own acts of translation. Unlike the free people of color, most of the enslaved blacks of Saint-Domingue did not speak or read French, and only a handful of them ever traveled to Europe. The leaders of the movement, however, were intelligent men who did not simply borrow ideas from France. Throughout the revolutionary period, they put forward their own visions of what a just society in Saint-Domingue should look like. Initially, before the French revolutionaries finally committed themselves to the abolition of slavery, the black leadership, including Toussaint Louverture, translated not the rhetoric of rights but instead the "throne-and-altar" language of the revolution's opponents into a program of their own. After the French National Convention passed its historic decree abolishing slavery in February 1794, the most important of the black leaders, Toussaint Louverture, adopted the language of French revolutionary republicanism. Forced after 1802 to fight against Napoleon's army to defend the freedom the French Revolution had given the black population, Louverture's successor Jean-Jacques Dessalines translated the French language of melodramatic vengeance into the bloody reality of the massacres that exterminated the white population in 1804.

From the beginning of the revolutionary process in France, the white colonists in Saint-Domingue had their own distinct idea of what it meant to translate the principles of the French Revolution to a colonial society based on slavery and racial hierarchy among the free population. During the pre-revolutionary period of 1787–88, the colonists and their supporters in France were among the most outspoken opponents of what they called "ministerial despotism," the arbitrary power of royal officials over the colonies. In September 1788, when numerous French provinces were demanding the restoration of their historic privileges, Gouy d'Arsy, a self-proclaimed spokesman for the Saint-Domingue colonists, wrote that "Brittany, Dauphiné, Provence, Béarn, have opposed all unconstitutional actions, and they have preserved and protected their constitution. Let their history be a lesson for our colony. If she shows the same firmness, the same unity, the same wisdom, she is sure of the same success" (AN, D XXV 13, September 30, 1788).

From the start of the revolution, whites in the French slave colonies repeatedly proclaimed themselves to be revolutionary patriots and even demanded natural rights for themselves while simultaneously insisting that the ideas of liberty and equality could not be applied to their slaves. In May 1789, Saint-Domingue's newspaper, the *Affiches américaines*, did not hesitate to publish the text of the "Instructions" written by the revolutionary pamphleteer Sieyès and sent by the duc d'Orléans to his representatives who participated in the drafting of *cahiers de doléances* for the Estates-General. This document included a sixteen-article draft of a declaration of rights whose first article read, "individual liberty will be guaranteed to all the French." In November 1789, the paper published a partial version of the official Declaration of the Rights of Man and Citizen, omitting those articles that "do not seem suitable for a country organized the way Saint-Domingue is," but praising those that promised to "guarantee forever all those who live under the government of the French empire from the tyrannical abuses of arbitrary power" (*Affiches américaines*, May 27, 1789; November 11, 1789). Among the articles of the Declaration that the paper decided to omit was the first one, which had emphatically announced that "all men are born and remain free and equal in rights."

Throughout the early years of the revolution, the colonists' defenders regularly cited the first sentence of Article 6 of the Declaration, which declared that citizens had a right to participate in the making of laws that affected them, in order to defend the proposition that no changes could be made in the institution of slavery or in the regulations concerning free people of color without the consent of the white colonists. The more militant colonists translated this principle into a demand that they be able to elect their own assemblies and legislate about the internal affairs of the colony. By the spring of 1790, Saint-Domingue had a network of local and provincial assemblies, all of them exclusively white, and a Colonial Assembly that took the self-government principle to the point of issuing its own constitution, claiming virtual autonomy for the colony.

The French authorities reacted strongly to what they saw as an infringement of the unitary national sovereignty proclaimed by the metropole's Constituent Assembly and dissolved the Colonial Assembly, but even as it scolded the colonists for defying the national government, the Constituent Assembly in October 1790 assured them that they would retain unrestricted power to legislate about what was euphemistically called "the status of persons," which included the questions of slavery and racial equality. To justify the denial of rights to persons of African descent, the colonists found ways to argue that they could not qualify as citizens. Underlying these arguments was a nascent biological racism that had been gaining strength in the eighteenth century as Enlightenment thinkers challenged the biblical account of a single human creation (Popkin, R. H. 1973). The claim that blacks were inherently inferior was sometimes crudely expressed, as in a pamphlet by a certain chevalier de Beauvois, who proclaimed blacks to be a species closer to orangutans than to whites, and sometimes more subtly, as in the elaborate racial classification scheme of Moreau de Saint-Méry, one of the colonial deputies to the Constituent Assembly. In addition, the defenders of slavery argued that it was a utilitarian necessity if the colonies were to continue to contribute to the national economy (Beauvois 1790; Garraway 2005).

When the Constituent Assembly appeared to violate its promise to let the colonies decide on "the status of persons" in May 1791 by passing a decree that granted rights to a small minority of the colonies' population of free people of color, the white colonists of Saint-Domingue reacted with violence, and in September 1791 their supporters in Paris succeeded in persuading the Constituent Assembly to reverse its decree. As the revolutionary legislators in France prepared to put the new constitutional monarchy they had designed into effect, the white colonists were confident that they had succeeded in blunting the potential dangers of a translation of the principles of 1789 to the colonial world. Instead, they had succeeded in getting the French revolutionaries themselves to endorse their own translation of the principle of representative government, a translation that guaranteed their right to exclude all individuals of African ancestry from any claim to citizenship and their insistence that the existence of the colonies required the perpetuation of slavery.

By the time the white colonists achieved this legislative victory in France in September 1791, however, the situation in the colony of Saint-Domingue had changed drastically: on the night of August 22, 1791, an uprising had broken out among the slaves in the colony's wealthiest sugar-growing district, the Plaine du Nord, and within a few days, hundreds of plantations had gone up in flames. The white colonists at the time, like many historians today, saw this movement as a straightforward translation of the French revolutionaries' ideas about liberty and natural rights into revolutionary practice. The black uprising was certainly a protest against oppression, but whether it was inspired by the ideas of the French Revolution is less clear.

Slaves could certainly have overheard some of the political discussions about the revolution among their white masters, and some slaves did know how to read. As of August 1791, however, there was no reason why slaves should have assumed that the revolutionary movement in France meant to do anything to improve their condition. Indeed, the vehemence with which whites in Saint-Domingue proclaimed themselves patriots and continued to denounce the power of the king may well have persuaded blacks that it was Louis XVI, rather than the revolutionary movement, who was on their side. During the early stages of the insurrection, whites reported that the blacks were convinced that the king had granted them three days per week to work for their own benefit and earn money to buy their freedom and that the white revolutionary government in France and the white colonists in the colony were refusing to publicize or implement this decree. Throughout the first several years of the insurrection, the black leaders, the self-proclaimed generals Jean-François Papillon and Georges Biassou and their ambitious subordinate, the future leader Toussaint Louverture, repeatedly affirmed their loyalty to the French monarchy and the Catholic Church. In reality, Louis XVI had never expressed anything more than a vague sympathy for the slaves, and he had certainly not issued an edict modifying the terms of slavery. Nevertheless, the royalism of the black insurgents in Saint-Domingue was not simply a mistranslation of French political ideas. As the historian of Africa John Thornton has shown, blacks shipped to the Americas as slaves brought with them their own ideas about political justice. Kingship was a fundamental institution in the African societies from which they came, as was the notion that society depended on a proper relationship with the sacred (Thornton 1993).

Whereas the French revolutionaries had done nothing to abolish or reform slavery, by 1791 they had taken measures that might well have struck people born in Africa and imbued with the values of their native societies as profoundly disturbing. Most obviously, the French government responded to the slave uprising by sending massive numbers of troops to fight the insurgents. The revolutionary tricolor flag was deployed in battle to defend slavery, not to overthrow it. In addition, the revolutionary campaign against the Catholic Church was already in full swing, and indeed leading French critics of slavery, such as Brissot and Condorcet, were among the most enthusiastic supporters of harsh measures against "refractory" priests who refused to accept the controversial Civil Constitution of the Clergy. In Saint-Domingue, where at least a few priests showed sympathy for the slaves, a campaign against religion was unlikely to win much support from the black population. The dethronement of Louis XVI in August 1792 and his execution in 1793 would also have been difficult for blacks to understand.

The inability of the French revolutionaries to translate their principles into a program that could convince the black insurgents in Saint-Domingue was made manifest in a long document written or dictated in August 1793 by the man who was on the verge of becoming the major black leader in the colony, Toussaint Louverture. Addressing the revolutionary civil commissioners Sonthonax and Polverel, who had already begun to emancipate sections of the black population, Louverture began, "Perfidious republicans! You try to convince us that justice and the Republic assure us liberty, in the midst of a free people among whom reigns a perfect equality. Did the Republic need to shed so much innocent blood to establish itself?" He demanded to know, "how far are you going to extend your tyrannical powers after having ordered your infamous supporters to lay waste to our lands, burn our houses, slaughter our women, our children, our parents?" The French had committed a great crime by executing their king: "What proof of criminality could you bring against his sacred person, in order to put him to death like the worst of villains? Did your powers extend to that point?" Louis XVI had been "the unshakable pillar of the church, which you have trampled under foot, impious as you are." In their efforts to force the blacks back into slavery, Toussaint complained, "you had us pursued like ferocious beasts." "You try to make us believe that Liberty is a benefit that we will enjoy if we submit ourselves to order," Toussaint concluded, "but as long as God gives us the force and the means, we will acquire another Liberty, different from that which you tyrants pretend to impose on us" (AN, AA 55, d. 1511, August 8–27, 1793).

Toussaint Louverture's lengthy statement summed up the reasons why the black insurgents had consistently refused to look to the French revolutionaries as their allies or to see their professed principles of liberty and equality as meaningful in the context of Saint-Domingue's slave society. It is true that neither Toussaint Louverture nor the other black leaders were entirely blind to the possible emancipatory potential of the revolutionaries' ideas. On the same day that he signed his lengthy denunciation of the French Revolution, Toussaint Louverture also wrote another document, often referred to as the "proclamation of Turel," in which he used the language of the French Revolution for the first time, writing that "I want liberty and equality to reign throughout St. Domingue" (Tyson 1973: 28). Striking as this employment of revolutionary language is, however, it is important to recognize that the so-called proclamation was actually a letter meant only for certain specific readers, that there was no evidence that it ever circulated in Saint-Domingue – indeed, it was apparently seized by the revolutionary commissioners Sonthonax and Polverel, who commissioned one of their own supporters to refute it – and that the rest of the letter attempts to persuade its unidentified addressees to fight against the French, as Louverture himself continued to do for another seven months (Popkin 2010: 275).

Toussaint Louverture changed sides and allied himself with the French republicans in the spring of 1794, eventually becoming the commander of the French forces and using that position as his springboard to power. Louverture proved to be an effective translator of French revolutionary principles, both to the population in the colony and eventually to that of the metropole as well. "We are republicans," he wrote in a proclamation in June 1795 to the population of the colony, "and consequently free according to natural right. It can only be kings . . . who dare to claim the right to reduce to slavery men like themselves, whom nature has made free" (Laurent 1953: 182). When elections in metropolitan France in April 1797 returned a majority of deputies hostile to the equality granted to blacks in the colonies in 1793 and 1794, Louverture sent a proclamation across the ocean reminding the government that "it was the blacks who, when France risked losing this colony, used their strength and their weapons to keep it for her" (Louverture 1797). Nevertheless, Louverture translated revolutionary principles in his own way. Among other things, he consistently announced his personal commitment to Catholicism, even during the Directory period when the French government was at its most hostile to the Church, and the constitution he issued for Saint-Domingue in 1801 made Catholicism the official religion of the colony.

In 1799, Napoleon Bonaparte seized power in France and began to translate the principles of the revolution in ways that sometimes amounted to a repudiation of them. His attitude toward the ideas of 1789 was symbolized by his decision to omit a declaration of rights from the new constitution he promulgated two months after the coup of 18 Brumaire. The new constitution of 1799 clearly indicated that the political ideas of the metropole would not be translated to the colonies: one of its articles declared that the overseas territories would now be governed by "special laws," a formulation that clearly opened the way for the restoration of slavery where it had been abolished in 1794 and for its maintenance in colonies such as Martinique, where it had never been done away with. In Saint-Domingue, Toussaint Louverture responded by issuing his own constitution in 1801, which provided his own translation of revolutionary principles into colonial law. Above all, the 1801 constitution attempted to make the abolition of slavery in Saint-Domingue irreversible by modifying the language of the 1789 Declaration of Rights to state that all the inhabitants of the island, regardless of their race or place of birth, were free and French. Whether this document was ever translated into Creole for the benefit of the black population is not known.

Translations could not bridge the gap between, on the one hand, Louverture and the Saint-Domingue population, determined to maintain the freedom from slavery they had achieved, and, on the other hand, Napoleon, bent on restoring unchallenged metropolitan authority and white supremacy in the colony. After Napoleon sent a military expedition of more than 20,000 soldiers to Saint-Domingue in early 1802, force replaced words in the struggle for control of the island.

The French arrested Toussaint Louverture in June 1802 and sent him to France, where he died in prison after dictating a lengthy self-defense in which he tried valiantly to show that his actions had been a faithful translation of French principles to the colonial situation. The arrest of Louverture was not enough to assure Napoleon's success, however. As disease decimated the French forces, black resistance stiffened, and by the end of 1803, the new black leader Jean-Jacques Dessalines compelled the last French troops to surrender.

The French defeat was the occasion for a series of new acts of translation that served, not to bring the now independent nation of Haiti closer to France, but to make the separation between the former colony and the metropole permanent. Following the precedent of the American revolutionaries of 1776, the victorious black leaders translated their military success into the world's second declaration of national independence, written, ironically, in the language of the French whose sovereignty they were rejecting. In words reminiscent of the violent rhetoric of the revolutionary anthem, the "Marseillaise," Louis Boisrond-Tonnerre, one of Dessalines's secretaries, promised that the citizens of the newly named nation of Haiti would defend their freedom against "anyone who is born French, and who would soil with their sacrilegious foot the territory of liberty" ("quiconque né français, souillerait de son pied sacrilege le territoire de la liberté") (Gaffield 2016: 243).

Whereas the "Marseillaise" had been written in 1792 to spur French citizens to fight against foreign troops invading the country, the Haitian declaration of independence appeared at a moment when the military threat to the country had been reduced to insignificance. The violent words of the declaration were soon translated into acts, however, as Dessalines directed the systematic massacre of the remaining French whites, both civilians and military prisoners who had been too ill to be evacuated with the departing army. The 1804 massacres interrupted negotiations between the British in Jamaica and the Haitians that had come close to granting the latter recognition by the world's major overseas empire; it would take Haiti a generation to recover the diplomatic ground lost because of them. Enemies of abolition seized on the massacres as proof that blacks were an inherently savage race, unfit for a place in the civilized world.

The massacre of the white population in Haiti in 1804 was less a reflection of a generalized black savagery than of Dessalines's personal penchant for violence, on the one hand, and, on the other, of the long history of bloodshed in Saint-Domingue, both during the regime of slavery prior to 1791 and during the struggle that followed the outbreak of the slave revolt in August of that year. But, as the words of the proclamation Dessalines issued on April 28, 1804 to justify the massacres show, the killings were also a translation of a melodramatic notion of irreconcilable conflict between good and evil that was rooted in the French Enlightenment and the French Revolution, whose proponents often proclaimed themselves advocates of all that was good, pure and rational, and denounced their opponents as enemies of mankind. That proclamation closely followed the celebrated lines that Diderot inserted into the 1780 edition of Raynal's *Histoire des deux Indes* predicting that the injustice of slavery would sooner or later provoke a violent uprising.

This passage was certainly known in the colony: when he returned to the burned-out ruins of his home after the insurrection of 1791, one colonist somewhat improbably claimed that he had found his "elegant in-quarto edition of Raynal . . . still on my acajou table, open to the page containing this phrase: 'And if the blacks take vengeance, the laws for the whites will be terrible'" (Le Clerc 1793, cited in Popkin 2007: 104). Dessalines's proclamation referred to his followers as forming a "torrent"; Diderot had already spoken of a movement "more impetuous than the torrents" which would "leave everywhere ineffaceable traces of their justified anger." The proclamation spoke of avenging America; the Diderot passage had promised that "the fields of America will be intoxicated by the blood that they have for so long awaited, and the bones of so many unfortunates, piled up for three centuries, will tremble with joy." Dessalines had anticipated the homage future generations would pay him; Diderot had forecast that "the name of the hero who reestablished the rights of the human race will be blessed everywhere, everywhere they will put up trophies to his glory." Finally, Diderot had written, "The *Code noir* will disappear, and . . . the *Code blanc* will be terrifying, if the victor is inspired only by the right of reprisal" (Raynal 1780: Vol. 3, 204–5; Popkin 2016). Thus even the most extreme manifestation of anti-French violence in the Haitian Revolution can be seen as an act of translation: the translation of the Enlightenment's principles of natural law into melodramatic punishment of those held responsible for violating those principles.

The concept of translation, both in a literal and in a metaphorical sense, is thus useful in many ways for understanding how the impulse of the French Revolution affected other parts of the world and even sections of the French population that did not always see themselves as included in the new community of revolutionary citizens. The act of translation always involves a change of meanings:

even the most scrupulous translation puts what is translated into new contexts and necessarily changes its significance. At the same time, translations may reveal unrecognized potentialities in the content that is translated, as Sonthonax and Polverel did when they translated Louis XIV's oppressive *Code Noir* into a gesture on behalf of rights for slaves or when Dessalines translated Diderot's imaginary act of racial vengeance into an actual massacre. Finally, the concept of translation reminds us of the strategic importance of translators, of those individuals who are in a position to decide what ideas will be transmitted from one context to another. As humanity continues the ongoing struggle to translate ideals such as liberty and equality from the realm of ideas to that of social reality, the many complexities of translation during the revolutionary era continue to have important lessons for us.

Bibliography

Affiches américaines (1789), Port-au-Prince: Mozard.
Ami de l'égalité (1793), Port-au-Prince.
Archives nationales (Paris) (AN): series D XXV, AA.
Beauvois, baron de (1790), *Idées sommaires sur quelques règlements à faire par l'Assemblée coloniale*, Cap Français: Batilliot.
Bonnet, Edmond (1864), *Souvenirs historiques de Guy-Joseph Bonnet, general de division des armées de la République d'Haïti*, Paris: Auguste Durand.
Gaffield, Julia, ed. (2016), *The Haitian Declaration of Independence: Creation, Context, and Legacy*, Charlottesville: University of Virginia Press.
Garraway, Doris (2005), *The Libertine Colony: Creolization in the Early French Caribbean*, Durham, NC: Duke University Press.
Laurent, Gérard M. (1953), *Toussaint Louverture à travers sa correspondance (1794–1798)*, Madrid: Industrias Gracias España.
Louverture, Toussaint (1797), *Réfutation de quelques assertions d'un discours prononcé au corps législatif le 10 prairial, par Viénot Vaublanc*, Le Cap: Roux.
Le Clerc (2007 (1793)), "Campagne de Limbé," in Jeremy D. Popkin, *Facing Racial Revolution: Eyewitness Accounts of the Haitian Uprising*, Chicago: University of Chicago Press, pp. 93–104.
Moniteur générale de la partie française de Saint-Domingue (1791–93), Cap Français: Batilliot.
Patterson, Orlando (1982), *Slavery and Social Death: A Comparative Study*, Cambridge, MA: Harvard University Press.
Popkin, Jeremy D. (2007), *Facing Racial Revolution: Eyewitness Accounts of the Haitian Uprising*, Chicago: University of Chicago Press.

Popkin, Jeremy D. (2010), *You Are All Free: The Haitian Revolution and the Abolition of Slavery*, New York: Cambridge University Press.

Popkin, Jeremy D. (2016), "Jean-Jacques Dessalines, Norbert Thoret, and the Violent Aftermath of the Haitian Declaration of Independence," in Julia Gaffield, ed., *The Haitian Declaration of Independence: Creation, Context, and Legacy*, Charlottesville: University of Virginia Press.

Popkin, Jeremy D. (2017), "Colonial Enlightenment and the French Revolution: Julien Raymond and Milscent Créole," in Damien Tricoire, ed., *Enlightened Colonialism: Civilization Narratives and Imperial Politics in the Age of Reason*, Basingstoke: Palgrave Macmillan.

Popkin, Richard H. (1973), "The Philosophical Bases of Eighteenth-Century Racism," *Studies in Eighteenth-Century Culture* 3, pp. 245–62.

Raynal, Guillaume (1780), *Histoire des deux Indes*, Geneva: Pellet.

Thornton, John (1993), "'I am the Subject of the King of Kongo': African Ideology and the Haitian Revolution," *Journal of World History* 4, 181–214.

Tyson, George F. (1973), *Toussaint L'ouverture*, Englewood Cliffs: Prentice Hall.

Chapter 5

Enlightenment Tropes in French Popular Theater on the Haitian Revolution in the 1790s

Anja Bandau

> "Revolutionary theatre was never truly popular. And popular theatre was never truly revolutionary."
> (Michèle Root-Bernstein 2004)

The metaphor of theater surfaces persistently in relation to the descriptions of revolutionary events throughout cultural and literary history. The stage seems to represent the external world: the world as theater and revolution as theater. With respect to the Haitian Revolution, we can trace the metaphorical use of theatrical space in several texts on the events in Saint-Domingue and later Haiti; this metaphor also confirms the importance of the theatrical institution as a political space at the time (Camier and Dubois 2007). In more general terms, Elizabeth Maddock Dillon argues in relation to the colonial Anglo-Atlantic context that "in the space of the theatre ... audience and actors form an assemblage [in B. Latour's terms] that both embodies and represents the collectivity of the people" (2014: 4). According to her study, eighteenth-century popular theater attracted masses throughout the colonial Atlantic and served as a space of political interaction and contestation.

As I will argue in this chapter, theater served an important role in re-presenting revolutionary events and ideas on stage while also shaping the conception of these events for European metropolises. Jenna Gibbs has pointed out that popular theater played an especially crucial role in shaping "how predominantly white audiences" in Europe and America understood slave-led revolution, since the ambivalent attitude toward slave revolution was often represented in the theater's highly over-determined portrayals of revolutionary leaders (Gibbs 2015: 631). Gibbs's findings on blackface pantomime in Great Britain and the U.S. also hold true for the French context: "Blackface rebels were plastic figures in whom playwrights could sublimate ideological contention over slave revolt as a site of, on one hand, retributive violence and, on the other, democratic rights and liberation" (2015: 628).

In the last decade of the eighteenth century, French popular theater quite frequently adapted contemporary novels about slave rebellions, and particularly the Saint-Domingue insurrection, for the stage. Popular theater's accessibility and strong visual symbolism (which did not require literacy) certainly made it a successful venture. Already in 1789, Lavallé's novel *Le nègre comme il y a peu de blancs* dealt with abolition and a slave revolt prior to the actual events in Saint-Domingue, and in January 1790 it was transformed into a one-act play with *divertissements*, which saw multiple performances at the Vaudeville theater L'Ambigu-Comique in Paris. In 1795, Lavallé's text as well as Raynal's *Histoire des deux Indes* inspired Pigault-Lebrun's drama *Le blanc et le noir*, actually set in Saint-Domingue. Béraud and Rosny transformed Jean-Baptiste Picquenard's colonial anecdote *Adonis, ou le bon nègre* into a play of the same title in the very year of its initial publication (1798). There were also a number of other plays on the subject written and performed during the last decade of the eighteenth century. Nevertheless, within Literary and Theater Studies, the question of how the reverberations between "home politics" and "Haiti" played out on the metropolis's boulevard theater stages has only recently become a subject of research.

The reverberations between the revolution in Saint-Domingue, known as the Haitian Revolution, and other metropolitan and non-metropolitan spaces have been an object of study in work on the circulation of revolutionary news, ideas and agents in the context of the interconnected revolutionary Atlantic. In addition, the revolution in Saint-Domingue has come to signify an important Caribbean counterpart to, and radicalization of, the French Revolution and its democratic implications, pushing the latter's supposedly universal notions of liberty and equality to the limit while challenging the colonial order, which the French Revolution did not question. The Haitian Revolution's crucial place in global history is highlighted by the shift from a center-periphery model that juxtaposes metropolis and colony to a model of entangled history, a history of the circulation of objects, subjects, cultural practices and, generally speaking, knowledge. This chapter will focus on the differing aesthetics of *Le blanc et le noir* and *Adonis, ou le bon nègre*, and will raise the question of how the revolution and figures of the racialized other are represented and circulated in these plays. Drawing on the concepts of the melodramatic, the sentimental and the family romance, my analysis explores the reverberations between different phases of the French Revolution, especially the aftermath of the so-called *régime du terreur* (French Terror), on the one hand, and different aspects of and developments in the colonial space of Saint-Domingue (from social upheaval and political reform to colonial independence), on the other.

Both plays were written after the Terror, during the Directory (1795–98). This period of heightened debate in colonial politics, particularly about the recognition of non-white people as citizens (Dorigny and Gainot 1998: 302ff.), put abolition officially on the political agenda and temporarily established it as the status quo. The climate was characterized by a short phase of confidence in the possibility of a resolution of the situation in the colonies and of a defusing of the revolutionary situation in Saint-Domingue. This confidence influenced the way in which transatlantic reality entered the metropolitan scene. The day-to-day political context – such as the trial against civil commissioner Sonthonax in 1795 in Paris and the news arriving in France from Saint-Domingue – made the intricate relationship between metropole and colony clear, and might have been the reason or occasion for the publication of the plays, as theater at the time was a space for political debate.

A comparative study of both plays enables us to pinpoint a shift in the aesthetics of representation from bourgeois drama toward melodrama, and to offer a subtler description of the shifting representation of black revolutionary figures as they mirror political discussions during the Directory. Looked at comparatively, these plays and their different aesthetics help us understand how the depiction of the conflict varied under changing political conditions. By addressing the moral legitimacy of slave revolution and the possibility of recognizing (former) slaves as citizens, these texts negotiate conviviality between Europeans and their various colonial subjects. Whereas *Le blanc et le noir* in 1795 still envisions a shared future on the plantation in the colony, *Adonis, ou le bon nègre* in 1798 no longer presents this as an option.

Drama, the Melodramatic Mode, Sentimental Figures and the Spectacular

The French Revolution witnessed an explosion of theatrical forms, which at once represented and brought about radical political change.

Lynn Hunt (1984), Robert Darnton (1995) and Rolf Reichardt (2008: 272–3) have pointed out that this rupture, and the implementation of a "new" order, had to be instantiated and visualized as symbolic acts. A strong emphasis on plurimediality, consisting of public bill-posting, pamphlet culture, public performance of songs and debates in political clubs and revolutionary festivities, rehearsed the break with the old order that lay at the heart of French revolutionary culture. Popular hybrid forms such as the *opéra comique* and later melodrama, which relied on performance, music, pantomime and dance, as well as farce, boomed and (re-)created "a spectacle of revolution" (Barbara Darby in Gibbs 2015: 631). Theatrical representation, in Maddock Dillon's view, is intertwined with the question of the political representation of the common people and develops a political force (following Jacques Rancière's notion of the political) (Maddock Dillon 2014: 9f.). Her notion of the "performative commons," a revised version of the public sphere that draws on the "mutually informing practices of embodiment and representation found at the theatre" (2014: 4), is useful here. It draws on the fact that the often-excluded multitudes are represented through the body of a demos, the political commons in Maddock Dillon's words, that is performatively constituted, enacted in public manifestations both on stage and in the confines of a theater (2014: 11–13).

The general development of drama during the eighteenth century was linked to the shift from the focus on action and Aristotelian principles of its development, toward the spectacular impact of one singular event that was not necessarily founded on the logical unfolding of a plot or embedded in the thinking and action of the characters. The premise of the tableau (vivant) toward the end of the eighteenth century, a development that was accelerated by opera and musical plays, was linked to this transformation. Cathérine Ailloud-Nicolas (2008) argues that the spectacular mode is linked to the search for pathos – the violent effect – and for an action that causes destruction and suffering. The bourgeois drama (Diderot) that emphasizes serious depiction of the bourgeois family, emotion and empathy, as well as often implausible positive resolutions of conflict, draws on elements of an aesthetics different from that of the reduced characters of popular melodrama; nevertheless, it prefigures aspects of the melodramatic mode that became vital only at the end of the eighteenth century.

Melodrama functions "as a symptom of the anxiety generated by a frightening new world in which the traditional patterns of moral authority have collapsed. The force of that anxiety is registered in the apparent triumph of villainy, and then dissipated in the eventual victory of virtue" (Donald 1992: 111). Its extremes of good and evil structure its fundamental underlying psychic relations and ethical forces. To achieve these clear-cut contrasts, plots and characters are stereotypical. Violence is represented through evil and monstrous figures associated with the gothic mode, and is witnessed through the victim's pain as well as through the spectator's emotions in response to this suffering.

The aesthetic strategies of what Lynn Festa calls the "sentimental figures of Empire" in British and French eighteenth-century texts make "sentimental identification the primary means of representing metropolitan relations with colonial populations" and "give unprecedented centrality to feeling as a form of social and cultural differentiation" (Festa 2006: 3). According to Festa, the sentimental mode enabled "readers to identify with and feel for the plight of other people while upholding distinctive cultural and personal identities." That is, it "consolidated a sense of metropolitan community grounded in the selective recognition of the humanity of other populations" (2006: 2); a "sentimental community" that "upholds a common identity, not by forging bonds directly between seemingly like individuals, but by creating a shared relationship to a common but excluded object about which the community has feelings" (2006: 4). Sentimental figures located and assigned emotion to particular characters, thereby producing an experience of intimacy between imperial subjects and colonial objects of emotion characterized by pity and, therefore, by a hierarchical, non-egalitarian relationship. Though it suggests the possibility of empathy, "sympathetic identification creates difference rather than similitude" in these works (Festa 2006: 4). And one last vital aspect for the discussed context here: "Sentimental depictions of colonial encounters . . . converted scenes of violence and exploitation into occasions for benevolence and pity" (Festa 2006: 2).

The literary transformation of political conflict into private concern pervades literary practice throughout the French Revolution. The intimacy that results from positioning opponents in a very close (family) relationship[1] makes the violence inflicted even more monstrous. As Daut shows in *Tropics of Haiti* (2015), in narratives of the Haitian Revolution, this constellation of conflict in intimate relationships is accompanied by the implementation of the category of race and race relations: Here, hybrid figures, such as the mulatto/a who seeks vengeance on their white father/lover or betrays him, function as metaphorical or metonymical representations of colonial conflict as family drama.

Pigault-Lebrun's drama *Le blanc et le noir* (1795)

Le blanc et le noir was presented at Paris's Théâtre de la Cité[2] on November 5, 1795, but was removed from the repertoire by the author himself after only three performances. The drama is set in Saint-Domingue and enacts the revolution as family drama: At the coffee plantation Beauval near Cap Français, the plantation owner's philanthropist son Beauval *fils* befriends and plans to free one of the slaves – Télémaque – along with Télémaque's beloved female companion Zamé, who is subject to repeated whippings. When the plantation's manager threatens to sell Zamé, Télémaque calls for a rebellion, and the young Beauval must choose between saving his father's life and the righteous cause of armed insurrection led by his friend. The successful slaves defeat the white colonists but in an act of mercy decide to spare Beauval senior's life and accept his invitation to forget the horrors of slavery and live and work as "friends" on the plantation.

The prologue to the printed version (1796) – penned by the author to explain his intentions to an audience that had not approved of his play on stage – consists mainly of a compilation of citations from the famous eleventh book of Raynal's *Histoire des deux Indes* (1780). Pigault's drama enacts Raynal's argument that the cruelty of the slave trade and the violent excesses of the plantation masters provoke vengeance and violence among the ill-treated slaves. According to this logic, Télémaque becomes the avenger of his brutalized beloved Zamé and leads the insurrection (Pigault-Lebrun 1796: 84).

One of the main conflicts of the play is the tension between the logic of profit, embodied by the plantation's manager Matthieu, who "knows how to calculate," and the logic of humanist reason, embraced by his opponent Beauval *fils*. The latter accuses his antagonist of having transformed his father into a barbarian: "vous seul l'avez rendu barbare" (34). The conflict mirrors the arguments of the pro- and antislavery factions, whose fierce confrontation the metropolitan audience of 1795 had just witnessed during the trial of the civil commissioners Sonthonax and Polverel, France's representatives in Saint-Domingue. Their introduction of abolition in the colony in 1793 had led to the proclamation of abolition by the Convention in 1794. Accusing political enemies of terror was common after the end of Jacobin rule, and their trial (on the charge of having led a terror regime in the colony) was an attempt by the pro-slavery representatives of the colonists (club Massiac) to influence transatlantic colonial politics and eliminate the commissioners. The trial ended in the summer of 1795 with the rehabilitation of Sonthonax (Polverel had died in the meantime).

The then-prevailing pro-abolition stance is present in Pigault-Lebrun's play. Through the eyes of the enlightened younger Beauval, the audience sees the misery inflicted on the slaves. When he accuses the Europeans of barbarism and warns his fellow Europeans of the impending revolt of the slaves, echoing Raynal's prophecy of slave rebellion, the play credits the revolting slaves with moral integrity. He positions himself "between Raynal and Jean-Jacques, these friends of virtue, these benefactors of the world" ("entre Raynal et Jean-Jacques, ces amis de la vertu, ces bienfaiteurs du monde") (51). His plea against the atrocities of slavery culminates in two long monologues that directly echo Diderot's famous condemnation of European colonialism in *Histoire des deux Indes*:[3] "Oh white men, white men! If these images cannot move you; if your soul does not rise against itself, if you do not feel the harrowing pang of regret, may lightning purge the earth of your detestable species!" ("O blancs, blancs! Si ces images ne peuvent vous émouvoir; si votre âme ne se soulève pas contre elle-même, si vous ne sentez pas le trait déchirant du remords, puisse la foudre purger la terre de votre détestable espèce!") (46). But this radical view is thwarted by a second discursive move when Beauval *fils* addresses the slaves using notions of love, friendship and patience to contain the conflict and to foreclose all violent action. He urges Télémaque to embrace friendship in the name of reason in order to "erase," that is, to put aside, and, supposedly, avoid all suffering and discomfort (23). Pigault represents on stage Raynal's main argument that while the excessive mistreatment of slaves causes an excess of violence, good treatment leads to "moral" behavior – that is, integrity and loyalty to the white masters.

Le blanc et le noir represents the political and ideological conflict as a private, ethical conflict between father and son. The not-quite-white son questions and subverts the enslaving paternal authority that represents the old absolutist power and replaces it with fraternity with the former slave. At the beginning of the insurrection, a conflict arises between father and son as well as between the two brothers/friends. Beauval *fils* accuses Télémaque of forcing him to commit patricide when he supports the slave revolt. Télémaque's response points toward the wider social dimension of that supposedly private conflict by alluding to the value of freedom: "The real patricide is the one that kills the liberty of nations" ("Le véritable parricide est celui qui tue la liberté des nations") (98). Beauval *fils*' inner conflict between support of the revolution and family loyalty not only leads to his ambivalent attitude toward armed insurrection but also culminates in treason. Having to choose between two crimes (100), Beauval *fils* betrays Télémaque's secret, his trust and their friendship when he warns his father of the insurrection. Beauval *fils*' conflictive persona is mirrored in Télémaque's character, torn between revolutionary violence and friendship. Ready to accept the consequences of his actions, Beauval *fils* puts his life in the hands of Télémaque, who in an act of mercy forgives him and places friendship and humanity above revolutionary violence and vengeance (107). This moment of heightened conflict prepares the play's peripeteia and its main statement: Betrayal of the revolution out of friendship and love seems forgivable, and friendship will always be rewarded (107).

The play's last act firmly establishes this moral law of love, friendship and mercy as the alternative to revolutionary violence and terror. From the perspective of the insurgents this development seems quite contradictory, since the armed insurrection has produced its first successes, and an independent existence of the revolutionary slaves has come into view for the first time. This independence is symbolized by the alternative space of a cave where the armed former slaves have set up their camp (108). When Télémaque plans to continue the battle and seeks revenge against his former master Beauval, his female counterpart and companion Zamé contradicts him. Zamé, the incarnation of innocence, defines the logic of the play: She condemns Télémaque's plans of continued violence, accusing him of being ruled by uncontrolled and therefore negative passions (such as vengeance). By contrast, she recommends mercy, a stance she herself considers morally superior (121). Indeed, during the rebels' retreat, Zamé plans to save the defeated Beauval *père* from the insurgents' vengeance. In the final scene, Beauval *père* is moved by his former slave's generosity and altruism[4] and invites all the former slaves and colonists to participate in a compromise that will resolve the conflict: "Let's forget that there existed masters and slaves at my plantation. Come, my friends, begin to build your fortune helping me to increase mine . . . Let's forget our past misfortunes" ("Oublions qu'il exista sur mon habitation un maitre et des esclaves. Venez, mes amis, venez commencer votre fortune en m'aidant à relever la mienne . . . oublions nos malheurs passés") (123). The audience is offered a solution involving an improbable act of mercy that is inspired by a sudden conversion and that requires a loss of memory. Amnesia and friendship are to enable the cohabitation between blacks and whites. A social consensus, a new coherence of society, is envisioned at the cost of forgetting the violent past – not only anticolonial violence but most importantly the violence of the colonial economic system, the overthrow of which Pigault-Lebrun's drama refuses to consider. In this final scene, the author stages his version of the sublime, one that had already been explicitly formulated in the play's prologue: The sublime lies in the slave's morally superior behavior, that is, his capacity to sacrifice his physical as well as moral integrity to his master's wellbeing in spite of the mistreatment he has experienced at the hand of the latter.

Télémaque, who had aspired to freedom and vengeance, experiences an equally implausible conversion. Convinced by Zamé's moral appeal, by Beauval *fils*' pleading to spare his father's life, and by Beauval's sudden conversion, he has the final say on stage and calls his fellow revolutionaries back to work on the plantation:

> Brave companions, let us hurry to prove to our enemies that idleness, robbery, injustice have not put weapons in our hands. Man is born to work. Let us return into the plain, let us fertilize the fields that we just devastated, and may the example of Beauval, by enlightening the colonists about their true interests, finally motivate them to secure their fortune through justice and humanity.

> Braves compagnons, hâtons-nous de prouver à nos ennemis que l'oisiveté, le brigandage, l'injustice, ne nous ont pas mis les armes à la main. L'homme est né pour le travail. Retournons dans la plaine, fertilisons ces champs que nous venons de ravager, et puisse l'exemple de Beauval, en éclairant les Colons sur leurs véritables intérêts, les déterminer enfin à consolider leur fortune par la justice et l'humanité. (123)

Télémaque not only misses the opportunity to gain liberty through armed revolt, he also conflates injustice, idleness and theft in his enumeration of possible motives for the insurrection in such a way that the legitimate cause – injustice – becomes illegitimate through its implied equivalence with the latter two. Instead of armed revolt, he relies on the justice and humanity of his former abusers to guarantee freedom. Revolution is discredited and rejected as a viable path toward emancipation.

This highly improbable resolution – one that dismisses anticolonial revolutionary violence by criminalizing it and condemning it as morally inferior, and that simply "forgets" colonial violence – appears necessary in the logic of colonial/racial drama because it is only through this strategic maneuver that cohabitation between metropolitans and colonial subjects, Europeans and former slaves, seems possible within the existing economic system. This constellation is reminiscent of the aftermath of Terror because it not only questions revolutionary violence at all costs but also proposes love and friendship as figures of healing the traumatic past. Thus, it mirrors the efforts to envision a possible way of future conviviality that emerged in the wake of the revolution. The new alliance between Beauval *fils*, Télémaque and Zamé and the transformed father Beauval – based on the principles of solidarity, mutual appreciation and respect – echoes not only the constitution of 1795 but also Rousseau's idea of a social contract that enables individuals to attain civil liberty, that is, a sense of justice and morality within this new community. But at the same time this social contract strangely obligates them to work and participate in the land's owner's "tak[ing] possession of . . . his ground by labour and cultivation" (Rousseau 2010: 10).[5]

"Ils sont comme nous"/"They are like us": The Slave as *Citoyen*

The new subject emerging from the French Revolution was the *citoyen*, who was represented as an *honnête homme*, a man of virtue. Pigault's *Le blanc et le noir* negotiates the subjects of colonial and racial revolution in the context of the young French Republic with the help of a plot that combines the notions of virtue, equality and education (as the means of gradual transformation and emancipation). Pigault-Lebrun's prologue portrays the slaves as subject to the same passions and sentiments as Europeans, but capable of extremely virtuous conduct that seems sublime in the metropolitan observer's eye. In his play, the moral virtue and superiority of the slaves serves as the main argument for their integration into the new society. Moreover, the slave leader's name, Télémaque, affiliates the character with a hero from ancient epic, an association that elevates him to a character of classical drama. Pigault's Télémaque is the embodiment of an educated slave, perfectly capable of reason, virtue, friendship and sensibility (Pigault-Lebrun 1796: 27). However, consonant with abolitionist arguments of the time, the political and moral education of the African slave was considered the result of a longer process that could only happen with the help of educated and enlightened members of society, equated mostly with Europeans. Consistently, in the play, the slaves get a glimpse of their rights and liberty only through the teachings of Beauval *fils* (89–91), and Télémaque becomes able to cite the enlightened philosophers by following in the footsteps of his white friend: "Europeans, it is at this price that you eat sugar . . ." ("Européens, c'est à ce prix que vous mangez du sucre . . .," Voltaire,

Candide, 1759).⁶ Another intertext supports this hierarchical mentor-pupil-relationship: In Fenelon's educational novel *Les aventures de Télémaque* (1695) the young Telemachos is undertaking a journey together with his mentor, the actual hero of the book, who teaches him enlightened ideals. The parallels between Fenelon's mentor figure (who turns out to be Minerva, goddess of wisdom) and Pigault-Lebrun's Beauval *fils* highlight the hierarchical relation between the latter and Télémaque in *Le blanc et le noir*.

It is through the character of Beauval *fils*, who from the start is presented as *honnête*, virtuous, that the audience is invited to perceive the slaves as equal. He observes that "They are like us" ("Ils sont comme nous"). This radical statement of equality is supported by Télémaque's portrayal as an equal of Beauval *fils*, his friend, worthy of being part of *la patrie*. This friendship, however, turns out to be defined by subtle differences, which ultimately undermine Télémaque's equality. The opponents of humanism, Beauval *père*, his plantation manager Mathieu and the slave trader Barthelemy, ridicule him and his companions as "negroes . . . scholars, . . . thinkers" ("nègres . . . savans, . . . penseurs") (10) and later as "philosophes" (19). Télémaque's unrestrained passions – vengeance, rage, jealousy – further endanger his moral superiority and become a potential threat to the family romance. Although his reactions are rendered understandable, his passions – reminiscent of the violent period of terror – are represented as potentially evil and must be disciplined.⁷ This aspect is crucial, because in the play's logic, it is why the insatiable passions that lie at the heart of armed revolution have to be eliminated through sudden conversion at the end of the play.

Furthermore, the representation of the slave characters makes it very clear that the educated and eloquent Télémaque is an exception in the slave population. As noted, education was considered a precondition for slaves' access to citizenship. In *Le blanc et le noir*, the majority of the slaves are depicted in a way that marks an enormous gap between their behavior and the position of the enlightened citizen. The naive, Creole-speaking character Scipion makes this clear as he lacks the sense of self-emancipation Télémaque has acquired: "I will do all that pleases Télémaque" ("Yo va fait tout ca qui plai à Télémaque") (85). In his case, the ambiguity of the practice of naming slave characters becomes obvious.⁸ His character is ridiculous not only by virtue of his naivety and his "deficient French," but also due to the striking difference between these characteristics and the heroic attributes of his namesake, the famous Roman general Scipion (235–183 BC), who defeated Hannibal in the war against Carthage and was given the epithet "Africanus" because he helped Rome to conquer Africa. The historical namesake Scipion had a heroic literary afterlife in Cicero (*De republica*), Plutarch, Petrarch, and in Haendel's opera *Publio Cornelio Scipione*. But Pigault-Lebrun refers to this literary tradition in a burlesque way. Obviously, his Scipion does not conquer Africa but, on the contrary, is fighting for liberation from slavery. We might assume that this fact and the difference in characterization when compared to Télémaque motivate the burlesque reference to antiquity/antique literary tradition.

By emphasizing the unsettling role of hybrid figures in the depiction of colonial conflict (Daut 2015), we can re-evaluate the position of enunciation that Beauval *fils* is accorded in the play. The non-white characters are not the only ones who must adapt to the new society (that is, conform to a white norm of civilization); the enlightened, philanthropical white protagonist is also positioned outside that white norm, though for other reasons. Because of his abolitionist attitude, the slaves on the plantation spare Beauval *fils* from their condemnation of white colonists and do not consider him white anymore (see Pigault-Lebrun 1796: 90ff.). His position is thereby shifted closer to that of the black slaves, opening the way for the utopian ideal of a new, reformed potential family by facilitating a union between "le blanc et le noir." At the same time, he embodies the gap between this utopian ideal and the current state of race relations in French society. His in-between status is in a telling way reminiscent of the in-between position that Saint-Domingue's *gens de couleur*/people of color assumed in the process of decolonization and abolition, having often enough been assigned the role of mediator between Europeans and black slaves.

From Bourgeois Drama to Sentimental Drama and Melodrama

The names of the protagonist slave-couple – Zamé and Télémaque – are too significant to overlook. I have pointed out the different implications of choosing a character from antiquity – in Scipion's case – or antique mythology – in the case of Telemachos. The female black character Zamé resonates with the protagonist of Saint-Lambert's moral tale *Ziméo* (1769), one of the rare texts that represent the leaders of slave rebellion in French literature. The character is also present in Zameo, the main character in August von Kotzebue's play *Die Negersklaven* (1796), clearly indebted to Saint-Lambert's story as well as to Raynal's *Histoire des deux Indes* and written shortly after Pigault's play. Whereas Télémaque's treatment in *Le blanc et le noir* points toward the elevation of the black character, Scipion's representation inclines more toward parody. The differing reference to tradition intensifies the ambiguity of the characters; in order to determine whether either of these tendencies predominates, one would have to take into account aspects of performance and production practice. These details would also be of importance for considering the status of melodramatic strategies in Pigault-Lebrun's play. The author himself deliberately used the term "drama" in his subtitle, thereby linking the play to a genre that deals with people from the new center of society, a genre that sought to create a new social consensus through the enactment of inner conflict followed by a resolution achieved through all-encompassing virtue and sentiment. If we take it seriously, Pigault's choice of genre goes hand in hand with the development of the characters and with his quite radical suggestion that the African revolutionary leader is part of this new social consensus. Nevertheless, *Le blanc et le noir*'s improbable ending, which forecloses revolution by appealing to notions of love and friendship, and dispels vengeance through forgetting, pushes the play's aesthetics nearer to the sentimental drama and the future melodrama than to the drama itself.

The status of melodrama in Pigault's play can be explored via a comparison with two other plays that clearly belong to the latter genre. One year after Pigault-Lebrun, the German playwright August von Kotzebue would focus on the display of the battered or mutilated enslaved man or woman on stage and visualize suffering in a melodramatic way, successfully bringing it close to the audience with the help of a mediating figure (William) who feels empathy and pity on behalf of the audience. In comparison to Kotzebue's and other adaptations of the abolitionist topic for the stage, one aspect of *Le blanc et le noir* stands out: its focus on the inner conflict of Beauval *fils* and Télémaque. Only to a very limited extent does it represent on stage the physical pain of the enslaved, using what Lynn Festa has called sentimental figures, which allow the European spectator to feel compassion from a distance. Despite the fact that Zamé's physical punishment is the decisive impulse in the play, in which – very much in the spirit of melodrama – the "evil" in the form of Mathieu's whipping of Zamé crosses a categorical border that triggers the insurrection and thus pushes ahead the conflict, this incident is the only moment where the physical effects of punishment are explicitly shown.

Another argument against categorizing the play as melodrama is Pigault's strategy of translating Raynal onto the stage mainly through monologues, thereby rendering visible Beauval's and Télémaque's inner conflict. This resists the stereotypical characterizations common in melodrama. William's mediating role in Kotzebue's play is in some ways quite similar to that of Beauval *fils* in *Le blanc et le noir*, but differs decisively with respect to his proximity to the black protagonist: In Pigault-Lebrun's drama Beauval *fils*' inner conflict and his overall character are much closer to those of the eloquent and passion-ridden Télémaque than is the case with William and Zaméo. The resemblance between Beauval *fils* and Télémaque, as I suggested above, enabled the utopian vision of a new French family, even if equality ultimately proves elusive. One could argue that Pigault-Lebrun's drama thus makes the closeness of the black and white protagonists too serious and substantial to maintain the unidirectional distance Festa sees at play in the imperial mode of sentimental figures. This is even more evident in the case of Beauval the father, where pity is directed at the white characters. Pigault-Lebrun's main black protagonist is, from this perspective, too complex a figure to elicit the pity and empathy that sentimental figures such as *le bon nègre* – which we will see in Rosny and Béraud's *Adonis* – can provoke.

The Melodrama Par Excellence: Béraud and Rosny's *Adonis, ou le bon nègre*

In contrast to Pigault-Lebrun, the authors Béraud and Rosny unequivocally use the melodramatic mode in 1798 to bring the events of the revolution onto the Parisian stage.[9] In their play *Adonis, ou le bon nègre*, subtitled "*a melodrama in four acts, with dance, song, Creole decor and costumes,*" musical mediation, living scenery (tableau vivant) and dance come to play a crucial role in channeling and transmitting emotion. Even more importantly, these elements make up for a reduced argumentative depth and illogical plot development typical of the melodramatic form emerging at the end of the last decade of the eighteenth century.

Béraud and Rosny's play is based on a novel by the same title, written by Jean-Baptiste Picquenard and published the same year. However, the adaptors made some significant changes concerning the aesthetics and the political implications of the plot: Whereas the novel relies on eyewitness accounts and hints at historical events in combination with a romance that complicates the question of whether to condemn or to justify slave revolution, the melodrama almost completely erases the historical context offered in the novel and reduces its evaluation of slave revolution to single-minded condemnation.[10] There are, however, references to current political discussions of colonial issues in the metropolis – e.g. the changing attitude toward Toussaint Louverture – and adaptations to the authors' political agenda – e.g. the condemnation of the Terror, and the enforcement of republican values. The plot is simple: The humane and philanthropic owner of a coffee plantation, d'Herouville, is attacked and imprisoned at the camp of revolutionary leader Biassou; he becomes an eyewitness to the latter's terror regime. D'Herouville's slaves defend him, and their leader, Adonis, saves the life of d'Herouville and his family with the help of his beloved Zerbine. In return, the slaves are granted freedom and the land as their *patrimoine*. Whereas in the short novel, d'Herouville's black and white family, which now includes Adonis and Zerbine, has to flee the island and live in exile in the United States,[11] in the play, Biassou is defeated and Adonis becomes the "savior of the colony." The fate of the colony seems in far less danger in the play than in the novel, and d'Herouville returns to republican France.

The first dialogue in the play between the exemplary plantation owner d'Herouville and the revolutionary leader Biassou recalls accusations against white plantation owners in Raynal and Pigault-Lebrun. Biassou questions d'Herouville's humanity – "You are white and you are human?" ("Tu es blanc et tu es humain?") – and states: "I purge the colony of these European barbarians who held us in shame and in slavery" ("Je purge la colonie de ces barbares Européens qui nous tenoient dans la honte, et dans l'ésclavage") (Béraud and Rosny 1798: 13). But Biassou, as the leader of the revolt, is unequivocally condemned and portrayed as barbaric, treacherous, bloodthirsty and ungrateful. When d'Herouville tries to reason with him, and in a philosophical speech tries to change his mind, he describes Biassou's actions as a reign of terror, punishing the innocent and destroying the colony's future:

> What did they do, those tender mothers, those faithful wives, those children whom you are killing ... You who anticipate nothing beyond today, what will be your fate, when you have pillaged, destroyed and burned everything? Even supposing that no white man escapes your fury, do you think that you will extinguish the race? ... abandon those who use your arm to satiate their hatred and their passions, become a man again, and you will find your recompense in the good that you will have done.

> Qu'ont fait ces mères tendres, ces épouses fidelles, ces enfans . . . que vous égorgez . . . Vous qui ne prévoyez rien au-delà du jour qui vous éclaire, quelle sera votre sort, lorsque vous aurez tout pillé, dévasté, incendié? En supposant qu'aucun blanc n'échappe à votre fureur, pensez-vous pour cela en éteindre la race? . . . abandonne ceux qui se servent de ton bras pour assouvir leur haine, leur passions, redevins homme, et tu trouveras ta recompense dans le bien que tu auras fait. (14)

In the play, the novel's testimonial mode yields to melodrama and pantomime, and the counterpart of Pigault's ambiguous revolutionary leader, Télémaque, is split into two unidimensional characters: Adonis – the good negro – and Biassou, the barbaric villain. In what is clearly a move from drama toward melodrama, Adonis embodies unconditional loyalty to his master and is prepared to give his life to save him. While the Adonis of the short novel engages in a philosophical dialogue with his master, questioning European humanist thought, this dimension is completely absent in the play. General Biassou, who is the opposite of the good-natured Adonis, represents the actual armed insurrection confronting the white population with a terror regime. Through Biassou's character, revolution is criminalized as robbery and inhumane violence. The two characters function in Manichean counterpoint; the sentimental figure versus the monstrous one, introducing the gothic mode, sentimentalism's antidote in melodrama.

Whereas the novel's Biassou seems to be modeled after the historical figure George Biassou, one of the leaders in Saint-Domingue's north during the early phase of insurrection, and a man described by several contemporary sources as cruel, the play takes a very different tack. Here, the character "Biassou" is quite openly linked to Toussaint Louverture, at that time the powerful leader of the revolt, who controlled Saint-Domingue and forced commissioner Sonthonax to leave in 1797.[12] With this conflation of the two historical figures, the melodrama *Adonis, ou le bon nègre* takes up current political events and alludes to the dramatically changed, negative image of Toussaint that Sonthonax put into circulation in his report to the *Conseil des Cinq Cent* in February 1798 in reaction to the events in Saint-Domingue. The powerful position that Toussaint Louverture acquired, moreover, was not merely discredited by the equation of Toussaint with the villain in the play; it also led to Biassou-Toussaint's presentation as an equal adversary, capable of using the enlightened language of his opponents. Interestingly, the character of Biassou-Toussaint is not belittled, but presented as a gothic figure embodying the monstrous. Whereas all other African-born characters speak a pseudo-Creole marked as a defective French, which effectively reduces the slaves to naive and childlike characters, Biassou does not speak Creole and acts autonomously.

In accordance with the melodramatic mode, the focus in Béraud and Rosny's presentation of the plot clearly lies on the performative aspects as well as on musical accentuation and mediation. A significant number of monologues and dialogues are sung and musical numbers are inserted. The first scene opens with the love banter between Lindor and Marinette, two slave characters who take the role of the comic and good-natured servants; they announce festivities in honor of Mme d'Herouville. Throughout two more scenes, the slaves play music, sing and dance; several local musical instruments and dances (such as bamboula, calebasses, the banza – a form of banjo, chica – a dance) are mentioned, which creates the local color promised in the presentation of the play. The happy setting of d'Herouville's plantation, where gratitude, love, friendship and mutual loyalty prevail, contrasts with reports of Biassou's massacres and his arrival at the end of the first act.

As we can see in the extensive stage directions, music serves as mediation and punctuation (Elsaesser 1972): The orchestra announces danger and underscores the emotional development on stage. Music comments, dramatizes and lends local color, but also provides a background. Elsaesser understands music as a form of punctuation that creates a specific mood – sorrow, violence, fear, suspense, happiness. But the stage directions also give precise details about action, body language and gesture. The performative force of the tableau vivant as well as that of the ballet create spectacular scenes. At the moments of crisis and climax – for example, when d'Herouville is captured by Biassou in the first act, and when Biassou is defeated and at the mercy of Zerbine and Adonis at the end of the play – the tableau creates pathetic moments in fierce scenes of fighting. Local color is emphasized through the use of Creole, adding to the exoticizing and belittling of slave culture. The argumentative logic may be weak, but the united force of visual effect, music, performance and discourse guarantee that the message is conveyed to the public.

Republican Citizenship Performed and Revolutionary Violence Condemned: Metropolis and Colony

Béraud and Rosny's play uses the two antithetical leaders to juxtapose two paths toward abolition and freedom: The first, embodied by Biassou-Toussaint, confronts us with self-determined but violent insurrection; the second, represented by the eponymous good negro Adonis, represents loyalty, devotion and patience – in short, dependency on the good will of the colonial master. In keeping with French enlightened ideas about virtue, a patriarchal relationship between owner and slaves persists throughout Béraud and Rosny's play: It is the individual plantation owner who grants the slaves their freedom, bequeaths to them the ownership of the land, and imparts to them the ethical rules of living together. The future citizens – that is the former black slaves – are integrated through the moral categories of friendship and love within the framework of the family romance. But are the slaves really integrated into a shared society?

D'Herouville and his extended family go back to France and grant freedom and property to their former slaves. When the slaves show their devotion and attachment in an excess of emotion and ask to leave with their masters, they are reminded that their homeland/*patrie* is on the island, where they should work and live in union and "happy harmony," a union guaranteed by the principles of a just society, virtue, friendship and love (Béraud and Rosny 1798: 10, 35–8). Adonis is invited as "friend and brother" into the new republican family, but the majority of former slaves stay home (on the island) and, more importantly, must create their home from the former colony. The negotiation of citizenship and conviviality as well as of the relation between metropolis and colony has only begun, and it is a premonition of the solutions to come: Metropolitan France and colony remain separate spaces, the majority of the slaves become part of the – largely abstract – *unanimité des français*. This is *fraternité* (33) at a distance.

If melodrama considers festivities as the highest moment of positive utopia (as Wehle 1983: 157 argues), the play begins with precisely this utopian moment at the plantation d'Herouville, which also introduces the privileged scene of hierarchized conviviality between white and black.[13] Armed insurrection shatters any chance of multiracial cohabitation. At this point, melodrama – while denying the legitimacy of slave revolution – takes into account the current political situation, the impossibility of peaceful conviviality in Saint-Domingue. What was still an option in Pigault's play – the maintenance of the colonial order and a cohabitation of black and white on the plantation, even if achieved only through a stabilization of the colonial system relying on a logic of implausible conflict resolution – no longer seems possible in Rosny and Béraud's *Adonis*: Whereas *Le blanc et le noir* in 1795 still envisions a shared future on the plantation in the colony, *Adonis, ou le bon nègre* in 1798 laments the loss of this harmonious state, and d'Herouville and his family leave the colony together with Adonis.

Looking at the ending of Béraud and Rosny's play, what seems clear at first sight ultimately remains peculiarly open and imprecise. The play does not specify what the title "savior of the colony," which Adonis is awarded in the end, actually means. It suggests several readings: Perhaps it implies that he has saved the colony from serious destruction, providing its future inhabitants – whether former colonists and former slaves, or only former slaves – a material basis on which to live and work in this rich and productive territory. But it could also mean that Adonis has secured France's colony by defeating Biassou, hand in hand with French soldiers.[14] Republican values, in this reading, triumph against revolutionary terror in France; armed revolution is from the start not an option because it threatens France's colonial and imperial claim. It is considered as being too close to the legacy of terror and therefore portrayed as not legitimate.

Conclusion

During the short period of abolition of slavery in eighteenth-century French colonies, especially under the Directory, popular theater took slave revolution to the stage in an attempt to make it palatable for metropolitan political and ideological tastes. Staging this colonial topic meant taking a position in current political debates while negotiating metropolitan concerns. Theater was conceived of as an alternative political space where current political debates were re-examined and where post-Terror metropolitan issues and the legacy of republican ideals were negotiated. Both the plays discussed here gave their audiences an opportunity to relive the threat of slave revolution, but they also attempted to provide a means to overcome the hostile situation with the help of a family romance based upon love and friendship and a sentimental drama employing the dynamics of melodrama. In this experimental phase of French popular theatre, different forms coexisted within the *ambigu comique*. While melodrama is distinguished by its use of music, (sentimental) drama creates characters and constellations very close to those of melodrama. Sentimental drama is steeped in sentimentality but preserves elements of tragedy

(Pigault-Lebrun tries to present the leader of the revolting slaves as a classical hero, equal to the white protagonists). The moralizing efficiency of the theatre that the authors tried to put in place during the revolutionary period must be considered if one wants to understand the plays in question. Like other contemporary authors (cf. Kjaergard 2018: 166), Pigault-Lebrun and Béraud and Rosny argued for the social inclusion of hitherto marginalized groups and relied on the paradigm of family responsibility as the basis for happiness. Both plays show that the new French republican order had constantly to negotiate the meaning of equality, fraternity and liberty, not only in the hexagon, but also in relation to colonial questions. Both texts envision the inclusion of non-white actors in the patriotic family. In this context, the representation of virtue – an important task of revolutionary theatre – plays a decisive role. At the same time, the texts introduce a transformed racial hierarchy, negotiated under the conditions of a very fuzzy picture of a reformed colonial order. Pigault's quite radical equation of the complex characters of Télémaque and Beauval *fils*, his black and his white protagonists, gives way to a re-enforced hierarchization in Béraud and Rosny's play and its reduced central figures Adonis, the good negro, and Biassou, the monster. Whereas *Le blanc et le noir* represents the rare chance of equality in 1795, this opening disappears with political change in both the metropolis and in the colony in 1798. The comparison of both plays shows different attempts at controlling colonial and racial revolution by taming, denying or criminalizing the violent revolutionary overthrow of the racial and colonial order in a fictional representation on stage. Both the (sentimental) bourgeois drama and the melodrama include non-white actors in the patriotic family, but at the same time re-establish the racial hierarchy and the colonial order. It is remarkable that in the new Republic they are subject to negotiation.

Bibliography

Ailloud-Nicolas, Cathérine (2008), "Scènes de théâtre. Le tremblement de terre de Lisbonne (1755) et *Le Jugement dernier des Rois* (1793)," in Anne-Marie Mercier-Faivre and Chantal Thomas, eds, *L'invention De La Catastrophe Au XVIIIe Siècle: Du Châtiment Au Désastre Naturel*, Geneva: Droz, pp. 403–17.

Bandau, Anja (2008), "'Unglaubliche Tatsachen': Die haitianische Revolution und die anecdote coloniale," in Sven Grampp, Kay Kirchmann, Marcus Sandl and Eva Wiebel, eds, *Revolutionsmedien – Medienrevolutionen*.

Die Medien der Geschichte 2 (Historische Kulturwissenschaft), Konstanz: UVK, pp. 573–96.
Benzhaken, Jean-Charles (2010), "Introduction générale," in François Marie Bottu and Jean-Charles Benzaken, *La liberté générale, ou, Les colons à Paris*, Paris: SPM, pp. 13–85.
Béraud de la Rochelle, Louis-Fr.-Guillaume and Antoine Joseph Nicolas de Rosny (1798), *Adonis ou le bon nègre: mélodrame en quatre actes avec danses, chansons, décors et costumes créoles*, Paris: Glisau, Pigoreau et Le Pan.
Brooks, Peter (1976), *The Melodramatic Imagination: Balzac, Henry James, Melodrama, and the Mode of Excess*, New Haven: Yale University Press.
Camier, B. and L. Dubois (2007), "Voltaire et Zaïre, ou le théâtre des Lumières dans l'aire atlantique française," *Revue d'Histoire Moderne et Contemporaine* 54:4, pp. 39–69.
Chappey, Jean-Luc (2009), "Les tribulations de Joseph Rosny (1771–1814). Questions sur le statut de l'écrivain en révolution," *Annales historiques de la Révolution française* 356, at <http://ahrf.revues.org/10625> (last accessed October 22, 2020).
Darnton, Robert (1995), *The Forbidden Bestsellers of Pre-revolutionary France*, New York: Fontana Press.
Daut, Marlene L. (2015), *Tropics of Haiti: Race and the Literary History of the Haitian Revolution in the Atlantic world, 1789–1865*, Liverpool: Liverpool University Press.
Donald, James (1992), *Sentimental Education: School, Popular Culture and the Regulation of Liberty*, London: Verso.
Dorigny, Marcel and Bernard Gainot (1998), *La Société des Amis des Noirs: 1788–1799. Contribution à l'histoire de l'abolition de l'esclavage, Mémoire des peuples*, Paris: Éditions UNESCO.
Elsaesser, Thomas (1972), "Tales of Sound and Fury: Observation on the Family Melodrama," *Monogram* 4, pp. 2–15.
Festa, Lynn (2006), *Sentimental Figures of Empire in Eighteenth-Century Britain and France*, Baltimore: The Johns Hopkins University Press.
Garraway, Doris (2009), "Of Speaking Natives and Hybrid Philosophers: Lahontan, Diderot, and the French Enlightenment Critique of Colonialism," in Daniel Carey and Lynn Festa, eds, *Postcolonial Enlightenment*, Oxford: Oxford University Press, pp. 207–39.
Gibbs, Jenna (2015), "Toussaint, Gabriel, and Three Finger'd Jack: 'Courageous Chiefs' and the 'Sacred Standard of Liberty' on the Atlantic Stage," *Journal of Early American Studies* 13:3, pp. 626–60.
Hunt, Lynn (1984), *The Family Romance of the French Revolution*, London: Routledge.
Kjaergard, Jonas (2018), *Reimagining Society in Eighteenth-Century French Literature: Happiness and Human Rights*, New York: Routledge.
Kotzebue, August von (1796), *Die Negersklaven. Ein historisch-dramatisches Gemählde in drey Akten*, Leipzig: Kummer.

Lavallé, Joseph (1789), *Le nègre comme il y a peu de blancs*, Madras et Paris.

Lecomte, Henry L. (1910), *Histoire des théâtres de Paris: Le théâtre de la Cité 1792–1807*, Paris: H. Daragon.

McClellan, Michael (2004), *The Revolution on Stage: Opera and Politics in France, 1789–1800*, at <https://www.nla.gov.au/harold-white-fellows/the-revolution-on-stage> (last accessed October 22, 2020).

Maddock Dillon, Elizabeth (2014), *New World Drama: Performative Commons in the Atlantic World, 1649–1849*, Durham, NC: Duke University Press.

Picquenard, Jean-Baptiste (2006), *Adonis suivi de Zoflora et de documents inédits présentation de Chris Bongie, Autrement mêmes*, Paris: L'Harmattan.

Pigault-Lebrun (1796), *Le blanc et le noir. Drame en quatre actes et en prose*, Paris: Mayeur et Barba.

Pigault-Lebrun (1822), *Oeuvres complètes de Pigault-Lebrun*, Paris: J.-N. Barba.

Popkin, Jeremy D. (2012), *A Concise History of the Haitian Revolution*, Malden: Wiley-Blackwell.

Raynal, Guillaume Thomas (1780), *Histoire philosophique et politique des établissemens et du commerce des européens dans les deux Indes*, Vol. 3, Livre XI, Geneva.

Reichardt, Rolf (2008), "Plurimediale Kommunikation und symbolische Repräsentation in den französischen Revolutionen 1789–1848," in Sven Grampp et al., eds, *Revolutionsmedien – Medienrevolutionen*, Konstanz: UVK, pp. 231–75.

Root-Bernstein, Michèle (1993), "Popular Theatre in the French Revolution," *History Today* 43, pp. 25–31.

Rousseau, Jean-Jacques (2010 [1762]). *The Social Contract*, ed. Jonathan Bennett, at <http://www.earlymoderntexts.com/assets/pdfs/rousseau1762.pdf> (last accessed June 30, 2020).

Wehle, Winfried (1983), "Französisches Populardrama zur Zeit des Empire und der Restauration," in K. Heitmann, ed., *Neues Handbuch der Literaturwissenschaft*, Bd. 15, Wiesbaden: Athenaion, pp. 153–71.

Chapter 6

Reverberations of the Haitian Revolution: Media, Narratives and Political Debates, 1791–1863

Florian Kappeler

The Haitian Revolution (1791–1804) is the prototype of a non-Western revolution that reverberated globally. The German reception of this revolution, as part of a broad transatlantic discussion on the successful liberation of the Haitians from slavery and colonial rule (Geggus and Fiering 2009; Daut 2015), is a particularly significant example of these repercussions. Although the German debates on the events in the former French colony Saint-Domingue are almost unknown today, they played a crucial role at that time (Schüller 1992; Gribnitz 2002; Blänkner 2013) and were regarded as a turning point in the history of colonialism, if not the history of mankind.

At the beginning of the last phase of the revolution, when the French attempted to restore colonial rule and slavery, Johann Friedrich Reichardt, the editor of the journal *Frankreich im Jahre 1802. Aus den Briefen deutscher Männer in Paris* (France in the Year of 1802. From the Letters of German Men in Paris), proclaimed: "During the entire French Revolution, anticipation was rarely higher than it is now with regard to the events in St. Domingo. Whatever does transpire, a crucial decision for mankind will come out of it" (*Frankreich* 1802: 72).[1] The Swiss periodical *Miszellen für die neueste Weltkunde* (Miscellanies of the Latest Global History) concurred on the importance of these events, stating that the Haitian slave liberation had an impact on the global system of European colonialism as a whole: "The declaration of independence of the slave population has been a blow to the cornerstones of the colonial system" (*Miszellen* 1807b: 274).[2]

The slave revolution in the French colony Saint-Domingue thus had great resonance and was regarded as an event of universal significance. Far from being "silenced" (Trouillot 1995), it was widely discussed and characterized as an event that had crucial repercussions for Europe. Therefore, this article will not deconstruct the ideological conditions of an alleged silencing or decipher hidden references to the Haitian Revolution, as Susan Buck-Morss did with the works of Georg Wilhelm Friedrich Hegel (Buck-Morss 2009). Rather, it will reveal an archive that was neither marginalized nor encrypted. This archive varies over time and across geographical borders: In France, publications on Haiti were censored after the defeat of the Napoleonic army in 1803, and it was only after the suspension of censorship in 1817 that it became a central issue again, especially in the context of the abolition of the slave trade in France in 1818 and the recognition of the Haitian state in 1825 (Lammel 2015: 126ff., 165f.). By contrast, in the German-speaking countries that were not directly involved in the Haitian Revolution there was a broader debate that started during the years of the revolution and continued unabated in the following decades.

The aim of this chapter is to outline reverberations of the Haitian Revolution in the German-speaking world until the mid-nineteenth century that have been understudied up to now. As these reverberations were connected to the transatlantic debate, the chapter is part of current research on global entanglements of revolutions in general and the transatlantic print culture of the Haitian Revolution as a central example of these interconnections (Nesbitt 2008; Armitage and Subrahmanyam 2010; Conrad 2012; Polasky 2015). However, its main focus is on the media that spread the news of the slave rebellion and on narratives of the revolution (Baker and Edelstein 2015) in the German-speaking world. The central question is which narratives of the Haitian Revolution emerged through different media, such as journals and history books, and what impact they had on public debates. Consequently, my approach is a narratological one. A narrative is not defined by specific words but, according to Hayden White, by "modes of articulation" in the arrangement of events (White 1973: x). Thus, narratives are conceived as patterns of connections of events that can be found in different texts.

The first part of the chapter shows that the press, particularly historico-political journals, publicized information on the Haitian Revolution mainly by translating and documenting a wide range of original sources from across the political spectrum. Thereby, they facilitated a nuanced political view of the revolutionary events in the public sphere. In addition, they built an archive of sources for future historians. The second part of the chapter demonstrates that history books did indeed use the journals as archives and integrated them into historical narratives. These narratives interacted with public debates and fundamentally challenged European ideologies such as colonialism, racism and eurocentrism. The article will show in what way narratives of the Haitian Revolution influenced public debates in the German-speaking world and how they changed up to the mid-nineteenth century.

Media: News and Archives of the Revolution

How did the news of the Haitian Revolution spread in the German-speaking world? In Heinrich von Kleist's famous story *Die Verlobung in St. Domingo* (Betrothal in Saint-Domingue, 1811), it is presumed that the readers have detailed information on the events that happened eight years earlier: "Now it is common knowledge that in the year of 1803, when General Dessalines was advancing on Port-au-Prince with 30,000 Negroes, everyone with a white skin rushed into the town to defend it" (Kleist 1985: 137).[3]

But how did this "common knowledge" come into existence? The *Miszellen für die neueste Weltkunde*, published by the influential historian and revolutionary Heinrich Zschokke, who was a friend of Kleist, gives a hint: "We don't want to recapitulate the fates of Haiti as reported in the official press" (*Miszellen* 1807b: 274).[4] The assumption is that the readers got their information on the Haitian events from the press. In fact, the revolutionary events were perceived as news of importance in German newspapers right from the beginning. On November 4 – ten weeks after the uprising of the slaves – *Der Baierische Landbot: Eine Wochenschrift für alle Stände* (The Bavarian Rural Messenger. A Weekly for all Estates) reported briefly: "A ship that arrived from Le Havre brought the news that the black slaves on the island of St. Domingo have risen up" (*Baierischer Landbot* 1791: 1489).[5] According to the *Landbot*, this news was a paraphrase and a translation of a message from Paris. In contemporaneous sources, "news" means a brief notification of a current event that can include a short contextualizing report but not a coherent story.

Before the revolution, news on political events in Saint-Domingue was published very rarely. Pre-revolutionary writings dealt with the geography, botany, zoology and population of the colony but did not address political transformations. Most of these writings were translations of French or English books; for example, Johann Friedrich Schröter's *Allgemeine Geschichte der Länder und Völker von America* (General History of the Countries and Peoples of America, 1752–53) is a translation of the English compilation *A New General Collection of Voyages and Travels* (1745–47; cf. also Hilliard d'Auberteuil 1779; Schlözer 1777: 523–32; Raynal 1788). In these books, individual slaves were portrayed only in exceptional cases, such as that of the legendary guerrilla leader François Mackandal, and were depicted not as political actors but rather as criminals (Archenholz 1790). However, with the Haitian Revolution, all this changed.

The most important sources for the German reception of the revolution appear not in newspapers but in historico-political journals. In general, the relevance of this medium increased in the German-speaking world of the late eighteenth century. Particularly in the context of the French Revolution, many new journals were founded, and their diversity, size and range established "a media culture that might have been unrivalled in its spread, frequency and diversity" (Fischer et al. 1999: 10; see also Buck-Morss 2009: 42f.; Blanke 2011: 153ff., 163ff.).[6] Their content was no longer restricted to military and diplomatic events; rather, they documented historical sources from all over the world. The Haitian Revolution is one of the first examples of this new global focus.

The most important historico-political journals that considered the events, effects and receptions of the Haitian Revolution for over half a century were *Politisches Journal* and *Minerva*. At that time, most journals lasted only briefly and had a circulation of only a few hundred copies (Fischer et al. 1999: 19; Blanke 2011: 154). With a circulation of 8,000 copies, the conservative *Politisches Journal nebst Anzeige von gelehrten und andern Sachen* (Political Journal with Announcement of Academic and Other Things) was, in contrast, one of the most widely read journals of the period; it published more than forty articles on Haiti in total (Popkin 1996). At 6,000 copies, the liberal *Minerva – Ein Journal historischen und politischen Inhalts* (Minerva – A Journal of Historical and Political Content) was similarly influential (Bovekamp 2009). Although *Minerva* carried only twenty-two articles dealing with the Haitian Revolution (from 1792 to 1835), these were distinctly longer (three to four times on average). The more short-lived and generally pro-revolutionary journals *Frankreich* and *Europäische Annalen/Allgemeine Politische Annalen* published a dozen articles each on the subject in the years 1797–1805 and 1802–25, respectively. Another that dealt with Haiti, though less frequently, was Zschokke's *Miszellen* (1807–13, six short articles). In addition, the journalist Friedrich Buchholz published several articles in various journals (D'Aprile 2013: 155–88).

For the historico-political journals, it was crucial to distinguish themselves from newspapers. Thus, Gottlob Benedikt von Schirach, the editor of the *Politisches Journal*, wrote in 1804 that, although people were aware of the new nation and particularly the ferociousness of the revolutionaries "from the fragments of narrations on the recent incidents in Domingo read in the official press," a "coherent historical narration of these events all the more so has to be part of our contemporary history" (*Politisches Journal* 1804: 845f.).[7] According to von Schirach, one could not fully understand the Haitian Revolution from only fragmentary news accounts; readers needed a coherent story. Nonetheless, most of the journal articles did not offer such stories: For instance, the *Politisches Journal* quotes or paraphrases primarily from newspaper reports. Until 1802–3, most of the reports originated in French newspapers, but with the Napoleonic censorship that sought to whitewash the complete defeat, French sources lost credibility, and German journals relied more on British, American and (after the fall of Napoleon) also Haitian sources such as the newspaper *La Gazette Royale d'Hayti* (*Europäische Annalen* (1815) and *Politisches Journal* (1816)). In short, journal articles were partly based on newspapers and used them as sources for a selective presentation.

Johann Wilhelm von Archenholz, the editor of the *Minerva* and a liberal opponent of the *Politisches Journal*, also states that a historical narrative distinctly differs from newspaper reports. In the first edition of his journal (1792), he sets out the standard to which he claims he will hold his journal: that the articles should be based on a critical form of reportage: "If I wish to provide more than news, I have to spend days listening, seeing and verifying before I am able to pick up the pen and apply myself to my work for a few hours to write down *truly historical* articles" (*Minerva* 1792a: 122).[8] Archenholz wrote these words while living in Paris during the French Revolution. But he was not an eyewitness to the Haitian Revolution, and the journals had no correspondents in Haiti at the time. Therefore, in the articles on Haiti, eyewitness reports are replaced by documentations of sources: "Above all, this work is dedicated to recent history, inasmuch as the fates of near and distant countries and the opinions and actions of their inhabitants are of interest for enlightened peoples. The articles will mostly be carefully selected materials for future historians" (*Minerva* 1792a: 1).[9]

According to Archenholz, then, historico-political journals do not produce historical narratives themselves but rather provide "materials" for coming historians. In fact, journals such as *Minerva*, *Frankreich* or *Europäische Annalen* include an archive of translated historical sources (or, mostly, excerpts of sources). Sometimes the editors comment on them briefly in an introductory note, but the sources are almost never incorporated into a historical narrative. Like the newspapers, the journals are committed to a principle of topicality. Yet the practice of building up an archive also implies a principle of delay: The sources are supposed to serve as a foundation for future historiographies.

The specific periodicity of the journals combines topicality and deferring. Their seriality made it possible to publish documents on the Haitian Revolution over a long period and to refer to earlier articles and – in some cases – to revise them. For example, Archenholz writes in a preliminary note to an excerpt from Marcus Rainsford's *Historical Account of the Black Empire of Hayti* (1805), the first text written by a European eyewitness who sympathized with the revolution and particularly with its leader Toussaint Louverture: "These detailed news assembled by an eyewitness with expertise and in an elegant style open the curtains to this Negro stage and give us a completely different view of the events" (*Minerva* 1805: 277).[10]

Not only do the journals revisit and reassess earlier articles, but they are also characterized by a synchronic principle of plurality: *Minerva*, *Frankreich* and *Europäische Annalen* include accounts of revolutionary agents (only men) from across the political spectrum. For instance, during the revolution, *Minerva* published proclamations by the French government that approved of the abolition of slavery but defended colonial rule and plantation work (*Minerva* 1796a and 1796b). Another article, written by the French historian Jean-Charles-Dominique de Lacretelle, rejects the first point, while the secretary of the commissioners Paul-François Barbault-Royer postulates that France should side with the "mulattoes," but not the "blacks" (*Minerva* 1797a and 1797b).

A compilation of "Actenstücke zur Geschichte der Revolution in St. Domingo" (*Minerva* 1804/5) (Documents on the History of the Revolution in Saint-Domingue), published in the *Minerva* after the end of the revolution in 1805 under the title "Zur neuesten Geschichte von St. Domingo" (On the Recent History of Saint-Domingue), contains a letter by a French clerk highly critical of the Napoleonic intervention, but also includes statements from the revolutionaries themselves: First, a letter by Joseph Bunel, a French-born trader living in Haiti who worked as a diplomat and military paymaster for Toussaint and Dessalines (Girard 2010), that criticizes the former colonial civil servants' anti-revolutionary resentments; and second a selection of writings attributed to Dessalines, Toussaint's successor. The latter counters the hegemonic European narratives that accused him of committing cruelties against "white" people: "[Indeed] I swore to persecute the French fiercely, but also promised to spare the blood of the innocents and all the unfortunate tools of a cruel government" (*Minerva* 1804/5: 507).[11]

Some journals (*Politisches Journal, Minerva, Frankreich*) also printed extracts from early books about the Haitian Revolution such as Louis Dubroca's pro-Napoleonic and anti-revolutionary biographies of Toussaint and Dessalines, while others quoted from Rainsford's book taking the opposite view (*Minerva, Europäische Annalen, Miszellen*). Ten years later, several journals of different political factions (such as the liberal *Neue Monatsschrift für Deutschland* (1820) and the conservative *Der Staatsmann* (1825)) published the anticolonial writings of the Haitian intellectual and politician Baron de Vastey. By translating and printing French, British, American and Haitian sources, the historico-political journals situated the German reception in the transatlantic discourse of the Haitian Revolution. Moreover, they offered heterogeneous perspectives from eyewitnesses. Thus, they provided a basis for German political debates on the revolution and related issues such as slavery, racism and eurocentrism.

Archenholz declares that the documentation should not privilege individual political positions: "Everybody knows the quarrels about the colonies inside the legislative corps; they give room to factionalism as the news about these distant possessions are usually as unilateral as they are insufficient" (*Minerva* 1797a: 403).[12] This implies the common Enlightenment view that a political position should be grounded on nuanced historical knowledge. The aim of the polyphonic documentation was not only to publish sources for future historians but also to provide enlightened readers with political information. The documentation of diverse political positions was a statement against censorship and a strategy to delegitimize the arcane praxis of absolutism (Fischer et al. 1999: 10ff.). Indeed, historico-political journals were received by a broad (bourgeois) public and served – with their ongoing and evolving documentation of a wide range of reactions toward the Haitian Revolution – as media of political debates.

Transforming Archives into Narratives: Debates on Slavery, Racism and Revolution

Let us now return to the other explicit objective of the historico-political journals – the providing of sources for historians – and the historiography of the Haitian Revolution in general. The German answer to the question how to write a history of revolution from afar was: A history of revolutions can *only* be written from afar. For instance, Johann Samuel Ersch, a professor and librarian in Halle, states in his article "Remarks on the Difficulties of Writing a History of Revolution While It Takes Place":[13] "In a revolution, the painting is too close before our very eyes; the impression of every single event is too strong to compare its causes and effects properly ... only from afar do you overlook ... the spectacle as a whole" (Ersch 1800: 550).[14]

According to Ersch, the history of revolution has to be written from a distance. Eyewitnesses such as the actors whose reports were documented in the historico-political journals are focused on the events they are in the middle of and therefore not able to take an overview of the succession of events and discern causal relations. If this is true, the Germans – who were not involved in the Haitian Revolution – must be good historians. The revolution took place far enough away to be the perfect object of German historiography. But it is vital to remember where these objective judges got their evidence from: the German historians of the 1820s and 1830s who considered the Haitian Revolution used the journals as archives. For instance, Karl von Rotteck, professor of history in Freiburg, lists *Minerva*, *Politisches Journal* and *Europäische Annalen* as sources in the bibliography of his book *Allgemeine Geschichte vom Anfang der historischen Kenntniß bis auf unsere Zeiten* (General History from the Beginning of Historical Knowledge Until Our Times), which includes a section on the Haitian Revolution. Von Rotteck states that, because of the "unreliability of journalists,"[15] "careful selection and critique"[16] of the sources is essential: "many witnesses have to be verified, brought together and only *then* can depictions of the whole be attempted" (Rotteck 1832: 12, 9).[17]

According to Rotteck, the integration of narrative fragments ("Theilgemälden") into a whole historical narrative is what transforms archives into historical books. Both in journals and in history books, a coherent narrative is conceived as a criterion for a professional writing of history (cf. also Meinicke 1831: VIII, 369). Accordingly, historico-political journals provide materials for historical books, and the latter try to integrate them into a coherent historical narrative. Thereby, narrative fragments that already were present in the journals are paraphrased or modified. On the one hand, such narratives are part of the documented sources: Rainsford's book, for example, was influential in establishing a narrative of Toussaint Louverture as a "Great Man" and a crucial agent of the revolution. On the other hand, the editors' preliminary remarks work as narrative frames. For instance, Archenholz claims in 1804: "The eyes of the world are now on St. Domingo and the negroes who dwell there – one can hardly call these hordes of furious blacks a republic – for the consequences of this dreadful state of affairs cannot be calculated" (*Minerva* 1804/5: 340).[18] This racist narrative suggests that revolutions with non-white actors lead to barbarity. Even the liberal Archenholz denies that the Haitian revolutionaries had the ability to organize politically in a progressive way and depicts them as furious hordes. Although the preliminary remarks give authority to the narratives of the editors, the documented sources are much longer and at times stand in stark contrast to them. For example, the elaborate and self-conscious letters of Dessalines conflict with the racist narrative of Archenholz's comment.

I will now examine the most important narratives that emerged in journals and historical books in the early nineteenth century. My thesis is that narratives of the Haitian Revolution were part of three crucial contemporary debates in the German-speaking world: The first dealt with whether slavery was a necessary condition for a prosperous economy. This debate can be interpreted as a reaction to the abolition of slavery after – and partly due to – the Haitian Revolution. The latter was narrated either as a destructive or as a productive force for the colonial economy. The second debate responded to the fact that racist ideologies were challenged by the undeniable political agency of people of color during the Haitian Revolution. The narrative of the "Great Man" recognized a capacity for political action only in extraordinary (male) individuals but not in the masses, while in another narrative, the Haitian Revolution figured as evidence of the fact that people of color in general are born equal. The third debate questioned the assumption that modern revolution is a phenomenon of European origin. While some texts described the uprising in Haiti as an imitation of the French Revolution, others narrated it as an independent, if not unprecedented, project.

First, I will address the debate on the relation of the Haitian Revolution and the economic regime of slavery. Before the revolution, several books legitimized slavery quite bluntly: "It is possible to suppress their vices with the whip in large part; but one has to repeat this frequently" (Schröter 1752/3: 646).[19] When the revolution started, this affirmation of the colonial regime culminated in a narrative that portrayed freedom as a destruction of economic productivity: "Back then, despotism acquired new and invaluable sources of prosperity – and freedom is now destroying them" (*Politisches Journal* 1791: 1283).[20] According to this vision, despotism is a *conditio sine qua non* for economic vitality, while revolutions are inherently destructive. Not all the journals use such frank words, but even the progressive *Europäische Annalen* characterizes Haiti as an "island" that "before the troubles that devastated it during the revolution . . . was the most prosperous amongst the Antilles" (*Europäische Annalen* 1802: 189),[21] implying that the colonial regime of slavery brought economic prosperity, while the revolution brought only destruction. This narrative of revolutionary destructiveness often coincides with the racist assumption that people of African descent are incapable of producing economic wealth because of an alleged hereditary sloth (see *Miszellen* 1807a: 100). However, this narrative is modified fundamentally in the following years. We find striking evidence of this shift even in the journals that defended despotism and slavery two decades earlier, such as *Politisches Journal*. In his article "Phantasie über die Zukunft Westindiens" (Imagination of the Future of the West Indies, 1815), Johann Nikolaus Gloyer, secretary of the Danish war chancellery, states: "Aside from the moral atrociousness of this trade, surely the only way to retain the West Indies for Europe is to abolish the slave trade in general and slowly assimilate the negroes to the state of the general free working class in Central Europe" (*Politisches Journal* 1815: 131).[22]

This apology for the abolition of the slave trade in Denmark (1803) and England (1807) must be read in the context of the Congress of Vienna (1815), where the abolition of the slave trade was on the agenda. In Gloyer's essay, the slave trade is seen as an obstacle to a profitable colonial economy since wage labor is more productive than slave labor. The argument is that without the brutal regime of slavery, the workers have an increased life expectancy, and this more than compensates for the shorter work days of free laborers. Therefore, the "blacks" should be assimilated to the European working class. Although this argument leaves the functional European (and capitalist) perspective intact, the economic narrative of the Haitian Revolution has clearly changed: The abolition of slavery was no longer seen as an economic catastrophe. One may explain this as a pragmatic reaction to the victorious Haitian Revolution that created a fait accompli. Thus, the revolutionary transformation of Haiti actually had an impact on German debates.

Twenty years later, the abolition of slavery was widely accepted, particularly in history books. In 1828, Alexander Lips, professor of political science in Marburg, predicted the global abolition of slavery and considered this to be a long-term consequence of the Haitian Revolution and particularly of the international recognition of the young nation in 1825: "As a result, the former slave system, in particular, will be shaken to its core. Thus, the emancipation of the negroes will occur everywhere" (Lips 1828: 403).[23] However, even for the writers of the 1820s and 1830s, economic profit for Europe – and now for Prussia – was essential. For instance, the Prussian officer Johann Valentin Hecke considers the sovereign state Haiti to be "necessary to the revitalization of Prussian commerce and manufacturing industry" (Hecke 1821: 192; see also Lips 1828: 10).[24] Hecke also mentions the central role of Prussian military and German merchants in Haiti (1821: 218, 235). The critique of slavery is thus combined with an attempt to open up new sales markets and therefore partly appears to be a justification of Prussian export strategies.

When Lips mentions the "emancipation of the negroes," he addresses the second major debate, relating to the reception of the Haitian Revolution: The issue of the so-called human "races" and their capabilities. The central political role of people of color during the revolution came into conflict with a racist ideology that denied their political agency. Initially, a narrative of the extraordinary "Great Man" (Gamper 2016) bridged the gap between the racist ideology and the undeniable agency of people of color. This narrative identified political agency in only one black man, Toussaint Louverture, who was singled out as "a genius amongst the negroes" (*Politisches Journal* 1799: 22f.).[25] Toussaint is the first non-white person who is accepted as a "Great Man" – an actor of great historical impact – in European history. A number of biographies of the revolutionary attest to this fact, amongst them the book *Toussaint Louvertures frühere Geschichte nach englischen Nachrichten bearbeitet* (Toussaint Louverture's Earlier History Adapted from English News, 1802) and the translation of a French autobiographical narrative (*Frankreich* 1802). Marlene L. Daut mentions sixty biographies and memoirs of Toussaint in English and French before 1865 – not including the press (Daut 2015: 380; on French literature see also Lammel 2015). The narrative of the "Great Man" allowed German writers to deny that there were in fact a great number of colored people acting as political subjects during the Haitian Revolution. Literacy served as a criterion for political engagement, and it was wrongly assumed that people of color were generally illiterate at that time. Therefore, Toussaint is "compared to 500,000 animal-like humans who never had any idea of the alphabet" (*Politisches Journal* 1801: 1105).[26]

Yet the narrative of the extraordinary "Great Man" implies a counter-narrative: If one colored slave is capable of climbing to a position of power, why shouldn't the others do the same? In the following thirty years, Toussaint would become, rather than an exception, a prototype of the agency of people of color. In the 1830s, even an author such as Karl Eduard Meinicke, who did not endorse Haiti's post-revolutionary regime – for him, it is a "licentious negro democracy" (Meinicke 1831: 374)[27] – concedes that "the long struggle formed advanced political views in many negroes" (410)[28] because of the "awareness that freedom wasn't given to them as a gift but had to be fought for" (376).[29] Thus the narrative of the extraordinary "Great Man" becomes an exemplary narration of subaltern emancipation. According to Hecke, the mere existence of the postcolonial state Haiti solved the "problem of his [= the Negro's] inferiority. Now we have uncontested evidence that the Negro does not at all lack higher intellectual gifts" (Hecke 1821: 195).[30] Such capabilities are no longer reserved for the "Great Man"; instead the new nation demonstrates the equality of people of color in general. For Hecke, the revolution is not only a proof of equality but also an anticipation of coming revolutions: "If revolutions bear such beautiful fruits, then one has to wish fortune and blessings to all the revolutions against slavery! What would this human class be today, if it still languished in slavery? And what is it now? And what will it be one day?" (Hecke 1821: 244).[31]

In Hecke's book, people of color are not addressed as a "race" but as a "class": They are portrayed as politicized and no longer as racialized subjects. The Haitian Revolution evidences the fact that all human beings are equal and is presented as the avant-garde of a serial production of revolutions. Another fact should not be overlooked: The emancipation of the slaves of Haiti is now clearly referred to as "revolution," and that means revolution in the modern sense. In Hecke's book, the Haitian Revolution is portrayed as an event (or series of events) that anticipates an unprecedented future, implies a collective process of self-emancipation, and acts as a prototype of further revolutions; all of these attributes characterize modern revolutions in general (Baker 1990: 214; Griewank 1992: 187, 190). A generation earlier, around 1800, however, this was not yet a common view: Newspapers and journals referred to the events in Haiti as an upheaval, uprising, indignation, rebellion, revolt or (civil) war, while the term "revolution" remained reserved for events in Europe and particularly the French Revolution. As the term "revolution" was used earlier in French and English publications, it percolated into German publications through translations. In history books of the 1820s and 1830s, it became more common: von Rotteck speaks of the "indigenous revolutions of the West Indies and particularly Domingo" (Rotteck 1832: 386).[32] In his book *Staatensysteme Europa's und Amerika's seit dem Jahre 1783* (State Systems of Europe and America since the Year of 1783, 1826), Karl Heinrich Ludwig Pölitz, professor of history and political science in Leipzig, specifies that in Haiti "a revolutionary storm flared up with the very specific character that the black slaves shook off the European yoke" (Pölitz 1826: 504f.).[33]

In early writings, in contrast, the upheaval of the slaves was still depicted as an effect of the French Revolution. This brings us to the third major debate surrounding the Haitian Revolution, which dealt with whether the modern revolution was an originally European phenomenon. Initially, eurocentric narratives of imitation or adoption dominated the debate. In 1792, a *Minerva* article on the events in Haiti stated that "with the news: the whole of France gained freedom through a revolution, the magic word of freedom inspired all minds, and the idea quickly traveled to them: to shatter their own chains as well" (*Minerva* 1792b: 298).[34] In this view, the basic event that provoked the upheaval in Saint-Domingue was the French Revolution. The medium that allowed the inhabitants of the colony to adopt the revolutionary words was – again – the dissemination of news. According to *Minerva*, it had an effect on the emotions ("Gemüther") first and then led to intentional political acts ("Vorsatz") by parts of the white population and soon also by people of color. Thus, the narrative of imitation facilitates a narrative of emancipation.

However, in some history books of the 1820s and 1830s, the narrative of the French Revolution as a model of the Haitian Revolution was challenged. In the first German monograph on the revolution, *Geschichte des Freistaats von Santo Domingo (Hayti)* (History of the Free State of Saint-Domingue (Hayti), 1826), Friedrich Philippi writes: "Even if the French government had not experienced an overthrow, the uprising in Saint-Domingue would have erupted anyway" (Philippi 1826: 51f.).[35] For Philippi, the French Revolution was not a necessary condition for the slave uprising at all. Other books even invert the eurocentric narrative: Pölitz calls the Haitian state a "negro and mulatto republic with constitutional principles and regimes that one would have hardly found in the most liberal constitutions of

European republics since the last decade of the eighteenth century!" (Pölitz 1826: 505, see also Lips 1828: 406).[36] Thus, the eurocentric narrative of imitation was supplemented by narrations of Haiti as a revolutionary avant-garde.

Most certainly, the revolution of the Haitian slaves was a turning point for German debates on slavery, "race" and modern revolution itself. Particularly in history books of the 1820s and 1830s that addressed the Haitian Revolution, racism, slavery and eurocentrism were challenged. Nevertheless, the history books increasingly addressed a professional audience and therefore did not influence public debates to the extent that the journals did. This anticipates a problem that we confront today: An academic audience is aware of the Haitian Revolution and its consequences for racist, colonialist and eurocentric ideologies, but not the wider public (Buck-Morss 2009: 50).

And even the academic knowledge disappeared between the mid-nineteenth and the mid-twentieth century: The Foundation of the German Reich, German colonialism, two German-induced world wars and National Socialism buried the kinds of narratives that criticized colonialism and racism. In the mid-nineteenth century, a new narrative of "racial conflicts" emerged, one that would be hegemonic at least until the mid-twentieth century. One can find this narrative in the *Essai sur l'inégalité des races humaines* (1852–54), published by the French diplomat Arthur de Gobineau, the grandson of a French woman from Saint-Domingue, or as early as 1846 in Wilhelm Jordan's *Geschichte der Insel Hayti und ihres Negerstaats* (History of the Island of Haiti and its Negro State), where the author, a liberal and at the same time racist and nationalist writer, cites a French colonialist named Daugy who postulated that "as soon as they were free, the existence of the negroes would be physically incompatible with the existence of their European brothers" (Jordan 1846: 251).[37]

The narrative of "racial conflicts" transforms the narration of the revolution as a struggle of classes or social groups into a necessarily violent war of alleged "racial" groups. Twelve years later, in professor Heinrich Handelmann's *Geschichte der Insel Hayti* (History of the Island of Haiti, 1856), the "war of the races" (Handelmann 1856: 33, 45)[38] is already a constituent part of the historical narrative that does not have to be explained specifically. In 1863, the annual report of a school in the city of Cologne includes an article written by teacher Leopold Contzen with the title "Haiti und seine Racenkämpfe" (Haiti and its War of Races). Contzen states that it can be considered "as in fact the only specificity" of the Haitian Revolution, "that the struggling parties were separated rather through race than through interests" (Contzen 1863: 5).[39]

In the following decades, the Haitian Revolution disappears from public debates. The reasons for this vanishing are open to research. However, for the first period after the revolution the story of an alleged silencing has to be replaced by research on narratives of the Haitian Revolution seen from afar: The external perspective of the German countries was regarded not as an obstacle, but as an advantage for a reliable historiography. On top of this, in the German-speaking world, narratives of the Haitian Revolution challenged ideologies such as racism and eurocentrism to a greater extent than in other parts of the transatlantic print culture (cf. Daut 2015).

Firstly, narratives of destruction and prosperity both arose as attempts to understand the significance of the abolition of slavery in Haiti. While abolition was seen as a destructive force at first, it became part of a narrative of modernization of capitalist and colonialist rule later on – a narrative that was part of the Prussian attempt to open up new sales markets in Haiti. Secondly, a narrative of the extraordinary "Great Man" bridged the gap between racist ideology and the undeniable agency of non-white people in the Haitian Revolution. However, in the following decades the emancipation of the slaves was more and more narrated as an example of the equality of people of color, while in the second half of the nineteenth century, a narrative of "racial conflicts" transformed the revolution into a violent war between so-called "racial" groups. Thirdly, narratives of imitation and adoption influenced the debate about revolution itself: The Haitian Revolution was seen as an imitation of the French Revolution until the 1820s, when it was depicted as an indigenous revolution with a specific character, or even as a revolutionary avant-garde. The intermittent changes of these narratives prove that the writing of history is not a way out of the darkness of ignorance into a bright present but a persistent struggle with interpretation and narration, yesterday and today.

Bibliography

Archenholz, Johann Wilhelm von (1790), "Merkwürdige Verschwörung eines Negers auf der Insel St. Domingo," *Neue Litteratur und Völkerkunde* 8, pp. 172–85.

Armitage, David and Sanjay Subrahmanyam, eds (2010), *The Age of Revolutions in Global Context, c. 1760–1840*, Basingstoke: Palgrave.

Baierischer Landbot (1791), "Auswärtige Nachrichten," November 4, p. 1489.
Baker, Keith Michael (1990), *Inventing the French Revolution: Essays on French Political Culture in the Eighteenth Century*, Cambridge: Cambridge University Press.
Baker, Keith Michael and Dan Edelstein, eds (2015), *Scripting Revolution: A Historical Approach to the Comparative Study of Revolutions*, Stanford: Stanford University Press.
Blanke, Horst Walter (2011), *Historiographiegeschichte und Historik. Aufklärungshistorie und Historismus in Theorie und Empirie*, Kamen: Hartmut Spenner.
Blänkner, Reinhard, ed. (2013), *Heinrich von Kleists Novelle "Die Verlobung in St. Domingo": Literatur und Politik im globalen Kontext um 1800*, Würzburg: Königshausen & Neumann.
Bovekamp, Boris (2009), *Die Zeitschrift "Minerva" und ihre Herausgeber Johann Wilhelm von Archenholz (1743–1812) und Friedrich Alexander Bran (1767–1831): ein Beitrag zur Kompatibilität von Militär, Aufklärung und Liberalismus*, Kiel: Ludwig.
Buck-Morss, Susan (2009), *Hegel, Haiti and Universal History*, Pittsburgh: University of Pittsburgh Press.
Conrad, Sebastian (2012), "Enlightenment in Global History: A Historiographical Critique," *The American Historical Review* 117:4, pp. 999–1027.
Contzen, Leopold (1863), "Haiti und seine Racenkämpfe," *Jahresberichte für die Realschule I. Ordnung zu Köln für das Schuljahr 1862–1863*, pp. 1–30.
D'Aprile, Iwan-Michelangelo (2013), *Die Erfindung der Zeitgeschichte. Geschichtsschreibung und Journalismus zwischen Aufklärung und Vormärz*, Berlin: Akademie Verlag.
Daut, Marlene L. (2015), *Tropics of Haiti: Race and the Literary History of Revolution the Haitian in the Atlantic World, 1789–1865*, Liverpool: Liverpool University Press.
Der Staatsmann: Zeitschrift für Politik und Zeitgeschichte (1825), "Ueber die Ursachen der Revolution und der Bürgerkriege in Hayti. Vom Baron de Vastey," Vol. 7, pp. 1–66, 99–164, 199–230, 305–25.
Ersch, Johann Samuel (1800), "Bemerkungen über die Schwierigkeiten, die Geschichte der Revolution während derselben zu schreiben," *Minerva – ein Journal historischen und politischen Inhalts* 3, pp. 546–53.
Europäische Annalen (1802), "St. Domingo," Vol. 1, pp. 189–204.
Europäische Annalen (1815), "Königliche Zeitung von Hayti," Vol. 2, pp. 113–23.
Fischer, Ernst, Wilhelm Haefs and York-Gothart Mix (1999), "Einleitung: Aufklärung, Öffentlichkeit und Medienkultur in Deutschland im 18. Jahrhundert," *Von Almanach bis Zeitung. Ein Handbuch der Medien in Deutschland 1700–1800*, Munich: C. H. Beck, pp. 9–23.

Frankreich im Jahre 1802. Aus den Briefen deutscher Männer in Paris (1802), "Toussaint Louvertures Bericht über die Begebenheiten, welche im nördlichen Theil von St. Domingo sich zugetragen haben," Vol. 2, pp. 72–86.
Gamper, Michael (2016), *Der große Mann. Geschichte eines politischen Phantasmas*, Göttingen: Wallstein.
Geggus, David Patrick and Norman Fiering, eds (2009), *The World of the Haitian Revolution*, Bloomington: Indiana University Press.
Girard, Philippe R. (2010), "Trading Races: Joseph and Marie Bunel, a Diplomat and a Merchant in Revolutionary Saint-Domingue and Philadelphia," *Journal of the Early Republic* 30:3, pp. 351–76.
Green, John, Thomas Astley and Antoine-François Prévost, eds (1747–49), *A New General Collection of Voyages and Travels*, London: Thomas Astley.
Gribnitz, Barbara (2002), *Schwarzes Mädchen, weißer Fremder: Studien zur Konstruktion von "Rasse" und Geschlecht in Heinrich von Kleists Erzählung Die Verlobung in St. Domingo*, Würzburg: Königshausen & Neumann.
Griewank, Karl (1992 (1955)), *Der neuzeitliche Revolutionsbegriff. Entstehung und Entwicklung*, Frankfurt am Main: Suhrkamp.
Handelmann, Heinrich (1856), *Geschichte der Insel Hayti*, Kiel: Verlag der Schwersschen Buchhandlung.
Hecke, Johann Valentin (1821), *Reise durch die vereinigten Staaten von Nord-America und Rückreise durch England. Nebst einer Schilderung der Revolutions-Helden und des ehemaligen und gegenwärtigen Zustandes von St. Domingo*, Vol. 2, Berlin: H. Ph. Petri.
Hilliard d'Auberteuil, Michel René (1779 (1776)), *Betrachtungen über den gegenwärtigen Zustand der Französischen Colonie zu San Domingo*, Leipzig: Johann Friedrich Junius.
Jordan, Wilhelm (1846), *Geschichte der Insel Hayti und ihres Negerstaats*, Vol. 1, Leipzig: Wilhelm Jurany.
Kleist, Heinrich von (1985 (1811)), "The Betrothal of St. Domingo," *German Romantic Novelas. By Heinrich von Kleist and Jean Paul*, The German Library, Vol. 34, New York: Continuum, pp. 136–65.
Lammel, Isabell (2015), *Der Toussaint-Louverture-Mythos. Transformationen in der französischen Literatur, 1791–2012*, Bielefeld: transcript.
Lips, Alexander (1828), *Statistik von Amerika: oder, Versuch einer historisch-pragmatischen und raisonirenden Darstellung des politischen und bürgerlichen Zustandes der neuen Staaten-Körper von Amerika*, Frankfurt am Main: Verlag von Heinrich Wilmans.
Meinicke, Karl Eduard (1831), *Versuch einer Geschichte der europäischen Colonien in Westindien, nach den Quellen bearbeitet*, Weimar: Im Verlage des Großh. S. pr. Landes-Industrie-Comptoirs.
Minerva – ein Journal historischen und politischen Inhalts (1792a), [no title], Vol. 1, pp. 1–2 and 121–2.

Minerva – ein Journal historischen und politischen Inhalts (1792b), "Historische Nachrichten von den letzten Unruhen in Saint Domingo. Aus verschiedenen Quellen gezogen," Vol. 1, pp. 296–319.

Minerva – ein Journal historischen und politischen Inhalts (1796a), "Proclamation des Bürgers Levaux, Generals und Gouverneurs von St. Domingo," Vol. 1, pp. 519–27.

Minerva – ein Journal historischen und politischen Inhalts (1796b), "Proclamation der Commissarien der französischen Republik in St. Domingo," Vol. 3, pp. 324–37.

Minerva – ein Journal historischen und politischen Inhalts (1797a), "Ueber den neuesten Zustand von St. Domingo: Von Barbault Royer. Geschrieben im Januar 1797," Vol. 1, pp. 403–8.

Minerva – ein Journal historischen und politischen Inhalts (1797b), "Lacretelle d.j. über die Colonien und Santhonax. (Zu Ende des Januars 1797 geschrieben.)," Vol. 1, pp. 408–13.

Minerva – ein Journal historischen und politischen Inhalts (1804/5), "Zur neuesten Geschichte von St. Domingo," Vol. 4/1804, pp. 340–57, 506–20 and Vol. 1/1805, pp. 133–57.

Minerva – ein Journal historischen und politischen Inhalts (1805), "Toussaint Louverture. Eine historische Schilderung für die Nachwelt," Vol. 4, pp. 276–98, 392–408.

Miszellen für die neueste Weltkunde (1807a), "Christoph, gegenwärtiger Beherrscher von Haity," Vol. 1, pp. 99/100.

Miszellen für die neueste Weltkunde (1807b), "St. Domingo und die Negersclaven," Vol. 1, pp. 273–4, 277–8.

Nesbitt, Nick (2008), *Universal Emancipation: The Haitian Revolution and the Radical Enlightenment*, Charlottesville: University of Virginia Press.

Neue Monatsschrift für Deutschland (1820), "Probe haitischer Geschichtsschreibung," Vol. 3, pp. 182–209.

Philippi, Karl Ferdinand (1826), *Geschichte des Freistaats von St. Domingo (Hayti)*, Dresden: P. G. Hilschersche Buchhandlung.

Polasky, Janet L. (2015), *Revolutions without Borders: The Call to Liberty in the Atlantic World*, New Haven: Yale University Press.

Politisches Journal nebst einer Anzeige von gelehrten und andern Sachen (1791), "Statistischer Werth des Verlustes der durch die Freyheit verwüsteten Insel St. Domingo," Vol. 2, pp. 1283–90.

Politisches Journal nebst einer Anzeige von gelehrten und andern Sachen (1799), "Statistischer Abriß der Wichtigkeit der von Frankreich nun unabhängigen Insel St. Domingue. Nachrichten vom Neger Toußaint l'Ouverture," Vol. 1, pp. 17–23.

Politisches Journal nebst einer Anzeige von gelehrten und andern Sachen (1801), "Toussaint-Louverture. Eine biographische Zeichnung," Vol. 2, pp. 1102–7.

Politisches Journal nebst einer Anzeige von gelehrten und andern Sachen (1804), "Neger-Scenen auf St. Domingo," Vol. 2, pp. 845–50.

Politisches Journal nebst einer Anzeige von gelehrten und andern Sachen (1815), "Phantasie über die Zukunft Westindiens. Vom Kriegskanzley-Secretair Gloyer," Vol. 1, pp. 131–8, 208–17.

Politisches Journal nebst einer Anzeige von gelehrten und andern Sachen (1816), "Authentische Nachrichten über die inneren Verhältnisse und die Organisation des Königreichs Hayti," Vol. 2, pp. 905–11.

Pölitz, Karl Heinrich Ludwig (1826), *Die Staatensysteme Europa's und Amerika's seit dem Jahre 1783, geschichtlich-politisch dargestellt*, Vol. 1, Leipzig: J. C. Hinrichssche Buchhandlung.

Popkin, Jeremy D. (1996), "Political Communication in the German Enlightenment: Gottlob Benedikt von Schirach's Politisches Journal," *Eighteenth-Century Life* 20:1, at <http://muse.jhu.edu/journals/eighteenth-century_life/v020/20.1popkin.html> (last accessed October 23, 2020).

Raynal, Guillaume-Thomas François (1788), *Die Uebersicht der politischen Lage und des Handelszustandes von St. Domingo*, Leipzig: Haugsche Buchhandlung.

Rotteck, Karl von (1832 (1826)), *Allgemeine Geschichte vom Anfang der historischen Kenntniß bis auf unsere Zeiten. Für denkende Geschichtfreunde bearbeitet*, Vol. 9, Freiburg i. Brsg.: Herder'sche Kunst- und Buchhandlung.

Schlözer, August Ludwig von, ed. (1777), *Neue Erdbeschreibung von ganz America*, Vol. 2, Göttingen und Leipzig: Weigandsche Buchhandlung.

Schröter, Johann Friedrich (1752/53), *Allgemeine Geschichte der Länder und Völker von America*, Halle: Johann Justinus Gebauer.

Schüller, Karin (1992), *Die deutsche Rezeption haitianischer Geschichte in der ersten Hälfte des 19. Jahrhunderts: ein Beitrag zum deutschen Bild vom Schwarzen*, Cologne: Böhlau.

Toussaint Louvertures frühere Geschichte nach englischen Nachrichten bearbeitet (1802), Fürth: Bureau für Litteratur.

Trouillot, Michel-Rolph (1995), *Silencing the Past: Power and the Production of History*, Boston: Beacon Press.

White, Hayden (1973), *Metahistory: The Historical Imagination in Nineteenth-Century Europe*, Baltimore: The Johns Hopkins University Press.

Chapter 7

Ribbons of Revolution: Tricolor Cockades Across the Atlantic

Ashli White

Tricolor cockades are one of the most iconic artefacts of the French Revolution, if not of the Age of Revolutions. The story goes that before storming the Bastille in July 1789, members of the crowd pinned bits of green ribbon to their hats or coats so that in the thick of battle, they could distinguish friend from foe. In the months that followed, revolutionaries rejected green cockades, citing the color's aristocratic overtones, and instead adopted a combination of red, white and blue. Soon, across France and the wider Atlantic world, people took to wearing tricolor cockades as visible signs of their enthusiasm for the revolution (Maxwell 2014: 125; Wrigley 2002: 98–100). Because it was a small item made of inexpensive material, the cockade was accessible to large swaths of the population – perhaps more so than any other revolutionary item.

For groups excluded from formal political life – women, average folk and people of African descent, these ribbons afforded one public means to display their sympathies and, thus, participate in politics. Accordingly, historians of the Age of Revolutions have used cockades as a way of gauging the spread of revolutionary sentiment and the engagement of various social sectors in political culture. In these interpretations, support for the French Revolution, as embodied in the tricolor cockade, maps onto extant political rivalries. In Britain and the United States, for example, scholars show how tricolor cockades became a mode through which political parties tried to whip up support among the populace and vanquish their adversaries (Auslander 2009; Branson 2001; Heuer 2002; Hunt 1984; Newman 1997; Wrigley 2002).

This, however, is only one way of interpreting the Atlantic resonances of tricolor cockades. Tracking the actual movement of tricolor cockades around the Atlantic provides insights into other important connections. As they proliferated and were disseminated during the 1790s, they took on complex, and sometimes contradictory, meanings. In fact, wherever it surfaced, the tricolor cockade generated controversy, triggering diverse associations that went beyond loyalty to the French Revolution and local party allegiances.

This chapter follows the routes of two travelers for whom tricolor cockades became a source of debate. While both men began their Atlantic journeys from Philadelphia in the 1790s, their backgrounds, itineraries and relationships with cockades differed. The first is Benjamin Johnson, a Quaker bookseller, who sailed to France in 1796 as part of a delegation sent to visit a group of fellow Friends in Montpellier. The entire journey he worried about his refusal to wear a tricolor cockade, commented on those who did, and tried to make sense of what other people thought about cockades. His observations show how previous connotations of cockades found new significance and power during the Age of Revolutions.

Around the same time that Johnson left for France, Crispin, an adolescent servant originally from India, embarked on a more clandestine journey. Indentured to the wealthy Philadelphia merchant Stephen Girard, Crispin ran away in the winter of 1794–95 and eventually found his way to revolutionary Saint-Domingue. Crispin wore a tricolor cockade before, during and after his flight, and actors at the time argued about what exactly his cockade signified. His story reveals how a wearer's racial categorization further complicated the implications of tricolor cockades, and when read together with Johnson's account, lays bare the instability of this emblem in an Atlantic context.

Benjamin Johnson took a circuitous route from Philadelphia to Montpellier, stopping in England, Germany and the Netherlands before finally reaching France. In his diary, Johnson appraised the social and political conditions he witnessed: he condemned the slave ships docked in Liverpool and lamented the poor conditions and low pay of factory workers in Manchester and Sheffield. He celebrated the extension of citizenship to Jews in Amsterdam and caught a glimpse of the British royal family who, it seemed to him, lacked "dignity or any extraordinary capacity" (Johnson Diary, June 18, 1796, p. 28; June 25, 1796, p. 34; July 2, 1796, p. 44; December 23, 1796, p. 284; and July 13, 1796, p. 65). All of his observations were in keeping with some of the most radical views of the revolutionary era.

As Johnson drew closer to his final destination, he grew agitated by the prospect of donning a tricolor cockade. When the ship prepared to dock at the coast, he noted that "every passenger on board," except for himself and his Quaker companions, had cockades with them, either on their hats or in their "pockets ready to put on." Some offered to share their extra cockades with Johnson. When he declined, they suggested that if he did not want to wear one, he should have at the very least "a bitt of three colored ribband" to show any official who might stop him. Johnson regretted that, "We were not able, for want of their language, fully to explain the reason of our declining this badge of war" (Johnson Diary, February 1, 1797, p. 307–8).

It is not surprising that a Quaker would refuse, for religious reasons, to wear a cockade, but the episode flags multiple associations with cockades that held true around the Atlantic regardless of religious affiliation. Johnson's exchange with other passengers points to three important aspects of tricolor cockades: they were at once commodities, military emblems and markers of political belonging. It is worth examining each of these facets in order to understand how they contributed to the circulation and meanings of tricolor cockades in the Atlantic world.

First, commodities. Johnson's account raises the question, how did his fellow passengers acquire the tricolor cockades they had at the ready? French consumers could purchase tricolor cockades in shops, by subscription and on the streets (Spang 2015: 143). They were in such demand that as early as the fall of 1789, the Anglophone press claimed that the French had spent "nearly a million livres" on cockades (*Herald of Freedom*, November 10, 1789). Although the total sum is probably hyperbolic, the economic trend makes sense in a national context: when the tricolor cockade became a legal requirement in France, people bought many cockades (Maxwell 2014: 127). Even during the Directory, when Johnson traveled to France, and when revolutionary fervor was no longer at a fever pitch, the tricolor cockade was still *de rigueur*, including for foreigners (Wrigley 2002: 113). For visitors who failed to procure one before arriving in France, vendors in port cities hawked them to newcomers as they disembarked (Spang 2015: 143). But most of Johnson's fellow travelers already had their cockades, with extras to spare; they came prepared and had the ability to do so because of the particular characteristics of cockades as things.

Cockades were steady business during the Age of Revolutions because they were affordable for many people. They were made of readily available and inexpensive wool or leather, and even the most precious material for cockades – silk ribbon – cost less than a shilling for a yard, a discretionary purchase possible for many English laborers, whose average annual household expenditures ranged from 500 to 1,000 shillings (Styles 2007: 8). The low price reflected a competitive market, in which both England and France supported robust ribbon manufactories in Coventry and Saint-Etienne respectively, supplying both home and empire (Dodge 1988; Marot 2014). Moreover, people at all social levels already incorporated ribbon in various guises in their dress – to decorate a cap, a sleeve, or a gown, to edge a handkerchief or a lapel, to adorn their necks (Styles 2010: 43). Consider the case of the enslaved, the group with the least purchasing power. In 1783 a German soldier passing through Saint-Domingue observed that slaves brought produce to market, and used their profits to buy "some finery, or other trinkets" like "the finest ribbon" which gave "them the satisfaction of being different from their poor comrades" (Acomb 1958: 318). Advertisements for runaway slaves in the Caribbean and the United States occasionally noted ribbon embellishments, such as one for an enslaved barber in Kingston, Jamaica, who wore a "fustian coattee lapelled and edged with blue ribbon" (*Daily Advertiser* (Kingston), March 22, 1791). Enslaved people had access to ribbon in stores and outdoor markets, and in the Caribbean, dry goods merchants sent out traveling salesmen, with trunks of goods, to hawk wares from plantation to plantation (*Daily Advertiser* (Kingston), November 29, 1791; Martin 2008: 145–72).

In light of its affordability, accessibility and pre-existing dress practices, cockades were articles with tremendous potential for popular appeal, and sure enough, they appeared everywhere from the United States to the Caribbean to Europe. It was, therefore, relatively easy for Johnson's companions, or for that matter anyone else, to buy or make tricolor cockades. Equally important, Johnson's shipmates knew that a tricolor cockade was an essential accessory for their journeys. As one of his associates put it, a tricolor cockade "was even more necessary than a passport" in order to travel safely throughout the Atlantic (Johnson Diary, February 1, 1797, p. 308).

That said, the rules around cockades changed frequently. This was especially the case in colonial contexts. In Martinique, for instance, in the late 1780s, "every person, American or native – to avoid incurring the displeasure of the people, are obliged to wear the National Cockade." A few years later, counter-revolutionary forces demanded that the white cockade be worn, only for the tricolor to be reinstated when republicans prevailed (*Massachusetts Centinel*,

November 11, 1789; *Connecticut Journal*, February 14, 1793; *Daily Advertiser* (New York), May 2, 1793). From the makers' point of view, the fickleness of cockades was not necessarily a liability. The industry was built on novelty and the ability to respond to the whims of fashion – political and otherwise. For the wearer, though, the changeability of cockades was cause for concern: the wrong cockade (or for Benjamin Johnson, none at all) could provoke outrage and even land one in prison. At one point in his journey, Johnson remarked drily, "My curiosity to see a little dirty Flemish town was not strong enough to overpower my apprehension of being insulted for not wearing a cockade, I therefore staid at home also, pretty much in our chamber" (Johnson Diary, February 6, 1797, p. 308).

The language surrounding cockades – that of "displeasure" and "apprehension" – points to a significant characteristic that set cockades apart from ribbons of fashion and that relates to the second important aspect of their transnational movement: it was a "badge" of war (Johnson Diary, January 14, 1797, p. 303). As a pacifist, Johnson was sensitive to anything that hinted at armed conflict, yet given the provenance of cockades, Johnson's observation is more representative than idiosyncratic. Cockades' first and firmest affiliation was with the military. At a time when uniforms were anything but uniform, armies and navies long relied on cockades as a quick and cheap way to identify soldiers and sailors (Maxwell 2014: 122). Prominently displayed cockades helped to distinguish allies from adversaries; or within one's own camp, to incorporate foreign mercenaries.

As cockades became a more visible presence among civilians during the Age of Revolutions, their military connotations persisted. The 1793 French Constitution proclaimed that "all French were soldiers," and this emphasis on the centrality of military service to citizenship continued through the Directory (Heuer 2002: 35). The tricolor cockade was a visible sign of the merging of the categories of "citizen" and "soldier." What's more, the National Assembly decreed, "every cockade, other than that with the national colors, is a sign of rebellion" (*City Gazette and Daily Advertiser*, September 26, 1792). During the Terror, when the revolutionary tribunal published lists of men and women condemned to the guillotine, they were often accused of, along with other crimes, "trampling the tricolor underfoot" (*Journal de Paris national*, no. 540, June 24, 1794, p. 2180). To dishonor the cockade, or to wear a different one, was treasonous and hence punishable by state-sanctioned violence and even death.

The militaristic associations of cockades had important repercussions in Benjamin Johnson's United States. Well before his trip to

France, Johnson had witnessed the polarizing and violent tendencies provoked by cockades among political parties at home. Many Democratic Republicans embraced the French tricolor cockade, while Federalists, especially as the decade wore on, called for the black – or as some claimed, the British – cockade. Although these cockades operated as symbols of political conflict, they also contributed to generating that conflict because of their association with war (Maxwell 2014: 124). Riots broke out in Charleston, Norfolk, Philadelphia and New York, when one group spotted the other's cockades and tried to remove or deface them (Heuer 2002: 30). Often the protagonists were sailors or soldiers; in other instances, they were American citizens, and this was problematic. Commentators on both sides of the political fence criticized this development: "Citizens have no business with cockades; it is a military emblem which ought only to be worn by a soldier. To wear it as a badge of distinction is indiscreet and improper, it ought to be discountenanced by the citizens at large" (*Carey's United States' Recorder*, May 10, 1798). Cockades were understood as provocations to violence, and if they spread among civilians, then civil war could result.

These examples of men donning cockades and taking to arms demonstrate the boldest translation of ideals into action. But for all the explosive potential of tricolor cockades, they also signaled, somewhat contradictorily, the limits of political identification. As Johnson's account makes clear, tricolor cockades were badges of conformity. When their vessel neared France, Johnson's shipmates put on cockades as a matter of course, regardless of whether they believed in and were willing to fight for the ideals and country associated with it. If the French government demanded that all foreigners wear the cockade while in the country and that people in all newly incorporated territories embrace the emblem, then there is, in the very absolutism of such decrees, a tacit recognition that the wearers may not espouse and defend its principles.

One could argue that these laws were didactic, designed to help the wearer inculcate the republican values that the tricolor cockade theoretically encapsulated. Pedagogy, however, often fell short, and throughout the period, commentators in Britain, France, the United States and the Caribbean noted the gap between the lofty ideals that the cockade was supposed to signify, and the behaviors of the people who actually wore it. Some mocked their own "*cockaded* heroes" who played the soldier but whose courage went no deeper than the ribbon they wore (*United States Chronicle*, October 7, 1784). Newspapers in the United States were littered with anecdotes of men who used cockades to cloak their misdeeds – to escape from prison, to take out credit, to steal, to seduce young women (*Daily Advertiser* (New York), September 19, 1794; *Columbian Centinel*, November 12, 1794; *Wiscasset Telegraph*, December 24, 1796). In these scenarios, a man's cockade helped him to inveigle his way into someone's confidence and to take advantage of him or her.

Cockades masked even greater abuses. After witnessing a Caribbean colonist beat a slave, one U.S. commentator remarked, "this Frenchmen appears to me to be one of those who, while they honor the republic with their mouth, and decorate their hats with the national cockade, retain all that despotism so predominant in the West Indies, in their hearts" (*Argus*, June 9, 1795). The author reprimands the master for hypocrisy and then uses the episode to call for gradual manumission in New York. No matter where one went in the Atlantic world, tricolor cockades were cause for suspicion, for they all too easily masked the ideological and moral failings of wearers.

While Johnson's journey from Philadelphia to Montpellier inspired his ruminations about tricolor cockades and their manifold meanings, his preoccupation with their possible dangers – both literal and ideological – was not unique. Given the pervasiveness of this inexpensive commodity, many people had the opportunity to buy a cockade and then lay claim to the principles and acts attached to it. Both within and outside of France, elites worried about the volatile nature of tricolor cockades as well as their ability to disguise ideological ambivalence and other offences. In an Atlantic context, the concern around tricolor cockades was heightened by their presence among men of color.

In contrast to Johnson's experience with cockades, we lack Crispin's first-person account. As is the case for so many people of color in this period, our understanding is informed by what others did – and did not – say about him and his tricolor cockade. Luckily, his master, Stephen Girard, left a long paper trail, corresponding with contacts in the United States and Caribbean for over three years, in an attempt to retrieve his prized servant. Unable to fathom that Crispin wanted to leave of his own accord, Girard believed that Crispin had been "enticed" by a French "rogue" named Joseph Larelle, and after Girard made his accusations public, Larelle sued Girard for defamation. These dramatic circumstances resulted in a good deal of discussion about Crispin and his motives that provides valuable insight into how the racial identification of wearers influenced associations with tricolor cockades.

Soon after Crispin fled, Girard placed advertisements in several newspapers, offering a twenty-dollar reward to whoever found and secured the indentured servant. True to the genre in the United States, the notice included a fairly detailed description of Crispin: his age (sixteen), height (5 feet 4 inches), hair ("straight black"), build ("slender" and "well made"), his gait ("walks upright") and language abilities ("speaks French and broken English") (*Herald and Norfolk and Portsmouth Advertiser*, December 10, 1794). Girard had a harder time pinning down Crispin's racial category because subcontinental Indians were unusual in the early United States. Crispin had most likely arrived in Philadelphia through Girard's trade connections in the East Indies. But when most locals heard the term "Indian," they thought of Native Americans (Bean 2001: 19). In their correspondence about the case, Girard and his contacts struggled to find a racialized shorthand to portray Crispin: they called him an "Indian," "mulatto," "Indian mulatto," "mulatto Indian," "Indian negro," "Indian or negro" and "swarthy young negro" – sometimes several different terms in the same letter (Jean Girard to Mr. Adam, Nov. 21, 1794; Paul Bentalou to Stephen Girard, Dec. 11, 1794; Stephen Girard to Gy. Lavaud, March 20, 1795; Stephen Girard to General Laveaux, June 21, 1795; Stephen Girard to Chauveau, Oct. 8, 1795; Stephen Girard Papers; hereafter abbreviated SPG, and Stephen Girard as SG). For the newspaper ad, Girard settled on "a kind of Mulatto East-India Boy," hoping that the gesture to both color and origin would be enough for others to identify him (*Herald and Norfolk and Portsmouth Advertiser*, December 10, 1794).

Despite the clumsy terminology, Girard and his cohort saw Crispin as someone who had more in common with people of African descent than with white men. This classification had important implications for another key component of the advertisement: the description of Crispin's clothing. As best Girard could recall, Crispin "had on when he went away an almost new black hat, new short Jacket, and a pair of French fashioned trousers with feet in them, made of grey coating with plated buttons, white shirt, French neck handkerchief, and an almost new pair of shoes tied with ribbon" (*Herald and Norfolk and Portsmouth Advertiser*, December 10, 1794). His attire indicated a certain degree of economic wherewithal and style. Three of the items were new or "almost new," and individual garments reflected *au courant* fashions. Tied (versus buckled) shoes were only recently in vogue, and the French provenance of some articles spoke to an awareness of cosmopolitan modes.

Masters across the Atlantic world sometimes dressed their domestic servants and slaves, especially young, "exotic" ones like Crispin, in elegant clothing, as further demonstration of their wealth and power (Molineux 2012). An immigrant to Philadelphia from Bordeaux, Girard had established a formidable mercantile firm with extensive connections in France's Atlantic and Indian empires (McMaster 1918). Crispin and his stylish garments made Girard's impressive reach manifest: if Girard could afford to procure a subcontinental Indian and clothe him in such finery, then, the implication was, his wealth was extraordinary. Although Girard never explicitly stated the nature of Crispin's work, his dress suggests duties that brought him into contact with visitors. In the summer of 1794, for example, a Baltimore resident posted a notice for his runaway servant, a man from Isle de France (present-day Mauritius), who worked as a "waiting boy," and perhaps Crispin performed in a similar capacity (*Baltimore Daily Intelligencer*, July 5, 1794; Allen 1999; Salinger 1987).

For all of his master's influence, Crispin's clothing was not necessarily Girard's doing alone. As several scholars have shown, unfree workers asserted their own senses of selves through dress whenever they could, not only choosing specific garments, but also combining, fastening, folding or tying items in ways that marked them as distinctive (DuPlessis 2016; Prude 1991; White and White 1995). A hint of this modicum of control comes through in the advertisement when Girard notes that Crispin "wears sometime a National Cockade" (*Herald and Norfolk and Portsmouth Advertiser*, December 10, 1794). Girard's brother Jean, who was enlisted to help find Crispin, described the cockade in detail, as one "made of ribbons cut out in the shape of a carnation"; clearly, it was a noticeable accessory (Jean Girard to Mr. Adam, Nov. 21, 1794, SGP). The qualifier of "sometime" in Girard's advertisement catches attention: Crispin had some control over his cockade, putting it on and taking it off, presumably at his discretion.

While Crispin exercised a degree of power over his cockade, it is unclear what inspired him to wear it in the first place. Stephen Girard was a steadfast Democratic Republican, and so perhaps, on his orders, his household staff were required to sport the tricolor cockade. William Israel, who was bound to Girard from 1797 to 1804, later recalled that his master "had a peculiar knack of having a control over everybody," and therefore, such a demand may not have been out of the ordinary (Deposition, William Israel, August 23, 1838). Even if Girard mandated the cockade, Crispin knew its political connotations. The Democratic Republican party was adept at taking their political sympathies to the streets, in the form of fêtes celebrating the French Revolution. These occasions attracted men and women of all ranks and races – many sporting the tricolor. In Philadelphia ecstatic throngs greeted Edmond Charles Genet, Minister Plenipotentiary of the French Republic, with cries of "liberty, equality, fraternity" when he arrived in the city to take up his post in May 1793. The following summer, they staged the "Feast of Reason," a grand procession of Frenchmen and Americans who marched through the city and capped off their parade with music, speeches and oaths in which they swore "to live free or die" (Newman 1997: 131, 145–6; Elkins and McKitrick 1993: 335–6).

Significantly, in February 1794, just months before Crispin fled, the French National Assembly met rebel slaves' demands in Saint-Domingue by abolishing slavery and granting citizenship to men of African descent. At this moment, the agendas of the French and Haitian revolutions merged, and the tricolor cockade became an emblem for both movements (Dubois 2004; Popkin 2010). This union was hard for most Federalists and Democratic Republicans to accept, given the persistence of slavery and racism in the United States. Nevertheless, the momentous shift was all the news in Philadelphia: sailors brought word about it to the docks, the press commented on it in detail, and refugees from the revolution who filled the city debated it in the streets (Branson 2001: 56–8; Branson and Patrick 2001; Dun 2016; Nash 1998; White 2010). Some of these exiles, including enslaved ones, lived in Girard's household during Crispin's indenture. In May 1793, Mr. Faurez in Cape Français sent his slave to Girard, warning that "this negro is not making this trip with the best will in the world, [and] it will be necessary to take some precautions to prevent him from reshipping for the Cape." Girard complained to a refugee about another enslaved Saint-Dominguan staying with him: "Your negro Paul is a worthless fellow and always disorderly . . . My negress followed his example, and ran away two weeks ago" (J. Faurez to SG, May 4, 1793; SG to Mr. Bacon, Sept. 9, 1793, SGP). With occasions for everyday contact with black Saint-Dominguans who resented their emigration, Crispin had plenty of opportunities to learn what the tricolor cockade signified in the French colony.

White Philadelphians – and white Americans more broadly – were unsure what to make of men of African descent wearing tricolor cockades. In light of their militaristic connotations, some worried that cockades would empower black men to resist subjugation with violence. Several newspaper reports listed tricolor cockades as part of the arsenal necessary for war in the West Indies. One from New York relayed that "a Conspiracy has been discovered among the blacks at Dominica [sic]. In possession of the Ring-leaders were found fire arms, ammunition and French cockades" (*The Herald*, April 25, 1795). Patriots in Martinique, according to a Rhode Island paper, hoarded "muskets, regimentals, and national cockades, which were to be distributed among the negroes they expected would rise" (*State Gazette*, February 4, 1796). These accounts described cockades as essential elements for armed rebellion – as crucial as guns and ammunition – and some observers feared the consequences of Caribbean examples for the United States. A man in Charleston, South Carolina, writing under the pseudonym "Caution," described how "some free negroes have been seen on board the French vessels with the national cockade; what effect must this produce on our slaves[?] ... Have we not every reason to fear it will make them very restless in their present situation?" (*Columbian Herald*, August 14, 1795). For white observers in the north and south, black men's tricolor cockades signaled not only their desire for liberty and equality, but also their willingness to act with force to realize them.

Although such warnings about the dangers of cockades appeared in the U.S. press, this language did not inform Girard and his correspondents' discussion of Crispin. They saw the tricolor cockade as fundamental to the servant's dress and to identifying him; for example, when a young subcontinental Indian was jailed in Norfolk, two of Girard's agents visited him and deduced that he was not Crispin, in part, because he did not wear a tricolor cockade (J. H. Roberjot to SG, March 7, 1795; Citizen Oster to SG, March 5, 1795; SG to Jean Girard, March 24, 1795, SGP). Despite the cockade's centrality to Crispin's physical identity, it, in Girard's view, carried none of the militaristic or ideological connotations attributed to tricolor cockades worn by other men. Girard insisted that a devious Frenchman had duped his servant into running away, rather than Crispin searching and fighting for liberty of his own accord.

Atlantic masters often turned to the excuse of "enticement" to deny the agency of runaway bondsmen and to save face as masters. But what is striking in this episode is how Girard willfully ignored the potential symbolism of Crispin's tricolor cockade. While Girard did not account for this denial, several viable explanations demonstrate the instability surrounding tricolor cockades, especially those worn by people of color. First, Girard and his cohort could have thought Crispin was too young to know and act upon his cockade, although at sixteen he was, in this era, practically a man. They may have been influenced by racial stereotypes that effeminized subcontinental men, and so doubted that Crispin had the wherewithal to put up a fight. Or like Johnson's fellow travelers to France who pinned on their cockades right before disembarking, Girard and his contemporaries saw Crispin's cockade as a marker of conformity – something he wore at Girard's behest.

Whatever the rationalization, Girard and his colleagues refused to ascribe any ideological weight to Crispin's cockade and, by extension, to the person who wore it. This de-politicization of one of the defining emblems of the age is thrown into even starker relief upon Crispin's arrival in Saint-Domingue. In 1795, Girard learned that Crispin had landed in Port de Paix, a seaport in the northwest region of the colony. Port de Paix was a French republican stronghold where residents fiercely repelled invading British forces. The port also provided a strategic harbor from which republican corsairs attacked British vessels. In such a contentious environment, the tricolor cockade mattered, helping to distinguish the supporters of the revolutionary government from its detractors.

When Girard learned of Crispin's whereabouts, he contacted French authorities on the island in an effort to retrieve him. Although neither side of the epistolary exchange mentioned Crispin's cockade specifically, they did debate one of the central ideals associated with it, namely "liberty," and whether it was a motivation for Crispin's flight. Despite his support for the French Revolution, Girard had nothing but disdain for the republican project in Saint-Domingue; in another venue, he had referred to the government there as a "band of ignorant men ruling over slaves" (SG to Aubert, Chauveau & Bacon, June 13, 1793, SGP). In his attempt to persuade the Governor General Etienne Laveaux to force Crispin's return to Philadelphia, however, he adopted a more measured tone. He highlighted Philadelphia's credentials as "the first to pass a decree in favor of universal liberty," a sleight of hand since abolition in Pennsylvania was gradual, not immediate. Girard professed that he sought Crispin's return to Philadelphia so that he could testify in the lawsuit with Larelle, the supposed enticer, and he pledged that Crispin could return to Saint-Domingue after the trial – a dubious guarantee, to say the least (SG to General Laveaux, June 21, 1795, SGP).

Laveaux saw the situation differently. Calling the servant "Citizen Crispin," he stressed how freedom was central to Crispin's decision to flee to Saint-Domingue: "In coming to Port de Paix [Crispin] has come to enjoy liberty. In Philadelphia he was a slave. Have I the right to order him to take up his chains again? Assuredly not." To do otherwise would violate "our Glorious Constitution," abrogating a citizen's right by forcing him "against his own will to leave the land of liberty where he has taken refuge" (Etienne Laveaux to Genty Lavaud, Sept. 9, 1795, SGP). But Laveaux's version of events reflected his desires rather than actual circumstances, as the French republican regime struggled to make good on its promises of liberty and equality. Many areas of the colony refused to adhere to the 1794 decree, and violence erupted even in republican cities, including Port de Paix. Additionally, newly liberated black Saint-Dominguans resented the French government's reinstatement of the plantation regime, albeit with wage instead of enslaved labor. In February 1796, not long after Laveaux wrote his reply to Girard, black plantation workers rebelled in the mountains around Port de Paix. In the following seven months, black Saint-Dominguans in the area revolted another five times, and only in November did Toussaint Louverture pacify the region (Geggus 1982: 71, 180, 203–4; Lundahl 1985: 122–38). For a regime wrestling with putting its lofty ideals into practice, Crispin's flight to Saint-Domingue and his tricolor cockade could be used as a reassuring example of French achievements, at a time when its success was compromised at best.

In the end, Crispin did not return to Philadelphia. At this point, the trail goes cold, and what Crispin did next is unknown. The temptation is strong to see his tricolor cockade as a clear indication of his support for the French revolutionary project in Saint-Domingue, and perhaps he realized the ideological and militaristic promises of his cockade, joining republican forces in Saint-Domingue. But the various associations with cockades suggest other alternatives. Maybe a few years later, if he survived the violence, he felt betrayed by the French tricolor and fought for Haitian independence against Napoleon's forces. Or perhaps Crispin saw his cockade as a badge of conformity – an accessory that helped a distinctive subcontinental Indian blend, as much as he could, in Girard's Philadelphia and in revolutionary Saint-Domingue. While a definitive reading remains elusive, the significance lies in the diversity of interpretive options, as sundry actors imparted meanings to his tricolor cockade that both celebrated and denied his allegiance to French and Haitian causes.

Taken together, Crispin and Johnson's experiences offer up a new understanding of tricolor cockades as emblems of the age. Rather than tidy encapsulations of French revolutionary principles, tricolor cockades took on a range of associations that defy simple categorization. They were bellicose declarations of forceful intentions, both genuine and superficial tokens of belonging, and everything in between. Their content depended on who drew the connections, how, and even where, and this process of making connections sparked controversy repeatedly.

The multivalent quality of the tricolor cockade has implications for our appraisals of politics in this era. For decades now, scholars have shown how the revolutions of the late eighteenth century politicized the stuff of everyday life. In their interpretations, things became conduits for inculcating new ideals and new senses of national identity. But the case of the tricolor cockade points to how material culture influenced the form and texture of revolutionary politics in ways that defied the confines of the nation. In so doing, these objects complicated, extended and sometimes even undercut what individual nations, like France, hoped to achieve. It is for this reason that the tricolor cockade stands as the iconic object of this era, for it made manifest the instability, ambiguity and tension of Atlantic revolutions.

Bibliography

Acomb, Evelyn M., ed. (1958), *The Revolutionary Journal of Baron Ludwig von Closen, 1780–1783*, Chapel Hill: University of North Carolina Press.

Allen, Richard B. (1999), *Slaves, Freedmen, and Indentured Laborers in Colonial Mauritius*, New York: Cambridge University Press.

Auslander, Leora (2009), *Cultural Revolutions: Everyday Life and Politics in Britain, North America, and France*, Berkeley: University of California Press.

Bean, Susan S. (2001), *Yankee India: American Commercial and Cultural Encounters with India in the Age of Sail, 1784–1860*, Salem, MA: Peabody Essex Museum.

Benjamin Johnson Diary, Downs Collection, Winterthur Archives, Winterthur DE.

Branson, Susan (2001), *These Fiery Frenchified Dames: Women and Political Culture in Early National Philadelphia*, Philadelphia: University of Pennsylvania Press.

Branson, Susan and Leslie Patrick (2001), "Étrangers dans un Pays Étrange: Saint Domingan Refugees of Color in Philadelphia," in David P. Geggus, ed., *The Impact of the Haitian Revolution in the Atlantic World*, Columbia: University of South Carolina Press, pp. 195–208.

Deposition, William Israel, August 23, 1838; *Mary Kenton v. Thomas P. Cope et al.*, executors of the last will of Stephen Girard, Narratives and Copy of Charges [Box A-4105], March term 1834, no. 76, District Court of the City and County of Philadelphia, Philadelphia City Archives, Philadelphia.

Dodge, Jenny (1988), *Silken Weave: A History of Ribbon Making in Coventry*, Coventry: Herbert Art Gallery & Museum.

Dubois, Laurent (2004), *Avengers of the New World: The Story of the Haitian Revolution*, Cambridge, MA: Harvard University Press.

Dun, James Alexander (2016), *Dangerous Neighbors: Making the Haitian Revolution in Early America*, Philadelphia: University of Pennsylvania Press.

DuPlessis, Robert (2016), *The Material Atlantic: Clothing the New World*, Cambridge: Cambridge University Press.

Elkins, Stanley and Eric McKitrick (1993), *The Age of Federalism: The Early American Republic, 1788–1800*, New York: Oxford University Press.

Geggus, David (1982), *Slavery, War, and Revolution: The British Occupation of Saint-Domingue, 1793–1798*, New York: Oxford University Press.

Heuer, Jennifer (2002), "Hats on for the Nation! Women, Servants, Soldiers and the 'Sign of the French,'" *French History* 16:1, pp. 28–52.

Hunt, Lynn (1984), *Politics, Culture, and Class in the French Revolution*, Berkeley: University of California Press.

Lundahl, Mats (1985), "Toussaint L'Ouverture and the War Economy of Saint-Domingue, 1796–1802," *Slavery and Abolition* 6:2, pp. 122–38.

McMaster, John Bach (1918), *The Life and Times of Stephen Girard: Mariner and Merchant*, Philadelphia.

Marot, Sylvie (2014), *The French Ribbon*, New York: Pointed Leaf Press.

Martin, Ann Smart (2008), *Buying into the World of Goods: Early Consumers in Backcountry Virginia*, Baltimore: The Johns Hopkins University Press.

Maxwell, A. (2014), *Patriots Against Fashion: Clothing and Nationalism in Europe's Age of Revolutions*, Basingstoke: Palgrave.

Molineux, Catherine (2012), *Faces of Perfect Ebony: Encountering Atlantic Slavery in Imperial Britain*, Cambridge, MA: Harvard University Press.

Nash, Gary (1998), "Reverberations of Haiti in the American North: Black Saint-Dominguans in Philadelphia," *Explorations in Early American Culture: A Special Supplemental Issue of Pennsylvania History* 65, pp. 44–73.

Newman, Simon (1997), *Parades and the Politics of the Street: Festive Culture in the Early American Republic*, Philadelphia: University of Pennsylvania Press.

Newspapers: *Argus* (New York), *Baltimore Daily Intelligencer*, *Carey's United States' Recorder* (Philadelphia), *City Gazette and Daily Advertiser* (Charleston), *Columbian Centinel* (Boston), *Columbian Herald* (Charleston), *Connecticut Journal* (New Haven), *Daily Advertiser* (Kingston), *Daily Advertiser* (New York), *The Herald* (New York), *Herald and Norfolk and Portsmouth Advertiser* (Norfolk, VA), *Herald of Freedom* (Boston), *Journal de Paris national*, *Massachusetts Centinel* (Boston), *Pennsylvania Gazette* (Philadelphia), *State Gazette* (Providence, RI), *United States Chronicle* (Providence, RI), *Wiscasset Telegraph* (Wiscasset, ME).

Popkin, Jeremy (2010), *You Are All Free: The Haitian Revolution and the Abolition of Slavery*, New York: Cambridge University Press.

Prude, Jonathan (1991), "To Look Upon the "Lower Sort": Runaway Ads and the Appearance of Unfree Laborers in America, 1750–1800," *The Journal of American History* 78:1, pp. 124–59.

Salinger, Sharon V. (1987), *"To Serve Well and Faithfully": Labor and Indentured Servants in Pennsylvania, 1682–1800*, New York: Cambridge University Press.

Spang, Rebecca (2015), *Stuff and Money in the Time of the French Revolution*, Cambridge, MA: Harvard University Press.

Stephen Girard Papers (SGP), American Philosophical Society Library, Philadelphia.

Styles, John (2007), *The Dress of the People: Everyday Fashion in Eighteenth-Century England*, New Haven: Yale University Press.

Styles, John (2010), *Threads of Feeling: The London Foundling Hospital's Textile Tokens, 1740–1770,* London: The Foundling Museum.

White, Ashli (2010), *Encountering Revolution: Haiti and the Making of the Early Republic*, Baltimore: Johns Hopkins University Press.

White, Shane and Graham White (1995), "Slave Clothing and African-American Culture in the Eighteenth and Nineteenth Centuries," *Past and Present* 148, pp. 149–86.

Wrigley, Richard (2002), *The Politics of Appearances: Representations of Dress in Revolutionary France*, Oxford: Berg.

Chapter 8

The Noble Turk: Estanislao de Cosca Vayo's *Grecia, ó la doncella de Missolonghi* (1830) and the Spanish Response to the Greek War of Independence

Elizabeth Amann

The Greek War of Independence (1821–29) inspired a vast body of Philhellenic literature in France, Germany, the United Kingdom and the United States, including poems, essays, plays and novels, many of which were written while the conflict was still ongoing, in an effort to attract European support for the uprising.[1] In Spain, however, the literary production around the war was much more limited. The Greek political movement began only shortly after Rafael del Riego's 1820 *pronunciamiento*, which reintroduced the liberal Constitution of 1812 and marked the beginning of the Liberal Triennium. The Spanish liberals who had come into power in 1820 welcomed the uprising, which they saw as part of the same revolutionary wave.[2] But when absolutist rule was reestablished in Spain in 1823 through the intervention of the Holy Alliance, the topic quickly became taboo. During the ten years between 1823 and Ferdinand VII's death in 1833 – the period known as the "ominous decade" – discussion of the Greek uprising was heavily censored, and very few texts addressed the topic directly (Morfakidis Motos 2014: 139–40). Estanislao de Cosca Vayo's two-volume *Grecia, ó la doncella de Missolonghi* (Greece, or the Maid of Missolonghi), published in Valencia in 1830, seems to be the only novel dedicated to the subject originally written in Spanish.[3] It therefore offers a unique vantage point from which to explore the reverberations of the Greek uprising in a Spain whose own liberal aspirations had so recently been crushed.

Within the larger canon of European Philhellenic literature, Cosca Vayo's novel is interesting for a number of reasons. The first is its unusual plot, which features a love story between a Greek woman and a Turkish man. As David Roessel observes, the "romance of Greek liberation" generally involved "a white man saving a lapsed white woman from the Turk, a brown man" (2002: 61). In such plots, the Greek heroine usually rejects "the threat of sexual domination" represented by the Ottoman and turns romantically to the West (60).[4] In Cosca Vayo's novel, however, the heroine Constanza rejects her Greek admirer Nicetas and falls in love instead with the Muslim Mahomet. Whereas many narratives about the conflict evoke a clash of civilizations and an unbridgeable divide between East and West, Cosca Vayo creates a plot in which these differences are represented as an accident of birth and are ultimately transcended. Second, the Spanish novel takes considerable liberties with the historical record, altering the chronology, outcome and actors at key moments in the war. Moreover, Cosca Vayo himself seems to draw attention to these discrepancies by including a lengthy introduction with a historical overview that is notably at odds with the plot of the novel. Morfakidis Motos has pointed to the strange disconnect between Cosca Vayo's "real knowledge of the facts" and the outlandish "distortion" of his tale (2014: 146) but does not attempt to account for these divergences.

This chapter will address the following questions: First, what is the function of the altered chronology in the main plot? Second, why is the hero of the novel a Turk rather than a Greek? And finally, what vision does the novel offer of the Greek uprising in general? What elements does the Spanish writer foreground or omit? And what, if any, adjustments might have been necessary to make the work acceptable in the context of the "ominous decade"? In what follows, I will argue that Cosca Vayo's reflection on the Greek Revolution is inflected by his view of Spain's own experience of Muslim domination. Although he expresses some ambivalence about the more revolutionary aspects of the war, his narrative is unusually progressive in promoting universal values that transcend cultural and religious differences.

Rewriting the Greek War of Independence

Most of the main characters in the novel are based on historical figures who are mentioned in the introduction to the work. Constanza Zacarías, the heroine, and Antinos, the bishop who gives her refuge in the second volume, are based on minor figures of Greek history.[5] As Morfakidis Motos notes (2014: 146–7), Cosca Vayo's account of them seems to be based on a paragraph in the

Compendio histórico del origen y progresos de la insurrección de los griegos contra los turcos (1828), by J. M. de San Millán y Coronel, who published under the pseudonym of Marcos Manuel Río y Coronel (see Río y Coronel 1828: I, 118). This passage is in turn an almost verbatim translation of a paragraph in Pouqueville's *Histoire de la régéneration de la Grèce* (1824) (see Pouqueville 1824: II, 351–2). In both San Millán y Coronel's and Pouqueville's texts, Constanza/Constance leaves aside her spindle to take up a sword and rallies the men and women of Laconia to the cause of Greek independence. After receiving the blessing of Antinos, the bishop of Hellos, she attacks the crescents of the mosques in Londari and then burns down the house of the *vaivode* (governor), killing him in the process. Cosca Vayo's account in his introduction (1830: I, xv) follows closely San Millán's diction but carefully omits the details about Constanza setting aside her spindle, brandishing a sword and rallying the men, as well as the description of her arson and murder of the *vaivode*. The Spanish novel, thus, offers a somewhat less militant representation of the heroine. Although early in the text Constanza imagines herself wielding "the sword instead of the spinning wheel" (I, 66–7), she ultimately rejects the idea of the female warrior. During the attack on Chios, she agrees to the creation of a female battalion only on the condition that it not be sent to fight, for a virgin's hand should be stained by the "carmine of the rose" rather than "the scarlet of blood" (I, 152). Although Cosca Vayo frequently describes other women taking up arms in the battle of Missolonghi and elsewhere, Constanza's role in the novel is to promote the Christian values of forgiveness and peace.[6] When the Greeks attack the Citadel of Chios, she urges them to show clemency, even as they are fired upon by the Turks. Cosca Vayo, thus, carefully distinguishes Constanza from the figure of the female warrior.

The two main Greek protagonists, Nicetas and Canaris, are based on more well-known figures. Nicetas, the Greek hero who falls in love with the heroine, is Nikitas Stamelopoulos, known also as Nikitaras or the "Turk-eater," who was famous for his upright character and for donating his sword to the cause of defending Missolonghi. Canaris is based on Konstantinos Kanaris, an admiral who daringly burned the Turkish fleet in revenge for the Chios Massacre (1822) and who carried out similar exploits in Tenedos and Samos. Once again, however, Cosca Vayo makes significant changes to the historical record. Although his introduction correctly attributes the burning of the fleet in Chios to Canaris, it is Nicetas who realizes this feat in the novel itself. Moreover, whereas in the introduction Canaris, "modest and religious," avoids the applause of the masses and goes instead to pray in a church after returning from his exploit, Nicetas, who is motivated less by patriotism than by ambition, cannot suppress his joy at the honors bestowed upon him by the Greeks. Far from a noble deed, the destruction of the ships is represented as an act of vanity and pride and as a sign of Nicetas's ingratitude toward the Turkish hero Mahomet, who had generously spared his life just hours before.

Why then does Cosca Vayo replace Canaris with Nicetas? The answer may have something to do with the treatment of the history of the war in the novel. In the introduction, Cosca Vayo offers an overview of the Greek War of Independence in strict chronological order beginning with the proscription of Ali Pasha, which created an opportunity for the Greek rebels, and ending with the Battle of Navarino (1827). The plot of the novel, however, rearranges the chronology of the war in a significant way. The novel opens on April 22, 1826 in the aftermath of the siege of Missolonghi, but then the action moves first to Chios and then to Samos and represents a series of events that closely resemble those of 1822 and 1824. Just as the Samians in March 1822 landed in Chios and burned the mosques, forcing the Ottomans to retreat into the Citadel, in the novel a Greek fleet invades the city, sets the mosques on fire, kills most of the Muslims and forces the survivors back into the Citadel. But whereas the Turks quickly recaptured the island and massacred its inhabitants, Cosca Vayo allows the Greeks to triumph. The subsequent burning of the ships is therefore not an act of revenge for the Massacre of Chios (as was the case with Konstantinos Kanaris's historical feat) but rather an attempt by Nicetas, who did not participate in the Greek attack on Chios, to claim for himself part of the glory. Cosca Vayo, thus, allows the Greeks the military victory but deprives them of the moral one, which belongs to Mahomet, who immediately forgives Nicetas's ungrateful act. The narrative then goes on to recount events resembling the unsuccessful Turkish attempt in 1824 to recover Samos, one of the first islands to embrace the cause of independence. Finally, in the second volume, Cosca Vayo mentions the siege of Athens, which seems to return us to the post-Missolonghi period. But once again there is a striking discrepancy. In the novel, the Sultan is eager for Mahomet to return to mainland Greece, "where the Greeks had Athens under siege, and where the most brilliant army had disappeared as if by magic, destroyed by the victorious arms of the Hellenes" (II, 91). The introduction, in contrast, recalls how Athens "too had to open its doors to the Muslims" (I, xli). Cosca Vayo, that is, is either rewriting the 1826–27 siege of Athens as a Greek victory or rewinding the historical clock even further to recount the siege of the Acropolis of 1822 in which the Turks were surrounded by the Greeks.

Some of these historical liberties might be attributed to the logic of Cosca Vayo's plot. The Turkish protagonist Mahomet is represented as necessary to the success of the Ottomans:

> The banner of the cross fluttered on the ramparts of Tripolitsa, of Modon and of Navarino, whose squares the Christians had quickly captured. No warrior could replace Mahomet: because experience had shown that the Turks who fought like lions seeing that courageous man in front of them, fled like cowardly sheep in the absence of the Muslim hero. (II, 91)

When Mahomet is not present, the Turks can only lose. Early in the novel, Mahomet disobeys the Sultan's instructions to rejoin the Ottoman troops in order to participate in a duel with Nicetas. It is precisely during his absence that the Greeks manage to take and hold Chios. The war in the novel, thus, is not a fixed historical backdrop but rather seems subject to change as a result of the action of the main plot.

The decision to put Missolonghi before Chios and Samos may in part account for the decision to make Nicetas the hero of the burning of the ships. As Nikitaras was the key player in the defense of Missolonghi, it makes sense (within the logic of the novel) that he should be the Greek suitor of Constanza, "the maid of Missolonghi," and that he should continue to play a heroic role in subsequent episodes. But why invert Chios and Missolonghi in the first place? After the fall of Missolonghi, the Turks considered themselves on the verge of victory. In the novel, indeed, Mahomet withdraws to Chios in part because he considers his work done on the mainland. The historical victory of the Greeks would ultimately come about only through the intervention of foreign powers in the Battle of Navarino, in which the Ottoman fleet was defeated. As Cosca Vayo recognizes in the introduction, that battle "decided in one day the future fate of Greece" (I, xliv). The plot of the novel, however, suggests a different causality. By placing Chios and Samos after the defeat of Missolonghi and rewriting Chios as a victory, Cosca Vayo represents the liberation of Greece as the result of a national effort rather than international intervention.

The decision to move the action toward the East, however, also suggests a classical subtext. Like Paris, who abducts Helen from Sparta to decadent Troy, Mahomet takes the Spartan Constanza from the West to an island off the coast of Asia Minor where she is surrounded by luxury. And just as Agamemnon, Hector and Achilles lay siege to and ultimately conquer Troy, Nicetas (referred to as "the modern Achilles") and Canaris attack and take hold of Chios. This focus on the Trojan past is somewhat unusual. As Roessel notes (2002: 27), Philhellenic literature usually privileged the Persian Wars as an analogue for the Greek cause. In keeping with this tradition, Cosca Vayo sporadically makes reference to Leonidas and Thermopylae and to Platea, Salamina and Marathon. The plot of the novel, however, seems to replay the Homeric romance. Cosca Vayo, indeed, frequently draws on epic conventions such as bird omens, Homeric similes and the celebration of public games after battles. This subtext shifts the focus away from the civilizational clash between East and West and suggests a conflict between likes with heroes on each side. Indeed, the friendship between Nicetas and Mahomet, despite the antagonism between their peoples and their rivalry for Constanza's affection, underscores the fundamental similarity between them as well as their common sense of honor and fair play.

Converting the Turk

The main curiosity of the novel, however, is the decision to make its hero a Turk. From the outset, Nicetas is consistently represented as morally inferior to Mahomet. Cosca Vayo draws the contrast between the two heroes through two parallel sequences of episodes. In the first, Nicetas disguises himself as a black eunuch and has himself sold to Mahomet in order to infiltrate his harem in Chios and recover Constanza. When Nicetas is discovered, Mahomet does not have him imprisoned but rather agrees to fight a duel on equal terms. Allowed to fire first, Nicetas shoots at Mahomet and misses, but the Ottoman, in a spontaneous act of generosity, declines his right to fire back and instead embraces Nicetas, declaring him a friend in life, if an enemy in battle. In the second sequence, the two men's roles are inverted. After the Greek conquest of Chios and the burning of the fleet, Mahomet trades clothes with Nicetas and enters Chios, now held by his enemy, in order to bid Constanza farewell. Still dressed in Greek attire, he wins all of the contests in the public games held to celebrate the Greek victory but disappears before he is given the laurels, for "relishing triumph ... was for weak and ambitious hearts" (I, 208). It is precisely this noble gesture, however, that leads to his discovery. The astute Canaris, recognizing that only Mahomet would forgo his prize, orders his capture. Ambushed by Canaris's soldiers, Mahomet refuses to draw his sword because he has promised Nicetas not to fight while dressed in the Greek's clothing. Nicetas makes a superficial attempt to save him from a death sentence but is soon distracted by self-interest when Canaris offers him a generalship. Through parallel sequences, Cosca Vayo thus draws a stark contrast between Mahomet's selflessness and Nicetas's ambition, between Mahomet's act of forgiveness and Nicetas's neglect, and between Nicetas's degrading role as a black eunuch and Mahomet's triumph as a Greek athlete.

This critical representation of Nicetas may be related in part to a common European view of the Greeks as degraded by the long centuries of Ottoman oppression and tyranny. Cosca Vayo echoes this commonplace in the introduction, precisely when he describes the great accomplishment of Nikitaras, the battle of Tripolitsa, and the Greek massacre of the Turks to which it gave way. Lamenting their brutality, Cosca Vayo observes that "Four centuries of slavery, of misery, of excessive labor had vilified to an extreme the Hellenic people" (I, xxi–xxii). Later in the novel, Cosca Vayo contrasts Mahomet's honesty with Nicetas's hypocrisy and explains the latter in similar terms: "the slavery of so many centuries had impressed on the Greeks distrust, and their labors, baseness" (I, 201).

In part because of the perceived degradation and weakness of the Greek male, Greece tended to be represented symbolically as a young woman in Philhellenic art and literature. European literature of the period features titles and subtitles such as "la vièrge de Ténédos," "l'orpheline d'Argos," "la vierge héroique," "the Maid of Scio," "the Maid of Athens," etc. The identification of Constanza with the Greek nation is clear not only in Cosca Vayo's title – "the Maid of Missolonghi" – but also in the opening pages of the novel. When Constanza encourages Nicetas to return to battle after his defeat at Missolonghi, he tells her that "The fatherland exists undoubtedly in you because you have had the power to ignite and to raise my spirit, rigid and battered by the reverses of fortune" (I, 11). Later in the novel, when the masses attack Constanza, some Greek leaders protect her because they consider "her defense as that of the nation's honor" (II, 47).

The freedom of the Greek nation, however, is represented in the novel not so much by Constanza's freedom as by her freedom of choice. This is made clear in an argument between Nicetas and Constanza in Chios in which he accuses her of loving an infidel. Rejecting his attempt to control her, she responds: "did you want to break the chains that Mahomet laid for me in order to bind me yourself with even heavier ones? How unhappy I am, for everyone conspires against my liberty and everyone seeks my slavery!" (I, 164). At this point, Mahomet, who has overheard the conversation, appears dressed in Nicetas's clothing and defends Constanza's freedom of choice: "Do you not claim to fight for your fatherland's freedom? Why then do you attack hers?" (I, 167). In this scene, Cosca Vayo turns the basic Philhellenic romance on its head: here, it is the dark man who saves the white woman from the white man. In choosing Mahomet, Constanza is opting for the hero who espouses (in Greek attire) the Greek value of freedom. From the beginning of the novel, indeed, it is Mahomet rather than Nicetas who is most associated with this principle. When Constanza is in his palace in Chios, he offers her her freedom (chapter 5). It is notable, moreover, that later in the novel, when Constanza is liberated from prison, it is not Nicetas but rather an unnamed Greek leader who takes the initiative to free her.

Nicetas's inability to be the liberator – he frees neither Mahomet nor Constanza – and his failure to reciprocate the Turk's generosity may be related to his narrow worldview. When Mahomet first saves Nicetas by declining to shoot in the duel, Nicetas immediately recognizes the Ottoman's moral superiority but feels unable to respond in kind: "If only you professed my religion," he tells him, "I would give you proof that I too know how to be generous, but as you are a Saracen, it is impossible!" (I, 113). As Nicetas's words suggest, what distinguishes Mahomet is his ability to see beyond differences of country and religion and to recognize a common humanity in the other. Throughout the novel, Cosca Vayo underscores the importance of transcending superficial party distinctions. This may be one reason that he does not give the Greeks a monopoly on spiritual virtues. The novel challenges readers' prejudice by showing that Christian values can exist outside of Christianity.

The figure who ultimately frees Mahomet and who most incarnates this open and humanitarian perspective is the heroine. Defying the Greek leaders, Constanza finds a way to enter Mahomet's prison cell and dresses him in her clothing so that he can escape. Mahomet's two exchanges of clothing – first with Nicetas and then with Constanza – might be considered the beginning of his spiritual journey toward Christianity. As he takes on their dress, he makes promises not to shed Christian blood, even though, as Constanza realizes, "this was the equivalent of a death sentence" (II, 70). When the Turks later attack Samos, Mahomet does not join them, fulfilling his promise. And after they are beaten back by the Greeks, he once again disguises himself as a Christian to distribute alms to the Samians who have lost husbands or sons in the battle. By representing the conversion as a process of swapping dress, Cosca Vayo suggests that cultural or religious identity is not innate but something that, like clothing, can be changed.

The next step in Mahomet's spiritual transformation is an intellectual shift, which begins with a conversation with Antinos in which the bishop attempts to convert him to Christianity. Interestingly, Antinos points not to Scripture or the life of Christ but rather to the glorious order of Nature – the law of gravity, the rotation of the stars – which suggests the existence of a "supreme mathematician, an eternal physicist" (II, 121). Antinos thus begins by grounding the love of God in man's instinctive admiration for Nature. He then argues that if the goal of man is happiness, it can be achieved only through reason, for "only enlightened reason draws us away from objects that can cause us disagreeable sensations" (II, 124). Christianity is the superior religion, he claims, because it "protects the Enlightenment that makes us more virtuous and lovable" (II, 125). Unlike Islam, which is based on hatred, war and ignorance – Antinos argues – Christianity is a religion of love, peace and reason. By this logic, Christianity is identified with European Enlightenment.

Reason, indeed, seems at times to stand in for Greece. Mahomet welcomes Antinos's spiritual guidance because he hopes that with such a "brilliant guide ... reason will recover its rights" (II, 104). In Mahomet's view, reason is, like Greece, controlled by another power – the passions – and struggling to recover its independence. From the beginning of the novel, Cosca Vayo establishes a distinction between the moderation and enlightenment of the Christians and the unbridled passions of the Muslim – a standard cliché in Orientalist discourse. The passion of the Turk is "violent and rash, and he would sooner end his own life than manage to moderate himself and control his emotions" (I, 63). Antinos describes Christianity as the only religion that can "confront the passions and rein them in when they are most at work and determined to make us fall" (II, 100). Mahomet's inner struggle between passion and reason is thus a symbolic reenactment of the conflict between the Turks and the Greeks. His conversion to Christianity represents the triumph of the latter.

The final step in the conversion of Mahomet is the imitation of Christ. When the Samian Christians begin to hunt for the Ottoman,

Antinos, who has been protecting Mahomet in his monastery, tells him that he will lead him to "the dwelling of peace" for "only the sepulcher can give you life" (II, 167). Antinos's words surprise Mahomet, because he interprets them as an allusion to death: "Lead me where you will, beloved Nazarene, for I will face death as I would happiness" (II, 167). The bishop, however, is using "sepulcher" only in its literal sense: in the underground vault of the monastery, Mahomet will be safe from his enemies. This misunderstanding suggests that Mahomet, by descending into the tomb, is symbolically dying to be born again in imitation of Christ. It is indeed while he is in the sepulcher that he finally converts to Christianity. Within the logic of the novel, this spiritual conversion represents the triumph of the Greeks. If Christianity is the religion of peace and Islam that of war, it is logical that the Greek victory over the Turks should be spiritual rather than military. Ultimately the Greeks triumph not so much through their military prowess as through their ability to disarm a more powerful enemy by drawing him toward a more peaceful faith.

In its representation of a romance between a Greek woman and a Turkish man, who converts to Christianity, Cosca Vayo's plot resembles that of *Les Amours d'un Turc et d'une Grècque, épisode de la guerre de 1821* (1822), which similarly focuses on the relationship between a Greek woman, Sophia, and a Turkish man, Osmandi.[7] As in Cosca Vayo's novel, the protagonists wed at the end of the work in an underground vault shortly before their death. In the French novel, however, the Ottoman is the son of a "Greek and Christian renegade." The heroine's father, Lokario, is optimistic that Osmandi "has conserved the precious memory of his race" (1822: II, 25). And, indeed, as expected, the hero returns to the faith of his ancestors at the end of the novel. Conversion in this story is actually reversion, a return to something racially innate. In Cosca Vayo's novel, in contrast, Christianity is a choice, a rational decision to break with the past and with tradition. Antinos underscores this when he asks Mahomet, "Why do you use bullets in combat, if your grandfathers fought with arrows?" (Cosca Vayo 1830: II, 128). If we choose to depart from our forefathers in our choice or weapons, he argues, why should we not do so in our reasoning (and religion) as well? Whereas Osmandi returns to tradition, Mahomet privileges reason over the values of his fathers and his fatherland. It is important to observe, moreover, that Osmandi has no Greek rival for the love of the heroine. The only threat to their relationship is an Ottoman *disdard* (governor), who corresponds to the stereotype of the Turkish sexual predator. In this sense, the French novel conforms much more to the Philhellenic romance identified by Roessel: the white heroine opts for the white Osmandi, who rediscovers his Greek values, rather than for the dark *disdard*.

In contrast with the Spanish novel, *Amours d'un Turc et d'une Grècque* pays little attention to the hero's spiritual transformation. In the fifth volume, Osmandi simply decides to defect from the Ottoman to the Greek army and to be baptized so that he can marry Sophia. Although there are several passionate arguments between Sophia and Osmandi on the subject of religion, there is no formal scene of conversion as in Antinos's conversation with Mahomet. Moreover, unlike Antinos, who demonstrates rationally the superiority of Christianity over Islam, the priest figure in the French novel, Paléologue, goes so far as to suggest that people of all faiths can be admitted to Heaven if they are virtuous: "to do good is the first thing and perhaps the only thing necessary to deserve Heaven" (D . . . 1822: V, 17). Both the French and Spanish novels share a focus on values such as goodness and generosity that transcend superficial cultural or religious differences. Paléologue's comment, however, diminishes the importance of Osmandi's spiritual conversion. In the French novel, the triumph of the Greeks is not the spiritual conquest of the cultural other – Osmandi is simply returning to his roots – so much as the triumph of love over a misguided sense of duty.

It is also instructive to compare Cosca Vayo's work to a novel that he drafted just one year later in 1831 and published in 1834: *Los expatriados, ó Zulema y Gazul, novela histórica original perteneciente al año 1254*, which deals with the expulsion of the Moors from Valencia in the thirteenth century. In the introduction, which was written in 1834, Cosca Vayo explains what led him to write about this topic and in so doing draws an analogy to the earlier work:

> I wrote this novel in 1831 in the hope of reminding Spaniards, through the expulsion of the Moors, of that other unfortunate expatriation that they have all witnessed. The portrait of entire cities fleeing their walls at the approach of an army that has proclaimed chains and tyranny; the heroic efforts of so many courageous men who faced death for freedom; and finally the immorality of certain men who, selling out their companions in misfortune, and dressing in various colors made all the more disastrous the death of the fatherland: I wanted to portray all of this in this little work, which I wrote, like the *Doncella de Missolonghi* and the *Conquista de Valencia por el Cid*, only to awaken national enthusiasm. (Cosca Vayo 1834: iii)

In this passage, Cosca Vayo draws an explicit parallel between the subject matter of his historical novels and the recent defeat of liberalism in Spain: both *Los espatriados* and *Grecia* represent nations struggling to assert their autonomy (the Moors, the Greeks) in the face of a military conqueror (the Christians, the Turks), just as the Spanish liberals sought to defend their government against the invading French army in 1823. Cosca Vayo goes on to identify himself as a liberal who lost everything for freedom during "the ten years of proscription that have just ended" (iv) – a clear reference to the "ominous decade." Cosca Vayo, thus, is clearly reading the Greek War of Independence through the lens of recent Spanish history.

As Nettah Yoeli Rimmer has observed, however, the passage establishes a somewhat surprising equation between the expulsion of the Moors and the exile of the Spanish liberals (2017: 110). Whereas Spanish ideology traditionally represented the Reconquista as a triumphant moment, Cosca Vayo draws his heroes from the losing side and laments throughout the novel the cultural and aesthetic loss involved in this victory. In the opening pages, indeed, the beauty and wealth of Valencia under the Moors is compared with that of ancient Greece: "the Edetani kingdom enjoyed a Golden age, under the African's dominating sword, just as Greece enjoyed one with the rule of just and admirable laws" (Cosca Vayo 1834: 4). Curiously, Cosca Vayo identifies the liberals' struggle with that of the Moors, even though their system of government represents opposite values.

Cosca Vayo's willingness to identify his own cause with that of the Moors may reflect his position as a Valencian author, who clearly inscribes himself in the romantic project of recuperating local traditions.[8] In a culture that was born from the fusion of Muslim and Christian civilizations, the East-West opposition was probably less categorical for a writer from the Spanish Levante. Indeed, although Cosca Vayo claims that his goal is to promote "national enthusiasm" and to condemn figures who cross the divide, the plots of his novels in some ways undermine this claim. Both works, indeed, advocate for a humanitarian perspective that transcends national distinctions and party loyalties. Gazul, in *Los espatriados*, is condemned when he is fanatically pro-Moor and kills his best friend for political reasons, but is celebrated when he puts aside his beliefs and encourages his army to surrender in order to save his beloved Zulema and to ensure a peaceful future for his people. As Yoeli-Rimmer points out, the novel insists on "natural laws" – bonds of kindship or a sense of humanity – which take precedence over the national sentiment that Cosca Vayo claims to promote (2017: 112). The same can be said of

Grecia, ó la doncella de Missolonghi. At different moments in the text, both Constanza and Mahomet betray their respective nations in the name of higher values. Constanza frees Mahomet from the prison on Chios as a humanitarian act, while Mahomet refrains from fighting in Samos in order to avoid shedding Christian blood. In both novels, indeed, it is in the act of wearing "various colors" that the heroes seem most human and heroic.

The Political Passions

In the final section of this chapter, I would like to consider how the Greek War of Independence is represented in Cosca Vayo's novel. As Roessel has observed, many Philhellenic writers projected political meanings onto the movement that had little to do with the Greeks' own objectives: "The 'revolutionizing' of the Greek insurrection was, to a large extent, itself a misreading, or Europeanization, of the goals and aims of the Greek insurrection by authors with their agendas" (2002: 29). *Les Amours d'un Turc et d'une Grècque* offers a clear example of this European vision in a passage in which Paléologue situates the Greek insurgents within a universal "family" of freethinkers: "The entire world wants only to form a great family, whose center will be liberty." Paléologue goes on to conflate the *carbonari*, the liberals and the "Teutonic radicals" into a single category: they "all have the same ideas, the same principles, they want freedom or death and they want only that" (D . . . 1822: V, 40).

Cosca Vayo, in contrast, generally steers away from representing the uprising as an economic or political revolution. His focus is the struggle for independence rather than democracy or representational government. To the extent that he makes historical analogies, it is to other instances of liberation from occupation:

> Innumerable armies of Saracens flood Spain, they oppress it for some time; but a shout cried out on the rocks of Asturias wakes a nation, which breaks its chains and hurls the barbarous conquerors to Africa. Napoleon, in front of thousands of soldiers, does not want Italy and Spain to be independent; and the victors of Austerlitz and Marengo open their own tombs in the fields of Bailén. This is the same as what modern Greece has done: conquered by Mahomet II, it has recovered its independence in the time of Mahamud, for there are no shackles strong enough to have the power to bind nations forever. (Cosca Vayo 1830: I, l-li)

These analogies focus on independence from a foreign oppressor rather than on the revolutionary politics of radicals or *carbonari*. In the 1834 introduction to *Los espatriados*, Cosca Vayo may align the struggle of the Greeks with that of the liberals who defended a constitutional government in 1823. But writing in 1830, during the "ominous decade," he is somewhat more cautious: the battlefield of Bailén during the war of Spanish independence (1808–14), which restored the rule of Ferdinand VII, is a much safer analogue.[9] Moreover, whereas many French Philhellenic writers emphasized the importance of Enlightenment ideas (often introduced by Greeks who had lived abroad) for the emergence of the movement, Cosca Vayo draws on Enlightenment thinking only to demonstrate the superiority of Christianity over Islam.[10] The uprising is portrayed not as a foreign import or the product of enlightened thought (the role of Phanariots or the Greeks abroad is completely neglected) but rather as a spontaneous reaction of an oppressed people guided by its spiritual advisors. In this respect, Cosca Vayo seems to rewrite the Greek War of Independence in the image of 1808 in Spain, a movement that drew its strengths from the people and the pulpit.

Many episodes in the novel, moreover, betray a certain anxiety regarding the political enthusiasm and extremism that the uprising introduced. At the beginning of Part II, when Canaris insists on a death sentence for Mahomet, the narrator observes:

> This is the justice of political passions whose doctrine is boiled down . . . in the barbarous maxim of Canaris: "May the enemies of Greece die and let us close our eyes to the way in which we make them perish." This infernal policy, this principle of proscription, has shed more blood in the world than the most famous wars. (II, 22)

Cosca Vayo goes on to mention several examples of political passions out of control, including the Reign of Terror in France (II, 22–3). The intransigent Canaris is represented as a Greek Robespierre, an incarnation of the excesses of revolution. Elsewhere, this political passion is embodied by the enraged masses – "the fury of the rebels" (II, 49), "irritated masses" (II, 112), "the out-of-control multitude" (II, 192) – who are invoked with Homeric similes about sparks igniting stores of gunpowder (II, 45) or rivers breaking through dikes (II, 48–9). When Constanza frees Mahomet, the "frenetic masses" attempt to invade the Citadel where she is held, and in the process unleash a day-long bloodbath. The narrator comments that "the rabble throughout the world is inconstant and cruel" (II, 42).

It is noteworthy that the political passions of the masses are identified in the novel with the figure of Nicetas, who rouses the mob to violence in a fit of jealousy: "Nicetas himself who had for some time restrained the multitude, then urged it to commit horrors. Some said that jealousy was egging him on; and that depriving him of reason had converted him into another man" (II, 108). Canaris, thus, represents a political expediency that is blind to humanity while Nicetas incarnates the unbridled fury of the masses. Though portrayed as heroes in the introduction of the novel, the two figures ultimately embody the excesses of revolution. Cosca Vayo's negative rewriting of the Greek heroes may suggest either an ambivalence toward the movement or an attempt to bypass censorship by condemning its excesses.[11] Bádenas de la Peña observes similar misgivings in Río y Coronel's *Compendio histórico del origen y progresos de la insurrección de los griegos contra los turcos*, Cosca Vayo's main historiographical source for the novel: "although in favour of the fair expectations of the Greeks, [Río y Coronel] showed his mistrust and his concern about the spreading of liberation ideals and popular revolts as well as the dangers of breaking the political status quo in Europe after the defeat of the Napoleonic system" (Bádenas de la Peña 2007: 117).

As we have seen, Cosca Vayo's representation of the Greek War of Independence is an unusual Philhellenic text. By representing the nobility and openness of the Turk, the novel avoids the Manichaean logic of many representations of the war and insists on moral values that transcend religious differences and the East-West divide. The strong epic overtones of the novel reinforce this vision by pointing to virtue and merit on both sides of the conflict. The universal values that Cosca Vayo supports, however, are not those of social revolution. The novel supports the liberty and independence of the Greek people and evokes a sort of fraternity between Mahomet and Nicetas – but it does not advocate for equality. Time and again, it insists on the fickle and violent nature of a rabble all too easily carried away by "political passions." The Spanish novel, thus, offers a somewhat muted and ambivalent reverberation of the Greek uprising, one that avoids the "revolutionizing" tendency of other Philhellenic texts.

Bibliography

Aggelomatis-Tsougarakis, Eleni (2008), "Women in the Greek War of Independence," in Mark Mazower, ed., *Networks of Power in Modern*

Greece: Essays in Honour of John Campbell, London: Hurst & Company, pp. 45–68.
Bádenas de la Peña, Pedro (2007), "The Peculiar Relations between Greece and Spain at the End of the Ottoman Rule," in Evangelos Konstantinou, ed., *Ausdrucksformen des Europäischen und Internationalen Philhellenismus vom 17.-19. Jahrhundert*, Frankfurt am Main: Peter Lang.
Cosca Vayo, Estanislao de (1830), *Grecia, ó la doncella de Missolonghi*, Valencia: Mompié.
Cosca Vayo, Estanislao de (1831), *La conquista de Valencia por El Cid: novela histórica original*, Valencia: Mompié.
Cosca Vayo, Estanislao de (1834), *Los espatriados, ó Zulema y Gazul: novela histórica original perteneciente al año 1254*, Madrid: Repullés.
D . . . (1822), *Les Amours d'un Turc et d'une Grècque, épisode de la guerre de 1821*, Paris: Keleffer.
D. P. M. (1840), *La doncella de Missolonghi, drama original en 5 actos*, Málaga: Imprenta del Comercio.
Droulia, Loukia (1974), *Philhellénisme: ouvrages inspirés par la guerre de l'Indépendance grecque, 1821–1833*, Athens: Publications du Centre de recherches néo-helléniques de la Fondation nationale de la recherche scientifique.
Gies, David T. (2009), "Spain," in Robert Justin Goldstein, ed., *The Frightful Stage: Political Censorship of the Theater in Nineteenth-Century Europe*, New York: Berghahn Books, pp. 162–89.
Hualde Pascual, Pilar (2013), "Ecos filohelénicos en la época del primer romanticismo español (1821–1840)," in Francisco García Jurado et al., eds, *La historia de la literatura Grecolatina en España: de la Ilustración al Liberalismo (1778–1850)*, Málaga: Servicio de Publicaciones, Universidad de Málaga, 2013, pp. 261–84.
Morfakidis Motos, Dimitris Miguel (2014), "La Revolución helénica de 1821 a través de la novela histórica de la España decimonónica: *Grecia o la doncella de Missolonghi* – *Amor y religión*, o *La joven griega*," *Estudios neogriegos* 16, pp. 139–60.
P. G.** (1821), *La Vierge héroïque, roman grec de ces dernières époques*, Paris: Pelicier.
Pouqueville, F. C. H. L. (1824), *Histoire de la régénération de la Grèce comprenant le précis des évènements depuis 1740 jusqu'en 1824*, Paris: Firmin Didot père et fils.
Rode, Guillermo (1849), *El héroe de la Grecia y su page, o sea, La doncella de Misolonghi, drama histórico, en verso y dividido en cuatro actos*, Mexico: Tipografía de R. Rafael.
Roessel, David (2002), *In Byron's Shadow: Modern Greece in the English and American Imagination*, Oxford: Oxford University Press.
Río y Coronel, Marcos Manuel [pseudonym of J. M. de San Millán y Coronel] (1828), *Compendio histórico del origen y progresos de la insurrección de los griegos contra los turcos desde el año de 1821 hasta la*

llegada a Egina del presidente actual de la Grecia, conde de Capio de Istria, Madrid: Ramos y compañía.

Sétier, Louis-Pascal (1826), *L'Athénienne, ou les Français en Grèce*, Paris: Libraires du Palais Royal.

Yoeli Rimmer, Nettah (2017), "Poder y resistencia en *Los espatriados, o Zulema y Gazul* de Estanislao de Cosa Vayo," in Alberto Ramos Santana and Diana Repeto García, eds, *Poder, contrapoder y sus representaciones*, Cadiz: Editorial UCA, pp. 109–17.

Coda: Frederick Douglass and the Wild Songs of Revolution

Michael Boyden

An oft-analyzed passage of *The Narrative of the Life of Frederick Douglass*, first published in 1845, reflects the significance of the slave songs on the plantation where Douglass spent his early life in bondage. On their way to collect their monthly allowance at the farm house, the slaves "would make the dense old woods, for miles around, reverberate with their wild songs, revealing at once the highest joy and the deepest sadness" (Douglass 1994: 23). These "wild songs," Douglass suggests, never failed to move those who cared to listen:

> If any one wishes to be impressed with the soul-killing effects of slavery, let him go to Colonel Lloyd's plantation, and, on allowance-day, place himself in the deep pine woods, and there let him, in silence analyze the sounds that shall pass through the chambers of his soul – and if he is not thus impressed, it will only be because "there is no flesh in his obdurate heart." (Douglass 1994: 24)

The songs that Douglass heard on the Maryland plantation where he grew up would continue to haunt him throughout his later career as an antislavery advocate and social reformer. Over the years, moreover, the songs would accrue new resonances and meanings. They reverberated in new, sometimes unexpected ways. By highlighting such shifting dynamics, this coda illuminates Douglass's enmeshment in transatlantic revolutionary cultures at a moment of transformative change on both sides of the Atlantic. Douglass's engagement with slave music has often been framed in terms of a nascent black aesthetic. But Douglass was also a preeminently international figure who was attuned to emancipatory endeavors outside of the United States and continually reinterpreted his antislavery activism in relation to these movements. Attending to such connections and the kinds of conundrums they produced, I suggest, is essential to a deeper understanding of Douglass's developing political identity. Douglass's reformism was embedded in an emergent media network that reverberated widely across the Atlantic space and far beyond. If Douglass's remarkable career inaugurated a black counter-tradition to modernity, it equally fed on, and derived legitimacy from, other emancipatory movements that dominated international politics in the Atlantic space toward the mid-nineteenth century.[1]

This coda should thus be read as an attempt to round out this volume by exploring revolutionary reverberations into the middle decades of the nineteenth century, when social upheaval combined with improved technologies produced what one might call a transatlantic, and potentially global, revolutionary culture. Furthermore, the case of Douglass brings out an element that the contributions in this volume touch on only tangentially but that nevertheless calls for further inquiry at the present moment, namely that social change is always as much a matter of the "flesh" as of the written word. While the development of new technologies in the course of the nineteenth century would prove vital in the spread of reformist ideals, it is easy to lose sight of the fact that the primary medium of revolution was often – and still largely remains – the body. As I write these words, massive antiracism protests following the death of George Floyd at the hands of the Minneapolis police on May 25, 2020, are reverberating across the globe. Such movements once more draw our attention to the bodily nature of revolution. Douglass's characterization of the plantation songs in his autobiography throws into relief how humanitarian ideals are often communicated through ritual performances, songs and socially acquired modes of comportment. In addition to exploring an example of cross-Atlantic reverberations in the context of the antislavery movement and the European revolutions of 1848, therefore, this coda points to possible avenues of research not explicitly pursued in this volume and that revolve specifically around questions of oral transmission and embodiment in the construction of revolutionary networks and movements.

In *How Societies Remember*, the late anthropologist Paul Connerton argued that social memory is often expressed through communally acquired habits. Characteristically, Connerton suggests, these practices develop in times of revolution, when a new system of governance is established on the ruins of the old. To establish its legitimacy, the new regime is compelled to return to the past it rejects by means of commemorative acts, as was the case, for instance, in the ceremonial killing of Louis XVI, or in the adoption of new fashions and deportments parodying or critiquing earlier ones in the aftermath of the French Revolution. According to Connerton, it is "non-inscribed" (i.e. non-written) practices and acts of this sort that sustain social memory in ways that the written word often fails to do. The power of writing and other dissemination media resides in the fact that they do not require the co-presence of the addressed public. As a result, such inscribed communication reaches far beyond the original face-to-face context in which it originates. But, as Connerton insists, the technology of writing also subjects communal memory to processes of economization and criticism that undercut its acceptance. Writing is more economical than oral communication because it does not depend on the mnemonic function of bodily participation and rhythmic repetition. The primary mechanisms of remembrance in oral communities, rhythmically repeated songs and chants demanding audience participation, largely fall away in print culture. This results in an economization of memory but also exposes the written word to comparison and, thus, criticism (Connerton 1989: 76). In contrast, rituals involving automatic bodily movements – what Connerton calls "incorporating practices" – resist such scrutiny. As we all know from experience, it is easier to recognize a given habit than to change it. This is what makes incorporating practices such potent means of remembrance. "Habit is a knowledge and a remembering in the hands and the body," Connerton asserts, "and in the cultivation of habit it is our body which 'understands'" (1989: 95). Recovering such non-inscribing practices allows us to correct the prevalent bias toward written records in the study of revolutionary cultures, and in modern hermeneutics generally.

Douglass's insistence on the effectiveness of slave songs in communicating antislavery thought can be read in light of Connerton's distinction between inscription and incorporation. "I have sometimes thought," Douglass suggests, "that the mere hearing of those songs would do more to impress some minds with the horrible character of slavery, than the reading of whole volumes of philosophy on the subject could do" (1994: 24). In this statement, Douglass explicitly opposes writing and oral performance as two modes of communicating abolitionist ideals. It is significant, moreover, that Douglass repeatedly employs the word "impress" to convey the impact of the slave songs on the mind of the listener. By the mid-nineteenth century, the association of this word with printing was largely obsolete, but the contemporary reader would have understood Douglass's point that the slave songs, in spite of their supposed inarticulacy and fleetingness, ironically leave a more lasting impression than the written word (1994: 23). In accounting for the marked impression these songs leave on the listener, Douglass emphatically dismisses the notion that they signal that the slaves are content with their condition. Rather, Douglass asserts, the songs are so gripping because they capture the lived, tragic experience of industrial slavery. In other words, the songs reflect the shared suffering of the slaves, which they express by engaging in communal performances. They do so, moreover, "consulting neither time nor tune" (23). This suggests that the songs reverberate precisely because they are unscripted and rely instead on incorporated, improvisational practices. As the late Barbadian poet Kamau Brathwaite put it, oral culture constitutes a "total expression" that relies on embodied practices and rhythms rather than books and museums for its remembrance (Brathwaite 1981: 25). Of course, the dynamic shifts once one leaves this total community behind, and this is evident in Douglass's reflections on the topic. As he insists in *The Narrative*, the songs' vitality only became apparent to him once he had extricated himself from the slave community and had transformed himself into an advocate for abolition. As a slave, he failed to "understand the deep meaning of those rude and apparently incoherent songs" (Douglass 1994: 24). At the same time, he insists that the songs, while seemingly devoid of significance to outsiders, are "full of meaning" to the slaves themselves. Douglass here appears to contradict himself by arguing that only insiders can grasp the meaning of the songs but that he himself, while an insider, could not truly fathom their significance. But I believe that Douglass is pointing to the different modes of understanding invoked by Connerton: one involving the mind, and the other the body. While the mind may "analyze" the sounds of the plantation songs, it is the body – the flesh of the heart – that registers the meaning of slavery on a more palpable level.

Douglass was keenly aware of the power of bodily practices in mobilizing support for the antislavery cause. His contemporaries primarily knew him as an orator on the lecture circuit, whose testimonies of the plantation galvanized the abolitionist movement. Commentators frequently mentioned Douglass's commanding presence and ability to mesmerize his audiences with his oratorical talent. For instance, Ottilie Assing, a German-Jewish journalist and refugee of the 1848 revolutions who was drawn to Douglass's politics and would eventually become his translator and lover, dwelled on Douglass's exceptional energy and rhetorical ability.[2] Douglass himself routinely sprinkled his speeches with literary allusions that made the cause come alive to his intended audience. The phrase from William Cowper's poem "Slavery" in the passage cited above – "there is no flesh in his obdurate heart" – is an example of Douglass's use of poetry and literary allusions in his lectures. He recited these texts for dramatic effect and to underscore his awareness of the cultural reference points of the dominant white community. In large part, therefore, Douglass's rhetorical effectiveness was a matter of embodiment. What made him a privileged spokesperson for the abolitionist cause was that he was himself, as William Lloyd Garrison put it in his prefatory remarks to *The Narrative*, a "hunted fugitive" who nevertheless spoke as eloquently as Patrick Henry (Douglass 1994: 4).

At the same time, however, Garrison's praise points to a structural irony in Douglass's public image. Douglass expressed his admiration for the plantation songs in a written, linear narrative of his journey from bondage to freedom. His privileging of embodied experience in communicating abolitionist ideas was mediated by print. In many ways, the abolitionist movement profited from new developments in printing, such as the rise of the penny press which made cheap copies of antislavery tracts and slave narratives widely available. Douglass was also well aware of the appeal of the new medium of photography, which he employed strategically as an instrument of self-presentation.[3] While these inscribing practices served to spread the abolitionist agenda far and wide, they also involved risks of co-optation. In his *Narrative*, Douglass represented his acquisition of literacy as a key moment in his escape from the "mental darkness" of slavery (Douglass 1994: 40). This association of literacy with upward mobility reveals his reliance on narrative models of the dominant culture that was at the same time responsible for denying him true personhood. Furthermore, Douglass's decision to entrust his story to print made it vulnerable to the suspicion that it was a fraud. William Lloyd Garrison's preface to *The Narrative* in which he lauds Douglass's oratorical abilities, along with a letter by Wendell Phillips, was designed to prove that Douglass was truly the author of the text – that it was, as the subtitle states, "written by himself." But by impressing their seal of approval onto the text, Garrison and Phillips also enlisted Douglass in the service of their specific abolitionist project, which was geared toward the peaceful dissolution of the Union, which in their view sanctioned slavery in its founding documents. Douglass's performances on the lecture platform provided living proof of the inhumanity of slavery. His written autobiography, in contrast, invited skepticism as to whether he was really the (sole) author of the text. The structure and reception of *The Narrative* thus reveal the complex enmeshment of inscription and incorporation at the heart of Douglass's antislavery activism.

This complex overlaying of incorporating and inscribing practices in *The Narrative* is by no means the only irony running through Douglass's career. The slave songs that, as Douglass phrases it, continued to "follow" him after his escape to the North began to resonate in unanticipated ways after his British lecture tour of 1845–47 (Douglass 1994: 24). This lecture tour was prompted in part by the fact that the success of *The Narrative* had exposed Douglass as a fugitive slave and thus put him at risk of being recaptured by his master in Maryland. The trip would prove transformative for Douglass in a number of ways. Not only did his English supporters purchase his freedom, thus removing the possibility that his master might legally reclaim him as his property; the confrontation with another society in which inequalities were distributed differently also impelled Douglass to align the antislavery cause with other rights struggles, such as the Irish struggle for national liberation. This refiguration of Douglass's antislavery politics is evident in *My Bondage and My Freedom*, the revised and extended autobiography that he published in 1855. As many scholars have noted, Douglass here speaks with a more confident voice that signals his political maturation. This new tone is already clear in the framing of the text: the prefatory documents by Garrison and Phillips included in *The Narrative* are replaced by an introduction by the black physician and race leader James McCune Smith. This change seems to indicate that Douglass had reached a stage in his career during which he no longer needed white patrons to authenticate his life story. On a deeper level, the paratextual changes mark Douglass's turn away from the anti-Constitution abolitionism propagated by Garrison and Phillips.

But, most crucially for the topic of this volume, Douglass's discussion of the plantation songs was now embedded in a broader emancipatory agenda: "I have never heard any songs like those anywhere since I left slavery," Douglass asserts, "except when in Ireland. There I heard the same *wailing notes*, and was much affected by them" (1994: 184; italics in text). Douglass arrived in Ireland at the height of the famine, which made him rethink his approach to American slavery. The songs of the starving Irish whom Douglass encountered during his lecture tour echoed those of the plantation. While circumstances on both sides of the ocean were vastly different, Douglass increasingly came to understand that these "wailing notes" responded in similar ways to structural inequities ingrained in the societies from which they emerged. As Cody Marrs notes, Douglass's awareness of such connections allowed him to articulate "a robust vision of nonlinear, transnational liberation" that led him not only to reject his earlier Garrisonian stance but also to insert the abolitionist struggle in the revolutionary movements that swept the European continent in 1848 (Marrs 2013: 457). *My Bondage and My Freedom* demonstrates this widened framework of action. Among other things, the buoyant reception Douglass received during the British lecture tour impelled him to revise his preconceptions regarding the inherent superiority of republics vis-à-vis monarchies. The people attending the antislavery meetings in England, Douglass mused, were:

> about as good republicans as the mass of Americans, and with this decided advantage over the latter – they are lovers of republicanism for all men, for black men as well as for white men. They are the people who sympathize with Louis Kossuth and Mazzini, and with the oppressed and enslaved, of every color and nation, the world over. (Douglass 1994: 378–9)

By invoking the revolutionary leaders Kossuth and Mazzini, Douglass here situates the abolitionist movement in the broader struggle for liberty and representation that shook the old European order in 1848. The discordant songs of the plantations in the American South had started to chime with the songs of the Irish poor – as well as the polkas, mazurkas and anthems of revolutionary Europe.

While Douglass's embrace of this transatlantic perspective added to the momentum of the abolitionist movement, it inevitably generated new contradictions as the conflicting interests behind what Metternich called the "Springtime of nations" became increasingly apparent. This is already evident in "The Revolution of 1848," a speech that Douglass delivered in Rochester in August 1848, at a commemoration of the tenth anniversary of the abolition of slavery in the West Indies. Douglass began this lecture by lauding recent developments in Europe, notably the decision of the provisional French government led by Alphonse de Lamartine to emancipate the slaves in the colonies. This joyful event, Douglass believed, afforded antislavery activists in the United States "a more extended view of the cause of human freedom" (Douglass 1999: 104). Douglass saw in the revolutions of 1848 the advent of a new era of transnational unity. "The magic power of human sympathy is rapidly healing all national divisions, and bringing mankind into the harmonious bonds of a common brotherhood," Douglass asserted confidently (105). At the same time, however, Douglass was obliged to note the irony that the enactment of the French emancipation decree coincided with a reactionary swing in French politics after the election of the Constitutive Assembly. Moreover, just at the moment when Lamartine's decree took effect, the bloody June Days uprising enthralled the French nation. While Douglass expressed a preference for gradual British reformism over the violence in the streets of Paris, he still believed the impulse behind the uprising was justified. The *Blouses* behind the barricades might have been "[w]rong in head," but they were "right in heart" (107). Nevertheless, the clashing impulses of head and heart considerably complicated Douglass's alignment of his abolitionism with the unfolding events in Europe.

It is possible that Douglass's early assessment of the 1848 revolutions led him to abandon the path of pacifist resistance that he had embraced while still under the wings of Garrison and Phillips (although, it should be noted, Douglass had not fully broken with Garrison at this stage and remained largely under the influence of the latter's anti-Constitutionalism). This shift toward a more radical politics shines through toward the end of the lecture, where Douglass implicitly references the Nat Turner rebellion of 1831. While misguided in its methods, this failed slave insurrection in Virginia, Douglass here suggests, sprang from a noble cause; it was "right in heart." The only option sometimes available to American slaves seeking their freedom, Douglass indicates, was "to march directly upon the bristling bayonets of the whole military power," the way the people of Paris had recently done during the June Days uprising (Douglass 1999: 110). Arguably, therefore, "The Revolution of 1848" already foreshadows Douglass's more militant anti-slavery position during the run-up to the Civil War. While this is an exciting line of argument to pursue for the student of American history, I will limit myself here to pointing out the role of embodied practices in Douglass's revisioning of his abolitionist struggle. That Douglass delivered his 1848 lecture at a celebration commemorating the emancipation of the slaves in the West Indies shows how revolutionary movements derive their legitimacy from commemorative acts and embodied performances. It reveals how liberation movements are grafted onto, and acquire new urgency from, comparable events elsewhere. If the plantation songs of Douglass's youth had resonated with the "wailing songs" of the Irish peasants during his British lecture tour, the revolutions of 1848 added a further layer of significance to these embodied practices. They now resonated more powerfully still, in a way that only the body can comprehend. As he put it after his reflections on the European situation: the "wails of bondmen are on my ear" (109).

No less importantly, however, the connections between the European revolutions and American abolitionism, as observed through the prism of Douglass's writings and speeches, reveal how reverberating mechanisms might dampen as well as amplify the message of liberation and reform. This is apparent, for instance, in the Kossuth "affair," which divided American abolitionists in early 1852. During a heavily mediatized fundraising tour in the United States, the Hungarian nationalist Lajos Kossuth failed to speak out on the issue of slavery, most likely to avoid alienating American supporters with vested interests in the institution. Antislavery activists, including Douglass, vociferously denounced the Hungarian leader's strategic silence on domestic American politics.[4] Douglass's stance in the Kossuth case, however, was complicated by his commitment to a transnational vision of liberation. In 1853 and 1854, the British abolitionist Julia Griffiths published a two-volume anthology entitled *Autographs for Freedom* to raise funds for Douglass's financially ailing newspaper *The North Star*. The collection included a variety of pieces by prominent antislavery activists, including Douglass's novella *The Heroic Slave*, inspired by the 1841 revolt on board the slave ship *Creole*. This story has often been interpreted as pivotal in Douglass's transition from nonviolence to radical militancy. What critics have tended to overlook, however, is that the story originally appeared back-to-back with a laudatory portrait of Lajos Kossuth by Douglass's close collaborator John Thomas. Thomas explicitly defends the Hungarian against the charge of hypocrisy regarding the issue of slavery, in fact saluting him, along with Mazzini, as the "twin apostle of liberty" (Thomas 1853: 173). Such inconsistencies, if that is what they are, reveal that reverberating revolutions do not always follow a clear script or the rules of musical harmony.

The clashing reverberations of 1848 are perhaps most evident in Douglass's relation to Irish nationalism. During Douglass's stay in Dublin, Daniel O'Connell famously welcomed him as "the black O'Connell" of the United States, thus underscoring the strong ties shared by Irish nationalists and American abolitionists (Douglass 1994: 682). This sense of brotherhood is evident in Douglass's lecture on 1848. When commenting on how the French example had lit the revolutionary fire across Europe, Douglass makes reference to the "martyrdom" of the Irish nationalist John Mitchel (spelled "Mitchell" in the print copy of the lecture published in *The North Star*). Mitchel was one of the leaders of the Young Ireland movement, which had been galvanized by both the famine and the events in France to seek the removal of the British yoke. This abortive revolution resulted in the deportation of Mitchel, along with two other leaders of the revolt, Thomas Francis Meagher and William Smith O'Brien, to Van Diemen's Land (soon after renamed Tasmania). All three Irish nationalists eventually ended up in the United States. While William Smith O'Brien would side with the Union in the American Civil War, Mitchel and Meagher supported the Confederacy (Rapport 2009: 97). Such ideological confusions were of course rife in antebellum America, at a moment when old and emergent political parties were defining themselves in relation to the slavery issue. While traditionally open to immigrant constituencies, the Democratic Party was increasingly dominated by Southern slave interests. The new Republican Party, in contrast, was more receptive to the abolitionist movement's demands while also drawing many anti-immigrant and nativist factions. For this reason, it should not surprise that revolutionary refugees coming from Europe often had to weigh conflicting values upon entering the domestic political arena in the United States (for the Irish-Americans specifically, see Allen 1994). Mitchel, however, seems to have openly flaunted his support of not just Southern independence but also the institution of slavery. For Douglass, this was nothing short of an embarrassment. His relation to the Irish-American community, which, as opposed to the Irish nationalists at home, was predominantly proslavery, would remain fraught for the rest of his career (Honeck 2011: 24–5).

Shortly before his death, Douglass would settle the score with Young Ireland in the third and final version of his autobiography, *Life and Times of Frederick Douglass*, published in 1893. After singing the praises of O'Donnell, who combined a firm commitment to abolitionism with exceptional eloquence – his "musical voice" would come down on the listeners "like a summer thunder-shower upon a dusty road" – Douglass denounced the succeeding generation of Irish nationalists, "the Duffys, Mitchells, Meaghers, and others, – men who loved liberty for themselves and their country, but were utterly destitute of sympathy with the cause of liberty in countries other than their own" (Douglass 1994: 682, 683). Apparently, the bonds of sympathy did not necessarily reverberate across generations. Douglass's troubled relation to Irish nationalism, moreover, informed his changing understandings of the plantation songs that continued to follow him in his later years. *Life and Times* leaves the 1855 version of *My Bondage and My Freedom* largely intact, but the tone is more retrospective and melancholy. Douglass now characterizes the slave songs thus: "Nowhere outside of dear old Ireland, in the days of want and famine, have I heard sounds so mournful" (1994: 502). In "The Revolution of 1848," Douglass had still put a lot of emphasis on the role of black laborers in building a great American republic and forging alliances with workers elsewhere. In the final installment of his autobiography, however, he seems to consign "dear old Ireland" to a bygone era, a moment when labor competition and ingrained prejudice had not yet dulled white ears to the wailing notes of the black population of the United States. The wild songs of the plantation still reverberated in multiple channels, but some clearly no longer resounded on the same bandwidth.

To conclude, Douglass's continual reinterpretation of the slave songs of his youth in light of broader humanitarian causes is an exemplary case of how revolutions reverberate in multiple ways. Focusing on such multidirectional movements has significant theoretical and methodological implications. To begin, it allows us to reconsider the significance of events such as the revolutions of 1848, which have often been considered a historical failure: the "turning-point when Europe failed to turn" (Taylor 1951: 68). As the case of Douglass reveals, however, even if the revolutions failed, they did reverberate widely, if not always in predictable ways. Going beyond founding ideas or immediate outcomes may thus occasion a revaluation of the significance of political events such as 1848. Further, the example of Douglass shows that revolutions often reverberate through bodily practices as much as through writings and other inscription media. However broadly conceived, the metaphor of revolutionary scripts, as proposed by Keith Baker and Dan Edelstein, fails to capture the complex ways in which revolutions continue to be mediated by non- or partly scripted events, including songs, visual caricatures, sympathy or protest marches, commemorating acts and the like (Baker and Edelstein 2015). In this volume, we have considered how revolutionary ideals and concepts travel beyond their original context through real and fictional translations, rewritings, sentimental narratives, icons, fashion items and so forth. Most of these mediations depend on scripts, but they also have a bodily dimension, as is perhaps clearest in White's chapter on the repurposings of the iconic tricolor cockade. But incorporating mechanisms are also visible, for instance, in Bandau's exploration of theatrical tropes in revolutionary France, and in the performative nature of translating practices as discussed by Griesse, Johns, Löffler and Popkin. Translation here appears as an embodied practice that "impresses" not merely through the economy of the written word but also by means of various modes of posturing and framing. The complexities surrounding the translation of the *Code Noir* into Creole, as discussed by Popkin, clearly illustrate the corporeal dimension of revolutionary movements.

Today's social media platforms reflect and engender specific corporeal attitudes. Consider, for instance, the "#ICantBreathe" hashtags currently appearing on protesters' T-shirts and banners in cities worldwide. Scholars of comparative revolutions might observe interesting continuities between the die-in protests of the Black Lives Matter movement today – in which protesters reenact the posture of victims of systemic police violence – and the ritual execution of Louis XVI as analyzed by Connerton (1989: 7–13). Connerton's interpretation of the ritual significance of the regicide relies heavily on Ernst Kantorowicz's work on the political theology of kingship (Kantorowicz 1957). But, as Eric Santner has argued, the symbolic structures of kingship survive today in conceptions of national sovereignty (Santner 2011). If the execution of Louis XVI was designed to relocate authority from the institution of kingship onto the category of the "People," today's die-in protests along with other modes of resistance serve to assert the inviolability of the body – as the bearer of modern sovereignty – in the face of racist police brutality. What connects the two patterns of behavior is the extent to which they rely on repeated bodily practices and commemorative rites to express revolutionary principles and ideals. Perhaps now more than ever, we are in need of a worked-out heuristic framework that is attuned to the incorporated nature of social remembrance. When the killing of George Floyd led protesters in Bristol to topple the statue of the slave trader Edward Colston, it was suggested that the statue should be recast as Frederick Douglass (Crace 2020). Such interventions foreground the incorporating practices that sustain communities and through which they resist and "recast" ascribed identities.

Finally, my example of Douglass's developing attitude toward the revolutionary significance of plantation songs might reflect certain limitations in recent theoretical approaches that seek to situate national revolutions in a broader transnational framework. While the so-called transnational turn in historical scholarship has generated powerful new insights, it has not always resulted in sustained attention to how revolutions reverberate not just outward in space, but also across time. In this way, as Cody Marrs suggests, the postnational paradigm betrays a "hidden synchronism" that leaves the temporal structures undergirding the modern nation largely intact (Marrs 2013: 460). To be sure, most of the scholarship on the 1848 revolutions is geared toward challenging exceptionalist national narratives (Bender 2006; Roberts 2009; Fleche 2012). Just as often, however, such scholarship indirectly reinstalls the nation, and its temporal consciousness, as the bedrock for critical reflection. This is clear, for instance, in studies focusing on contributions made by given revolutionary groups to political debate in another state, for instance those of German (Levine 1992; Nagel 2012) or Italian (Gemme 2005) revolutionaries to political debate in the United States during the Civil War. The nation here remains the primary focus. Something similar can be argued regarding literary-historical scholarship on how the authors of the American Renaissance processed the events in Europe (Berthold 2009; Reynolds 1988). Though illuminating, these and other studies do not fundamentally challenge received classifications, spatial boundaries and temporal categories. While this danger may be inherent in any comparative approach, placing multidirectional reverberations, and their odd effects, front and center allows for a more insightful inquiry into revolutionary dynamics. The concept of reverberations brings out the discontinuous temporalities of revolutionary movements and performative rituals in ways that have so far remained insufficiently explored. While they retain their primary focus on the Age of Revolutions as traditionally defined, the contributions in this volume constitute a modest effort to fill that gap.

Bibliography

Allen, Theodore (1994), *The Invention of the White Race*, Vol. 1, London: Verso.
Assing, Ottilie (1860), "Vorrede," in *Sclaverei und Freiheit: Autobiographie von Frederick Douglass*, Hamburg: Hoffmann und Campe, pp. ix–xiv.
Baker, Keith Michael and Dan Edelstein, eds (2015), *Scripting Revolution: A Historical Approach to the Comparative Study of Revolutions*, Stanford: Stanford University Press.
Bender, Thomas (2006), *A Nation Among Nations: America's Place in World History*, New York: Hill and Wang.
Berthold, Dennis (2009), *American Risorgimento: Herman Melville and the Cultural Politics of Italy*, Columbus: Ohio State University Press.
Brathwaite, Edward Kamau (1982), "English in the Caribbean: Notes on Nation Language and Poetry," in Leslie A. Fiedler and Houston A. Baker, Jr., eds, *English Literature: Opening Up the Canon*, Selected Papers from the English Institute, 1979, Baltimore and London: Johns Hopkins University Press, pp. 15–53.
Connerton, Paul (1989), *How Societies Remember*, Cambridge: Cambridge University Press.

Crace, John (2020), "Could the Colston Statue Be Recast as Social Reformer Frederick Douglass," *Guardian*, June 12, at <https://www.theguardian.com/politics/2020/jun/12/could-edward-colston-statue-be-recast-as-social-reformer-frederick-douglass> (last accessed October 23, 2020.)

Douglass, Frederick (1853), "The Heroic Slave," in J. Griffiths, ed., *Autographs for Freedom*, Vol. 1, Boston: John P. Jewett, pp. 174–239.

Douglass, Frederick (1950), "Letter to Kossuth," in *The Life and Writings of Frederick Douglass*, Vol. 2, New York: International Publishers, p. 171.

Douglass, Frederick (1994), *Autobiographies*, New York: Library of America.

Douglass, Frederick (1999), "The Revolution of 1848," in P. S. Foner and Y. Taylor, eds, *Frederick Douglass: Selected Speeches and Writings*, Chicago: Lawrence Hill Books, pp. 103–10.

Fleche, Andrew M. (2012), *The Revolution of 1861: The American Civil War in the Age of Nationalist Conflict*, Chapel Hill: University of North Carolina Press.

Gemme, P. (2005), *Domesticating Foreign Struggles: The Italian Risorgimento and Antebellum American Identity*, Athens: University of Georgia Press.

Gilroy, Paola (1993), *The Black Atlantic: Modernity and Double Consciousness*, Cambridge, MA: Harvard University Press.

Honeck, Mischa (2011), *We Are the Revolutionists: German-Speaking Immigrants and American Abolitionists after 1848*, Athens: University of Georgia Press.

Kantorowicz, Ernst H. (1957), *The King's Two Bodies: A Study in Medieval Political Theology*, Princeton: Princeton University Press.

Levine, Bruce (1992), *The Spirit of 1848: German Immigrants, Labor Conflict, and the Coming of the Civil War*, Urbana: University of Illinois Press.

Marrs, Cody (2013), "Frederick Douglass in 1848," *American Literature* 85:3, pp. 447–73.

Meehan, Sean Ross (2008), *Mediating American Autobiography: Photography in Emerson, Thoreau, Douglass, and Whitman*, Columbia: University of Missouri Press.

Moten, Fred (2003), *In the Break: The Aesthetics of the Black Radical Tradition*, Minneapolis: University of Minnesota Press.

Nagel, D. (2012), *Von republikanischen Deutschen zu deutsch-amerikanischen Republikanern: ein Beitrag zum Identitätswandel der deutschen Achtundvierziger in den Vereinigten Staaten 1850–1861*, Röhrig Universitätsverlag.

Rapport, Mike (2009), *1848: Year of Revolution*, New York: Basic Books.

Reynolds, Larry J. (1988), *European Revolutions and the American Literary Renaissance*, New Haven: Yale University Press.

Roberts, Timothy Mason (2009), *Distant Revolutions: 1848 and the Challenge to American Exceptionalism*, Charlottesville: University of Virginia Press.

Santner, Eric L. (2011), *The Royal Remains: The People's Two Bodies and the Endgames of Sovereignty*, Chicago: University of Chicago Press.

Sinha, Manisha (2016), *The Slave's Cause: A History of Abolition*, New Haven: Yale University Press.
Taylor, A. J. P. (1951), *The Course of German History: A Survey of the Development of German History Since 1815*, 2nd edition, London: H. Hamilton.
Thomas, John (1853), "Kossuth," in J. Griffiths, ed., *Autographs for Freedom*, Vol. 1, Boston: John P. Jewett, pp. 166–73.

Notes

Introduction

1. For the concept of "transculturation," see Pratt 2008, and for that of "counterpower" see Negri 1999. Paul Gilroy's important work (1993) on the Black Atlantic as a "counterculture" to modernity displays a similar revisionist agenda.

Chapter 1

1. My first reflections on the topic of this article have been published in Griesse 2017. While some of my earlier arguments are summarized here in a rather condensed form, new dimensions have been introduced especially with respect to the global entanglements of revolt perceptions in this Age of Revolutions.
2. The newest synthetic study of the uprising is Трефилов 2015. See also Alexander 1973; Longworth 1974; Natalizi 2011; Peters 1973.
3. The term media-hype has been used in Maier and Schumacher 2009.
4. "On garde le plus qu'on peut, le silence sur les courriers qu'on expédie à Casan, et qu'on en reçoit. A l'égard des lettres particulières de ces Contrées, il est rare qu'elles échappent aux soins qu'on prend de les supprimer." Ambassador Durand de Distroff from Petersburg to the Duc d'Aiguillon (French foreign minister), February 1774, Archives diplomatiques du Ministère aux Affaires Etrangères (MAE), Correspondance Russie 95 (1774 janvier-juin), f.100 verso.
5. Significantly, the decree "О Высочайше дарованных разным сословиям милостях, по случаю заключенного мира с Портою Оттоманскою" [On the grace and mercy granted by Her Majesty to the different estates, at the occasion of the Peace treaty concluded with the Ottoman Porte] hides the very issue of the uprising behind the Russo-Turkish War. See (Полное собрание законов Российской империи. [Собрание 1-е. С 1649

no 12 дек. 1825 г.] 1830, vol. 20 [С 1775 по 1780 = № 14233–15105], sec. 14.275).
6. Not surprisingly, the few studies that deal with the work are in general by literary scholars. See Günzerodt 1958; Степанов 1991.
7. However, in contrast to the recyclers of the French "biography," these accounts do not plagiarize the narrative published in Büsching's *Magazine*. They rather take it as a starting point in order to comment on or correct certain features on the basis of their personal experience and eye-witnessing, since the German authors have either been involved in the repression of the uprising, or affected by it during their sojourn in Russia. See [Bellermann] 1792; Freymann 1794.
8. Other historians who followed Blok include Hoffmann and Schützler 1962; Hoffmann 1975; Donnert 2008.
9. This is the conclusion reached by Kamenskij, who did not find any documents on the Pugachev uprising in Müller's archives (Каменский 1989: 154). In contrast, Hoffmann asserts that the documents were transferred to Petersburg in the 1820s, when Pushkin was commissioned to work with them for his history of the uprising (Hoffmann 2005: 163).
10. On Müller's biography cf. Hoffmann 2005.
11. "Cet Couvrage seroit piquant, curieux & recherché, si l'on pouvoit se persuader qu'il offre l'Histoire réelle de l'Aventurier qui a fait tant de bruit dans ces dernier temps; & qui après avoir causé de justes inquiétudes, a fini comme tous les rebelles, qui courent au trône & arrivent à l'échaffaud. Malheureusement celle que nous annonçons porte par-tout des caracteres de fausseté qui ne permettent pas au Lecteur de se faire illusion; on l'annonce comme traduite du Russe; nous ignorons si ce Roman a paru en effet dans cet Empire, entier ou en partie; il est très vraisemblable, qu'il n'y a jamais été publié. Ce n'est pas dans cet Empire que l'on auroit osé mettre au jour cette Vie du Rebelle Pugatschew; dans laquelle on ne laisse pas d'exalter des actions faites pour le degrader. On paroît avoir écrit ceci d'après la relation que la Cour de Pétersbourg fit publier de la rebellion, & de la maniere dont elle l'a appaisée; l'Auteur, quel qu'il soit, a brodé sur les faits principaux tout ce que son imagination lui a suggéré; elle lui en a fourni aussi un grand nombre, & le plus grand nombre certainement . . ." (Anon. 1776).
12. On the genre of pseudotranslation, see Toury 1995; Kupsch-Losereit 2014.
13. "Notre Héros voulut connaître les hommes; s'instruire des moeurs & des coûtumes de tous les Peuples. La Politique, la Guerre, le Commerce, les différentes branches de l'Administration publique, tout entrait dans le plan qu'il s'était formé; & éclairé des lumiéres de son ami Boispré, il espérait voyager en Philosophe, & mettre même à profit jusqu'aux folies des Hommes. Il serait difficile de dire jusqu'à quel point il a poussé ses progress dans une étude aussi difficile. L'essai malheureux qu'il vient

de faire des leçons qu'il a puisées dans ses voyages, & des principes que lui a inspires son ami, est un préjugé peu favorable à sa prétendue Philosophie. Peut-être aussi que s'il avait réussi dans son coupable dessein, on l'aurait vu racheter tous ses crimes par toutes les vertus qui caractérisent les grands Princes. Auguste Triumvir fut un monstre de cruauté; Auguste Empéreur mérita l'admiration de l'Univers entier."

14. "si c'était moi que la violence & l'intrigue eussent couronné, & que cette élévation illégale divisât mes Sujets, je déposerais & sceptre & couronne entre leurs mains, est leur dirais: *'Mes Frères, je me suis laissé entrainer à l'idée que, placé sur le Trône, je pourrais vous rendre tous heureux; l'expérience prouve que je me suis trompé. Je devais savoir que le droit d'y monter ne pouvait m'être donné que par vous; je l'ai usurpé ce droit; je vous le rends, content d'être cotre égal, & prêt à obéir à celui que vous voudrez honorer de votre choix, & que vous croirez plus digne que moi de commander à des hommes justement jaloux de leur liberté.'* Crois-tu, mon cher Boispré, que si le Comte Poniatowski, s'appercevant des troubles qu'allait causer son intrusion au Trône, avait parlé ainsi aux Polonais, ils ne se fussent pas tous réunis pour affermir sur sa tête une Couronne, qu'il mérite peut-être, mais dont alors il aurait été doublement digne?' Lorsque Jemeljan s'exprimait avec tant de grandeur d'ame, il ne pensait pas sans-doute qu'il était lui même à la veille, non pas de prendre un sceptre qu'une partie de la Nation qu'il voulait s'asservir lui aurait présenté; mais de renverser de son Trône une Souveraine, sa Souveraine légitime, que le vœu unanime de tous ses Peuples y avait placée."

15. The plural (peoples) is always employed when the entire population of Russia is meant, which shows to what extent contemporaries were aware of the multiethnic composition of the Russian Empire.

16. On the use of pseudotranslation for political criticism in eighteenth-century France see Kupsch-Losereit 2014. On the shift in widespread stereotypes of Russia from barbarism to backwardness (that introduced the temporal dimension of a civilizational process) see Griesse 2016.

17. In her correspondence with Voltaire, for instance, she repeatedly called Peter the Great her "grandfather."

18. Peter I had tried at the beginning of the eighteenth century to petition the Emperor along these lines. He wanted to get rid of a work he considered offensive to his government, since it depicted a recent uprising in an illicit way. See Griesse 2014.

19. On the impact of Raynal's work in Catherine's Russia see Лехтблау 1939; Старцев 1940.

20. In the *Histoire* there are only few references to Russia, which seem to have been written in the first place by Diderot, who had sojourned in Russia at Catherine's invitation and received a considerable pension from her. Catherine did not know about Diderot's co-authorship and in her letters to Grimm she complained about Raynal, who would distort

the facts in alleging that her reform projects hardly ever succeeded. See Madariaga 2014: 233–5.
21. On political liberty with regard to the American War of Independence see especially "Livre 18, XLII. Les colonies étaient en droit de se séparer de leur metropole, indépendamment de tout mécontentement," in Raynal 1780: 390–403.
22. In Russia the Trevogin case has attracted researchers of eighteenth- and nineteenth-century utopias. For a recent study with further references see Ростовцева 2014.
23. He was apparently inspired by an opera, *La reine de Golconde* by Monsigny and Sedaine, written in 1766, which was performed in Paris at that time. Moreover, he had found out during his library studies that hardly anything was known about Borneo, which fired his imagination, since he could not be proved wrong, if only his story was consistent. He even invented a language and concomitant scripture, Golkondish, as he called it.
24. Trevogin's autobiographical account written in prison has been published in Курмачева 1983: 336–40.
25. Natan Eidel'man juxtaposed Denis Fonvizin's and Trevogin's perception of prerevolutionary France, see Н. Я. Эйдельман 1989: 47–52.
26. Quoted from Pushkin 2017: 4–5. The translation dates to 1875.

Chapter 2

1. "Das Schnepfenthal-Projekt konnte als nationales Basismodell für sittliche Erziehung der zukünftigen Tugendelite wirken ... für das geregelte Zusammenleben von Menschen verschiedener Konfessionen und Nationalitäten und damit ein Modell für die kosmopolitische Erziehung des Menschen."
2. "Die Mrs. Wollstonecraft verzeihe mir, dass ich hier widersprechen muss. Jeder Geschäftsmann wird es fühlen, dass er die Pflichten gegen seine Kinder nicht so erfüllen kann, als er wünscht; wenn nun auch das Weib an der Regierung des Staats Theil nehmen wollte: was sollte denn aus den Kindern werden. O, ein Weib das die Pflichten als Mutter erfüllt, und ein Paar gute Bürger und Bürgerinnen erzieht, erwirbt sich Verdienst genug um den Staat, und hat auch so vielerley Geschäfte, dass ihm wohl schwerlich Zeit zur Theilnahme an der Regierung übrig bleiben möchte."
3. For an example of Wollstonecraft's "exaggerations" see the two-part review in the *Neue Allgemeine Deutsche Bibliothek* IX:1, Part 1 (1794), pp. 126–32, and XVII:1, Part 2 (1795), pp. 66–71.
4. "Im Englischen wurde zuerst von jedem Schüler ein auswendig gelerntes Pensum vorgetragen; dann aus den Elements of morality vorgelesen und übersetzt, und zuletzt ein in Teutscher Sprache vorgelesener Brief mündlich ins Englische übertragen."

5. "Es muss jedem Menschen erlaubt seyn, seine Glückseligkeit zu suchen, worin er sie suchen will, sobald er den Gebrauch der Vernunft hat, und sobald er dieser zu Folge sein Wohlseyn nicht in etwas Unsittlichem sucht"; "Die Glückseligkeit des Weibes ist allein auf häusliche Freuden beschränkt"; "Auch in der häuslichen Gesellschaft ragt der Mann als das Haupt hervor, wie in der bürgerlichen"; "Habet nur Muth stark zu seyn, und Ihr werdet es seyn! Suchet das zu werden, was Ihr seyn sollet; und man wird gezwungen seyn, Euch das zu geben, was man Euch schuldig ist! Lernet Eure Pflichten kennen: und man wird Euch Eure Rechte nicht vorenthalten können!"
6. "verbunden mit den fürchterlichsten innerlichen und äusserlichen Kriegen"; "könnet Ihr es . . . noch nicht wagen, diese Rechte für Euch sogleich zurück zu fordern: so suchet wenigstens der Nachwelt das zu erringen, worauf Ihr selbst noch Verzicht thun müsset! Bildet Eure Töchter besser, als Ihr gebildet wurdet; und bahnet diesen dadurch den Weg, die Ihrigen einst noch besser zu bilden! Eine späte, glücklichere und bessere Nachwelt wird Euch einst dafür segnen; und das Bewusstseyn, etwas Gutes für die Zukunft vorbereitet zu haben, wird Euch die Leiden der Gegenwart erleichtern!"
7. *A Picture of England* was translated from the first part of the French edition that appeared in Gotha, Germany, in the neighborhood of Salzmann's *Erziehungsanstalt*: *Tableau de L'Angleterre et de L'Italie* (Gotha: Charles-Guillaume Ettinger, 1788); see also the English excerpt printed in the *Lady's Magazine* 21 (1790), p. 721, and Maurer 1987: 187.
8. The editing of the *Annalen*'s literature section was farmed out to well-respected literary figures: first to Georg Forster (until page 215 of volume 9:8) and then to J. J. Eschenburg. Wollstonecraft receives two notices by Eschenburg covering, first, the *Vindication of the Rights of Woman*. She is called "a woman of spirit and courage" helping her sex gain "general respect and independence" with her "lively" arguments against prejudices, the poor education of women, and "against the delusion [*Wahn*] that the main purpose of women's existence should solely be to please the male sex"; *Annalen der brittischen Geschichte des Jahrs 1792* 9:8 (1794): 282–3. The second review covers Wollstonecraft's *Letters of a Short Residence in Sweden, Norway and Denmark* which "do honor to the right feeling and power of observation of this author; however, she appears to have seen many objects too fleetingly, or even heard them only halfway correctly, about which she nonetheless allows herself to give a rather decided opinion"; *Annalen der brittischen Geschichte des Jahrs 1795* 16:7 (1799), p. 38. (These reviews are erroneously indexed in the general *Register* of the *Annalen*, Volume 20, as on page 295 of volume 9 and page 43 of volume 16. The review of the Scandinavian *Letters* interestingly appears in the volume covering 1795, the year Wollstonecraft

completed her travels, rather than in the volume covering 1796, when her published version of the *Letters* first appeared.)
9. Rauschenbusch-Clough (1898: 200–2) cites Schlabrendorf's remarks to his close friend Carl Gustav Jochmann; see Jochmann 1836: I. 193–8.
10. The passages Archenholz translates are from Wollstonecraft (1794): Book III, Chapter 3, pp. 299–305, 306–7, 308, 309; Book IV, Chapter 1, pp. 330–1, 354–7; Book V, Chapter 3, pp. 483–5, 486; and Book V, Chapter 4, pp. 502–4, 507–8.
11. "durch ihre Schriften berühmte Engländerin"; "Sie ist Verfasserin einiger Romane; auch hat sie über die Erziehung, über die Moral, und über die Rechte der Weiber geschrieben."
12. "Ueber die Franzosen und ihre Regierungs-Veränderung."
13. "da Selbstsüchtigkeit mit ausgedehnten, lobwürdigen, edlen Absichten unvereinbar ist, so darf man sich nicht wundern, wenn man die Schwäche des National-Characters vor Augen behält, daß bei der ersten National Versammlung ein jeder Deputirter eigne Plane [sic] vorzulegen hatte. Diese wurden jedoch von den Häuptern nicht geachtet; und da diese untereinander nicht einverstanden waren, so stritt man um die Wette, wer die heftigsten Maaßregeln vorschlagen sollte, weil diese nach dem Grade ihrer Heftigkeit den meisten Beyfall fanden ... hätten die damit begabten Männer sich vereinigt, und, geleitet durch eine wahre Liebe ihres Vaterlandes, auf einem Punct gearbeitet, so würden alle die Unfälle, die das Reich verheerten, und die Ruhe von Europa vernichteten, nicht die Sache der Freyheit geschändet haben. Eine jede große Reform erfordert ein systematisches Betragen; denn die friedlichen Fortschritte einer Revolution müssen großentheils in der Mäßigung der Aufopferungen, und in den dabey beobachtenden gleichartigen Schritten aller handelnden Theile bestehn ... Es war durchaus nöthig eine solche Coalition zu machen, um den gefährlichen Folgen alter Vorurtheile entgegen zu arbeiten; denn es war moralisch gewiß, daß die hartnäckigen Gewohnheiten solcher Menschen, die durch persönliches Interesse an ihren Standpunct gefesselt waren, den ruhigen Gang der Revolution aufhalten würden."
14. It must be noted that Wollstonecraft's attitude appears to have evolved after she witnessed the upshot of the French Revolution; she had earlier, in the *Vindication of the Rights of Woman*, depicted the citizen-mother as unacknowledged legislator, a portrayal that contains some of the theoretical spirit of the finished blueprint. See my *Bluestocking Feminism* (Johns 2014: 72), which notes how Wollstonecraft superimposes a Biblical "millennial vision onto her model of social existence," coming to conceive of "the model mother-instructor" as "governor of a microstate" that is the family, with repercussions on the macro-state, the country. Her time in France appears to have changed her approach.
15. "Die brittischen Tugenden, die sonst durch ihre Masse in der Sittengeschichte Europens so vorzüglich Glänzten, haben größtentheils aufgehört, ein Gegenstand der Bewunderung der Nationen zu seyn."

16. *New-Yorker Criminal-Zeitung und Belletristisches Journal* VII:47 (11 February 1859), p. 740, and *New-Yorker Criminal-Zeitung und Belletristisches Journal* VII:48 (18 February 1859), p. 758–9.
17. *New-Yorker Criminal-Zeitung und Belletristisches Journal* VII:50 (4 March 1859), np.
18. *New-Yorker Criminal-Zeitung und Belletristisches Journal* VIII:Nn (8 April 1859), pp. 42–3.
19. *New-Yorker Criminal-Zeitung und Belletristisches Journal* VIII:Nn (1 July 1859), p. 238, and *New-Yorker Criminal-Zeitung und Belletristisches Journal* VIII:Nn (8 July 1859), p. 254.
20. Indeed, she deepened her connection to Wollstonecraft in the next generation by naming her own son after Percy Shelley, who had married Wollstonecraft's daughter Mary.

Chapter 5

1. See Lynn Hunt (1984) on the transposition of the political conflict between old and new order into a family conflict in the literature written in the context of the French Revolution.
2. Théâtre de la Cité was a popular theatre that opened in 1792 with a revolutionary piece and a play also by Pigault-Lebrun, a successful theater author of the time (Lecomte 1910: 3–4). It seated 1,800–2,000 people. Its interior was a mixture of royalist and republican décor (such as the statue of liberty) and its repertory included "pièces consacrées mêlée avec les nouveautés, la plupart politiques" (Lecomte 1910: 8) – a Jacobin anti-clerical canon as well as reactionary and Napoleonic pieces (3–4) – and lighter fare such as songs, dances, pantomimes and comedies (7).
3. Diderot, one of Raynal's numerous collaborators, was responsible for some of the more radical passages of anticolonial critique in the 1780 edition of Raynal's widely translated and highly influential socio-political text.
4. "Sensibility, charity, generosity, all that men honor, you unite in yourself. Such greatness does overwhelm me, such virtue confounds me" ("Sensibilité, bienfaisance, générosité, tout ce qui honore les hommes, tu le réunis en toi. Tant de grandeur m'accable, tant de vertu me confond") (116).
5. Regarding Rousseau's model of political contract, Hardt and Negri rightly conclude: "The contract of association is intrinsic to and inseparable from the contract of subjugation" (Hardt and Negri cited in Maddock Dillon 2014: 9).
6. The ventriloquist quality of these enlightened African or indigenous figures that articulate Western thinking has been pointed out by Doris Garraway (2009).
7. According to Wehle (1983), this follows a melodramatic logic.

8. It refers to the frequent practice of slaveowners to name their slaves for famous historical figures from antiquity. Several slaves with the name Scipio Africanus who lived during the eighteenth century as servants can be found and might have also served as reference.
9. Joseph Rosny was a former member of the military who during the Directoire entered administration and simultaneously tried to establish himself as a writer in several different genres (from memoirs to drama). He was interested in republican ideals and in educating the new citizens (see Chappey 2009). There is no information on Louis-François-Guillaume Béraud de la Rochelle in the relevant sources, but if we take his surname literally he had a link to the Atlantic port town La Rochelle, which might be interesting in connection with the topic.
10. This development is followed in a later version of the novel where the historical context is also erased. Similarly, the revolutionary content of Pigault-Lebrun's *Le blanc et le noir* is reduced in a complete edition of Pigault's work in 1822. The author introduces a fable titled "Le solitaire et le brigand" to the paratext: It represents the revolting slave as a criminal (*brigand*) and the philanthropic and pro-abolitionist son of the plantation owner as a misguided "solitary" (*solitaire*). The bandit/robber/slave is portrayed as living only for his pleasure and unwilling to work. This further criminalization and effacing of virtue on the side of the revolutionary slave as well as the discrediting of the abolitionist philosopher's vision of building a black and white patriotic French family speak a clear language. The fate of the play is shared by other similar texts whose authors intend to reduce and belittle the revolutionary character and mirror French colonial forgetfulness, as Yves Benot labeled the progressive silencing of the events of the revolution in Saint-Domingue during the period of restoration.
11. See my article on Picquenard's prose text and the function of anecdote in the colonial context (Bandau 2008).
12. Various hints support this reading: "le camp Brida" (43) refers to Toussaint's headquarters and the former plantation where he once worked. Toussaint, who had once been seen as a positive figure supporting French politics, fell into discredit after coming into power in 1798: "Tu traites les Français de barbares, toi qui jadis fus bien reçu dans leur patrie!" ("You treat the French as barbarians, you who were once well received in our country") (13). His great political abilities as well as the importance he gave to communication are mirrored in the character.
13. Here we are also introduced to the enlightened model of conviviality the play favors and proposes to the freed slaves at the end. When it becomes clear that Mme d'Herouville has to leave the country to be saved, the slaves do not seek material goods for their future but insist on the sentimental gift of their "good master's" portraits. This move symbolically prolongs the presence of the latter in the colony and the play takes it even one step further: the former slaves' harmonious living together shall be guaranteed symbolically by these portraits.

14. An outcome that French colonial administrators as well as other actors envisioned – and that Toussaint in his very strategic behavior tried to convey, though his actions spoke another language, that of independence.

Chapter 6

1. "selten war wol während der ganzen französischen Revolution die Erwartung gespannter, als jetzt . . . über den Ausgang der Begebenheiten von St. Domingo. Wie er auch sey: Eine für die Menschheit wichtige Entscheidung wird aus ihm hervorgehen." All translations are the author's unless otherwise indicated.
2. "Die Freierklärung der Sklaven . . . erschütterte die Grundpfeiler des Kolonialsystems."
3. "Nun weiß jedermann, dass im Jahre 1803, als der General Dessalines mit 30000 Negern gegen Port au Prince vorrückte, alles, was die weiße Farbe trug, sich in diesen Platz warf, um ihn zu verteidigen."
4. "Wir wollen hier nicht die Schicksale Haity's aus öffentlichen Blättern wiederholen."
5. "Ein aus Havre angekommenes Schiff hat die Nachricht gebracht, daß die Negersclaven auf der Insel St. Domingo sich empöret hätten."
6. "eine Medienkultur, die in ihrer Ausbreitung, Dichte und Differenziertheit konkurrenzlos gewesen sein dürfte"
7. "aus den in einigen öffentlichen Blättern gelesenen Bruchstücken von Erzehlungen der neuern Vorfälle auf Domingo, . . . Eine zusammenhängende geschichtliche Schilderung dieser Ereignisse . . . gehört um so mehr auch für unsre Zeitgeschichte."
8. "Will ich mehr als Zeitungsnachrichten liefern, so muss ich ganze Tage hören, sehen, lesen und prüfen, ehe ich die Feder in die Hand nehmen und einige Stunden der Arbeit widmen, *wahrhaft historische* Beyträge niederzuschreiben."
9. "Dieses Werk ist vorzüglich der neuesten Geschichte gewidmet, in so ferne die Schicksale naher oder ferner Länder, und die Meynungen und Handlungen ihrer Bewohner für aufgeklärte Völker Interesse haben. Die Aufsätze werden größtenteils sorgfältig gewählte Materialien für zukünftige Geschichtsschreiber seyn."
10. "Diese mit vielen Details und Sachkenntnis von einem Augenzeugen in einer angenehmen Schreibart aufgestellten Nachrichten, ziehen gleichsam den Vorhang vor dieser Neger-Bühne weg, und geben uns eine ganz andre Ansicht der Dinge."
11. "[Zwar] schwor ich, mit Grimm die Franzosen zu verfolgen, versprach aber auch . . . das Blut der Unschuldigen und aller unglücklichen Werkzeuge einer grausamen Regierung zu schonen."
12. "Man kennt die Streitigkeiten im gesetzgebenden Corps über die Kolonien; sie geben dem Partheygeist umso größern Spielraum, da

die Nachrichten über diese entfernten Besitzungen gewöhnlich eben so einseitig, als mangelhaft sind."
13. "Bemerkungen über die Schwierigkeiten, die Geschichte der Revolution während derselben zu schreiben."
14. "Bey einer Revolution hat man das Gemälde zu nahe vor den Augen; jedes Ereignis macht einen zu starken Eindruck, als daß man die Ursachen und Folgen desselben gehörig miteinander vergleichen könnte ... erst in der Ferne übersieht man das Ganze des ... Schauspiels."
15. "Unzuverlässigkeit der Journalisten"
16. "sorgfältige Sichtung und Kritik"
17. "viele Zeugen müssen noch ... geprüft, zu richtigen Theilgemälden zusammengetragen, und *dann* erst die Schilderungen des Ganzen versucht werden"
18. "Die Augen der Welt sind jetzt auf St. Domingo und die dort hausenden Neger – eine Republick kann man diese zusammen gerotteten rasenden Schwarzen wohl nicht nennen – gerichtet, da die Folgen dieses Unwesens nicht zu berechnen sind."
19. "Man kann einen guten Theil ihrer Fehler durch die Peitsche abstellen ...; man mus solche aber oftermalen wiederholen."
20. "Die Despotie erwarb damals neue, unschätzbare Quellen des Wohlstandes, – und die Freyheit zerstört sie jetzt."
21. "vor den Umständen, welche sie während der Revolution verheerte, die blühendste ... unter den Antillen war"
22. "Abgesehen von der ganzen moralischen Scheußlichkeit dieses Handels, bleibt es sicher das einzige Mittel, Westindien den Europäern zu erhalten, wenn man unter gänzlicher allgemeiner Aufhebung des Sclavenhandels, die Neger nach und nach ... dem Zustande der gemeinen, freyen, arbeitenden Volksclassen im mittleren Europa nähert."
23. "Besonders wird das bisherige Sclavensystem in seinen Folgen erschüttert..... Allmälig muss so überall die Emancipation der Neger eintreten."
24. "zum Wiederaufleben des preußischen Handels und der Manufaktural-Industrie sehr wesentlich nothwendig"
25. "ein Genie unter den Negern"
26. "mit 500'000 thierischen Menschen verglichen ..., die niemals nur irgend einige Idee vom Alphabet gehabt hatten"
27. "zügellose ... Negerdemocratie"
28. "viele Neger ... durch den langen Kampf schnell für höhere politische Ansichten gebildet [wurden]"
29. "Bewußtsein, die Freiheit nicht als Geschenk erhalten, sondern sich erkämpft zu haben."
30. "Problem über seine Inferiorität ... Wir haben jetzt unbestrittene Beweise, daß es dem Neger gar nicht an höheren Geistesgaben mangelt."
31. "Wenn Revolutionen solche schöne Früchte tragen; dann muß man jeder Revolution gegen Sklaverei Glück und Segen wünschen! Was

wäre diese Menschenklasse heut, wenn sie noch in der Sklaverei schmachtete? Und was ist sie heut? Und was wird sie einst werden?"
32. "einheimischen Revolutionen Westindiens und vor allen Domingo's"
33. "ein Revolutionssturm mit *dem* ganz eigenthümlichen Charakter aufbrausete, dass … die schwarzen Sklaven das Joch der Europäer abschüttelten"
34. "bei der Nachricht: ganz Frankreich habe sich durch eine Revolution Freiheit errungen, das Zauber-Wort Freiheit alle Gemüther … beseelte, und schnell den Vorsatz zur Reise brachte, auch ihre Fesseln zu zersprengen"
35. "Wenn übrigens die Regierung in Frankreich auch keinen Umsturz erfahren hätte, so wäre darum die Empörung auf St. Domingo doch ausgebrochen."
36. "Neger- und Mulattenrepublik mit Verfassungsgrundsätzen und Regierungsformen, wie sie kaum in den freisinnigsten Constitutionen der europäischen Republiken seit dem letzten Jahrzehnt des achtzehnten Jahrhunderts angetroffen wurden!"
37. "das Dasein der Neger, so bald sie frei wären, physisch unverträglich sei mit dem Dasein seiner europäischen Brüder"
38. "Racenkampfe"
39. "als durchaus einzige Eigenthümlichkeit [der Haitianischen Revolution], dass weniger von den Interessen als von den Racen die streitenden Parteien geschieden wurden"

Chapter 8

1. For a bibliography of Philhellenic literature, see Droulia 1974.
2. A writer for the *Nuevo Diario de Madrid*, for example, observed that "The volcano has erupted in many places at once, proof that the channels are branching out and that they form a system … the shouts that resound on the banks of the Eurotas will make an excellent duo with the ones that are continually intoned on those of the Tagus" (22 April 1821, cited in Hualde Pascal 2013: 266). All translations in this essay are my own.
3. The only other novel published in Spanish on the topic during the period, *Amor y religión, o la joven griega* (1830), is a translation of Adèle Daminois' novel *Alaïs, ou la Vierge de Ténédos* (1826). See Morfakidis Motos 2014: 151–7. As Pilar Hualde Pascal points out, however, several works engaged the war indirectly by focusing on analogous historical situations such as the struggle against the Turks in the seventeenth century (e.g., Ramón López Soler's *Kar-Osman, memorias de la casa de Silva*, 1832) (Hualde Pascual 2013: 270–1). It is interesting to note that Cosca Vayo's work was converted into

a play, which follows quite closely its plot and transcribes verbatim numerous passages: *La doncella de Missolonghi, drama original en 5 actos compuesto por D. P. M.* (1840). Another play with a similar subtitle – Guillermo Rode's *El héroe de la Grecia y su page, o sea, La doncella de Misolonghi, drama histórico, en verso y dividido en cuatro actos* – was performed in Mexico in 1849. Its plot, however, is significantly different from that of the Spanish novel.

4. A typical example is *La Vierge héroïque, roman grec de ces dernières époques* (1821), in which the Greek heroine, symbolically named Hélène, escapes from a lascivious Ottoman chieftain and ultimately marries a Greek raised in Vienna with Enlightenment values.
5. According to Aggelomatis-Tsougarakis (2008: 61), Konstantina Zacharia is mentioned in French but not in Greek sources. Her role seems more important in Philhellenic literature than in the war itself.
6. The image of the female warrior was a commonplace of Philhellenic discourse. For an example, see Louis-Pascal Sétier's *L'Athénienne, ou les Français en Grèce* (1826) in which the Greek heroine Mira adopts male dress to participate in the defense of Missolonghi.
7. The author of the novel is identified on the title page as "M^e D . . ., avocat à la Cour Royale de Paris" and elsewhere as "F. D.***" (D . . . 1822: I, 2).
8. One of his novels, for example, deals with the Spanish hero El Cid from a specifically Valencian perspective: *La conquista de Valencia por el Cid: novela histórica original* (1831). As he states in the introduction, his goal is "to sketch as exactly as possible not only some of the singular customs of the Valencians but also the fertility and beauty of its countryside" (Cosca Vayo 1831: I, xi–xii). As Nettah Yoeli Rimmer observes in his discussion of *Los espatriados*, Cosca Vayo "makes use of the Moorish history of Valencia to subvert the power structures of the Spanish empire" (2017: 116).
9. A similar analogy appears in the Mexican play by Guillermo Rode in which Nicetas falls in love with a Spanish woman named Isabel, who draws a parallel between the Greek cause and her own country's struggle against the French: "My country as well, yes, beautiful Spain, / was oppressed by the daring Frenchman; / and it rejected the yoke with noble rage" (Rode 1849: 47).
10. For an example of the Philhellenic discourse on the Enlightenment, see *Les Amours d'un Turc et d'une Grecque*, D . . . 1822: I, 162–3 and V, pp. 22–3.
11. After the intervention of the Holy Alliance in 1823, Ferdinand VII abolished the freedom of the press and introduced a rigorous system of censorship. Writers were prohibited from using pseudonyms, and all texts criticizing the Church, the monarchy or the government were forbidden (Gies 2009: 166).

Coda

1. For the idea of a black counter-tradition and Douglass's role in it, see Gilroy 1993. On Douglass and black music, see particularly Moten 2003.
2. As Assing states in the preface to her translation of *My Bondage and My Freedom*, Douglass's second autobiography which I will discuss below: "Alles in ihm ist frisch, ächt, wahr und gut" (Everything in him is vigorous, real, true and good) (Assing 1860: xiii). Insisting on his noble "white" features, Assing's characterization of Douglass further highlights the racialized discourse operative at the time.
3. See Meehan 2008, chapter 4, for Douglass's relation to photography.
4. See Douglass's "Letter to Kossuth" in Douglass 1950: 171. For a synoptic account of the Kossuth affair, see Roberts 2009, chapter 7, and Sinha 2016: 366–7.

Index

Note: page references with 'n' indicates chapter notes.

abolition of slavery, 49, 52, 80, 82–3, 88, 95, 98–9, 104, 111, 116, 120, 123–5, 129, 143, 146
abolitionist movement, 82, 102, 167–76
absolutism, 58, 99, 121, 139, 150
Affiches américaines (newspaper), 83–4
Aggelomatis-Tsougarakis, Eleni, 193n
Ailloud-Nicolas, Cathérine, 96
American Civil War of 1861–65, 174, 176, 179
American Revolution of 1775–83, 24–6, 57, 61–3, 70, 72
Amours d'un Turc et d'une Grècque, Les, épisode de la guerre de 1821, 159–60, 162, 193n
Anderson, Bonnie S., 53
Annalen der brittischen Geschichte (periodical), 44–5, 48–9, 186n
Anneke, Mathilde Franziska, 8, 36, 49–52, 188n
Archenholz, Johann Wilhelm von, 36, 44–9, 119–20, 121, 123
Arendt, Hannah, 1
Arsy, Gouy d', 83
Assing, Ottilie, 170, 194n
Aston, Louise, 50

Baierische Landbot, Der (newspaper), 117
Baker, Keith, 5, 177
Bammer, Angelika, 43
Bank, Michaela, 49
Bar Confederation, 14, 19
Barbault-Royer, Paul-François, 120
Barnes, Edward, 67
Basedow, Johann Bernhard, 37
Beerbohm, Julius, 42
Béraud de la Rochelle, Louis-François-Guillaume, and Antoine Joseph Nicolas de Rosny, *Adonis ou le bon nègre*, 94–5, 106–12, 189n
Biassou, Georges, 86, 107–12
Bible, 58
Bibliothek der pädagogischen Literatur (journal), 42
Black Lives Matter movement, 10–11, 178
blackface pantomime, 94
Bloch, Ernst, 43
Blok, Georgij, 16
Boisrond-Tonnerre, Louis, 89
Bonnet, Guy-Joseph, 81
Botting, Eileen Hunt, 40
Bowdler, John, *Reform or Ruin. Take Your Choice!*, 68, 69
Brathwaite, Kamau, 170
Brockhaus family, 42

Buchholz, Friedrich, 119
Buck-Morss, Susan, 116
Bunel, Joseph, 121
Büsching, Anton Friedrich, *Magazin für die neue Historie und Geographie*, 16, 23–4, 27, 183n

Catherine II of Russia, 13–15, 17–29, 182n, 184n
Catholicism, 59, 60, 86–8
censorship, 6, 39–40, 46, 116, 119, 121, 129, 164
 damnatio memoriae policy on the Pugachev Rebellion of 1733–75, 14–17, 21, 22, 24, 25, 29, 182n
Charles II of England, Scotland and Ireland, 57
Chios Massacre of 1822, 152, 153
Christianity, 152, 157–60, 163; see also Bible; Catholicism; Protestantism
citizenship, 84–5, 95, 103, 110–11, 138, 143, 145
cockade, tricolor, 9–10, 134–47
Code Noir of 1685, Creole translation of, 77–81
colonialism, 6, 78, 80–5, 93–5, 97–102, 104, 107, 110–12, 115, 117, 128
Colston, Edward, Bristol statue of, 178
comparative revolution studies, 5
 source- and target-oriented approaches, 4–6
Congress of Vienna of 1815, 124
Connerton, Paul, 168–70, 178
constitutional monarchy, 26, 59, 63, 64, 85
constitutions, 25, 26, 83, 84, 88–9
Contzen, Leopold, 128–9
Cosca Vayo, Estanislao de
 Grecia, ó la doncella de Missolonghi, 10, 150–64

 Los expatriados, ó Zulema y Gazul, novela histórica original perteneciente al año 1254, 160–1, 163, 193n
Cossacks, 13–15, 18
Cowper, William, "Slavery", 171
Creole language, 78–80, 103, 109
 translation of *Code Noir* of 1685 into, 77–81
Créole patriote (newspaper), 82
Crispin (indentured Indian servant), 135, 140–6
Cylch-grawn Cynmraeg, Y (journal), 65

Darnton, Robert, 96
Daut, Marlene L., 97, 125
Davies, David, 66, 67, 69
Davies, James, 60–1
Davies, Walter, 68
Decembrist uprising of 1825, 26, 27
decolonization, 104
Denmark, 40, 124
despotism, 21, 83, 124
Dessalines, Jean-Jacques, 83, 89–91, 117, 121, 123
Deutsche Frauen-Zeitung (newspaper), 50
Diderot, Denis, 90, 91, 96, 99, 184n, 188n
Dillon, Elizabeth Maddock, 93, 96
Distroff, Durand, 14
Douglass, Frederick, 10, 167–79
 British lecture tour of 1845–47, 172, 174, 175
 The Heroic Slave, 175
 Life and Times of Frederick Douglass, 176–7
 My Bondage and My Freedom, 172, 176, 194n
 The Narrative of the Life of Frederick Douglass, 167–72
 The North Star, 175

Dubois, Laurent, 6
Dubroca, Louis, 121

Edelstein, Dan, 177
education, 27
　Erziehungsanstalt school, Schnepfenthal, Germany, 37–8, 40–2
　slaves', 102, 103
　women's, 40–1, 43, 51, 52
　see also literacy
Elizabeth of Russia, 17
Ellis, Thomas Edward, 71
Elsaesser, Thomas, 109
embodiment, 168–71, 177, 178
Enlightenment, 6, 19, 21–2, 25, 27, 43, 57, 62, 84, 90, 109, 121, 158, 163
epic, 155, 163, 164
equality, 9, 43, 77, 78, 80, 82–4, 87, 94, 102–3, 106, 112, 123, 126, 129, 145–6, 164, 173
Ersch, Johann Samuel, 122
Erziehungsanstalt school, Schnepfenthal, Germany, 37–8, 40–2
Esprit des journaux, L' (journal), 17–18, 22
Eurocentrism, 117, 121, 127–9
Europäische Annalen (journal), 118, 119, 120, 121, 122, 124
Evans, Thomas, 66, 67, 69
Evans, William, 68, 69
eyewitness accounts, 106–7, 119–20, 122

feminist philosophy, 36–8, 40–3, 48–53
Fenelon, François, *Les aventures de Télémaque*, 103
Festa, Lynn, 97, 105
First League of Armed Neutrality of 1780–83, 24, 26

Fleetwood, William, Bishop of Ely, 59–60
Floyd, George, 11, 168, 178
Fonvizin, Denis, 26
Fonvizin, Mikhail, 26
Frankreich im Jahre 1802 (journal), 115, 118, 120, 121
free people of color, 78, 80, 82, 84, 85
Freemasons, 37–8, 44
French Constitution of 1793, 138
French Declaration of the Rights of Man and Citizen of 1789, 6, 67, 77, 78, 83–4, 88
French Directory of 1795–99, 67, 88, 95, 111, 136, 138
French popular theater depictions of the Haitian Revolution, 9, 93–112
　Béraud and Rosny's *Adonis ou le bon nègre*, 94–5, 106–12, 189n
　Pigault-Lebrun's *Le blanc et le noir*, 94–5, 98–106, 111–12, 188n, 189n, 190n
French Revolution of 1789–99, 6, 21, 24, 26, 36, 44–8, 56–7, 63–9, 70, 72, 77, 81–3, 85, 87, 90, 94–7, 101–2, 111, 115, 123, 127
　Reign of Terror, 45, 95, 101–2, 107, 138, 163
　tricolor cockade, 9–10, 134–47
Fuller, Margaret, 50, 51, 53

Galbaud, François-Thomas, 80
Garrison, William Lloyd, 171, 172, 173, 174
Geggis, David P., 6
Genet, Edmond Charles, 142–3
George I of Great Britain and Ireland, 59, 60

George III of Great Britain, 24
Germany, 15, 16, 29, 179
  reception of Mary
    Wollstonecraft's writings in, 8,
    36–53
  reception of the Haitian
    Revolution in, 9, 115–29
Gibbels, Elisabeth, 39–40
Gibbs, Jenna, 93–4
Gilroy, Paul, 182n
Girard, Stephen, 140–6
Glorious Revolution of 1688,
  59–63, 66, 67, 69–70, 72
Gloyer, Johann Nikolaus, 124
Gobineau, Arthur de, 128
Godwin, William, *Memoirs of the
  Author of* A Vindication of the
  Rights of Woman, 36–7, 38
Great Britain, 37, 48–9, 52, 58–9,
  94, 134, 139
Greece, ancient, 155, 161
Greek War of Independence of
  1821–29, 10, 150–64, 192n
Griffiths, Julia, ed. *Autographs for
  Freedom*, 175
Gruffydd, William John, 71
GutsMuths, Johann Christoph
  Friedrich, 42

Haiti and the Haitian Revolution
  of 1791–1804, 6
  debate in German-speaking
    countries on, 9, 115–29
  depictions in French popular
    theater, 9, 93–112
  translation of French
    revolutionary concepts to, 8–9,
    77–91
  tricolor cockades in, 135, 143–6
Handelmann, Heinrich, *Geschichte
  der Insel Hayti*, 128
Hecke, Johann Valentin, 125, 126
Hemans, Felicia, 50, 51
historiography, 6, 122–9
Hobsbawm, Eric, 3, 4–5

Hoffmann, Peter, 183n
Hualde Pascual, Pilar, 192n
humanism, 103, 108
Hungarian nationalism, 175
Hunt, Lynn, 96

Irish nationalism, 172–7
Israel, William, 142

Jacob, Margaret, 38
Jacobite rebellion of 1715, 59, 60
Jamaica, 89, 137
Johnson, Benjamin, diary of
  (Quaker bookseller), 135–40,
  146
Johnson, Joseph (publisher), 37,
  45
Johnson, Samuel, *Dictionary of the
  English Language*, 62
Jonas, Alexander, 49
Jordan, Wilhelm, *Geschichte
  der Insel Hayti und ihres
  Negerstaats*, 128

Kantorowicz, Ernst, 178
Kirkley, Laura, 40
Kleist, Heinrich von, *Die
  Verlobung in St. Domingo*, 117
Knott, Sarah, 3
Koselleck, Reinhart, 8, 56–9, 62,
  64, 69–72
Kossuth, Lajos, 173, 175
Kotzebue, August von, *Die
  Negersklaven*, 104–6

Lacretelle, Jean-Charles-
  Dominique, 120
Lamartine, Alphonse de, 173–4
Latour, Bruno, 3, 93
Lavallé, Joseph, *Le nègre comme il
  y a peu de blancs*, 94
Laveaux, Etienne, 141, 145–6
Lempa, Heikki, 40–1
Lewis, Titus, 69–70
Lexow, Rudolph, 50

Lips, Alexander, 125
literacy, 94, 126, 171
Louis XVI of France, 77, 85–7, 169, 178

manifestos, 14, 28, 53
Marrs, Cody, 173, 178
Martinique, 88, 137, 143–4
Meagher, Thomas Francis, 176
Meinicke, Karl Eduard, 126
melodrama, 95–7, 104–9, 111
memory, social, 168–9, 178
Millet, Thomas, 79
Milscent, Claude, 82
Minerva (journal), 44, 45, 47, 118–22, 127
Miszellen für die neueste Weltkunde, 115, 117, 119, 121
Mitchel, John, 175–6
More, Hannah, *Village Politics*, 67
Motos, Morfakidis, 151
Müller, Gerhard Friedrich, 16–17, 22–4, 27, 29, 183n

Nat Turner rebellion of 1831, 174
Netherlands, The, 40
New Yorker Criminal-Zeitung und Belletristishes Journal (newspaper), 50
North Star, The (newspaper), 175
Novikov, N. I., 25

O'Brien, William Smith, 176
O'Connell, Daniel, 175
Ogé, Vincent, 82
Old Believers, 23
Ottoman Empire, 14, 21, 153, 154
 Turkish men in Philhellenic literature, 151, 155–62, 193n
Owen, John, 66

pacifism/peaceful revolution, 44–9, 46, 53, 60, 138, 174, 175; *see also* violence, revolutionary

Palmer, Robert Roswell, 4
Panin, Nikita, 26, 29
Panin, Peter, 26
Papillon, Jean-François, 86
Paris Commune of 1871, 70
Parnasskie Vedomosti (journal), 27
Paulson, Ronald, 1, 5
peaceful revolution *see* pacifism/peaceful revolution
Persian Wars of 5th century BC, 155
Peter I of Russia (Peter the Great), 21, 184n
Peter III of Russia, 13, 21–2, 23
Pettitt, Claire, 3
Philhellenic literature, 150–1, 155, 160, 162–4, 192n, 193n
Philippi, Friedrich, *Geschichte des Freistaats von Santo Domingo (Hayti)*, 127
photography, 171
Pigault-Lebrun, *Le blanc et le noir*, 94–5, 98–106, 111–12, 188n, 189n, 190n
Poland, 14, 19–20
Politisches Journal (newspaper), 118, 119, 121, 122, 124
Pölitz, Karl Heinrich Ludwig, 127–8
Polverel, Etienne, 77–8, 80–1, 82, 86, 87, 98–9
polysystem theory, 6
Pouqueville, F. C. H. L., *Histoire de la régéneration de la Grèce*, 152
Price, Richard, *Discourse on the Love of our Country*, 63–4, 65
property, theory of, 6, 25, 26
Protestantism, 59–61, 65, 72
Prussia, 125, 129

Pugachev Rebellion of 1733–75, 7, 13–31
  damnatio memoriae policy on, 14–17, 21, 22, 24, 25, 29, 182n
  Le Faux Pierre III (The False Peter III, biography, Anon.), 15–16, 17–22, 23, 24, 27, 28, 29, 30, 183n
  Reliable News of the Insurgent Emeljian Pugachev and the Rebellion he Instigated (Anon.), 16–17, 22–9, 183n
Pushkin, Alexander
  The Captain's Daughter, 15, 29–31
  History of the Pugachev Rebellion, 15, 16, 29–30

Radishchev, Alexander, *Journey from Petersburg to Moscow*, 25–6
Rainsford, Marcus, *Historical Account of the Black Empire of Hayti*, 120, 123
Rauschenbusch-Clough, Emma, 41
Raymond, Julien, 82
Raynal, Guillaume, *Histoire des deux Indes*, 90, 94, 98, 99, 104
  Révolution de l'Amérique, 25–6, 184n
Razin rebellion of 1670–71, 14
Reichardt, Johann Friedrich, 115
Reichardt, Rolf, 96
republicanism, 111, 173
reverberation, concept of, 2–4
revolution, concept of, 1–4, 57–8, 127–8
Revolutions of 1848, 49, 51, 70, 168, 173–5, 178
Rhys, Morgan John, 65, 67
Richards, William, *Geiriadur Saesneg a Chymraeg* (English and Welsh dictionary), 69, 70
rights, 20, 25, 102
  of slave, 9, 78–9, 83
  of women, 44, 49
Río y Coronel, Marcos Manuel (J. M. de San Millán y Coronel), *Compendio histórico del origen y progresos de la insurrección de los griegos contra los turcos*, 152, 164
Rosny, Antoine Joseph Nicolas de, and Louis-François-Guillaume Béraud de la Rochelle, *Adonis ou le bon nègre*, 94–5, 106–12, 189n
ritual, 168–9, 178, 179
Rode, Guillermo, 193n
Roessel, David, 151, 155, 160, 162
Rotteck, Karl von, 122, 127
Russo-Turkish war of 1768–74, 14, 182n

Saint Petersburg Gazette (newspaper), 25
Saint-Domingue *see* Haiti
Salzmann, Christian Gotthilf, 37, 38–41
  Moralisches Elementarbuch, 8, 37, 38, 41, 44
Santner, Eric, 178
Schaubs, Christine, 37–8
Schirach, Gottlob Benedikt von, 119
Scott, Sarah, *Millenium Hall*, 48
serfdom, 13, 14, 25
Skocpol, Theda, 5
slave revolution, 93–5, 99–100, 106–7, 111, 116
slave songs, 167–72, 176–8
slavery, 9, 25, 78–87, 90, 104, 121, 122–9; *see also* abolition of slavery
Smith, James McCune, 172

Smith, William, *Sermon on the Present Situation of American Affairs*, 62
social media, 178
Sonthonax, Léger-Félicité, 77–8, 80–1, 82, 86, 87, 98–9, 108
sovereignty, popular, 20–1, 24, 25
Spanish liberalism, 150, 161, 162, 163
Spanish response to the Greek War of Independence of 1821–29, 150–64, 192n
Spanish war of independence of 1808–14, 163
spirituality, 157–9
Stuart, James, 59

Tanguy-Laboissière, Claude-Corentin, 79
Taylor, Barbara, 53
Thomas, John, 175
Thornton, John, 86
Toussaint Louverture, 83, 86–9, 107, 108, 120, 121, 123, 125–6
translation, 4, 6, 177–8
  of French revolutionary concepts to Haiti, 77–91, 178
  on the Haitian Revolution into German contexts, 116–18, 120, 121, 125, 127
  Mary Wollstonecraft's writings into German, 36–53
  representations of Pugachev Rebellion of 1733–75, 15–16, 18–20, 25, 29, 30
  of "revolution" into Welsh, 56–72
Trevogin, Ivan, 27–9, 185n
Trouillot, Michel-Rolph, 6

Ukraine, 27
United Kingdom *see* Great Britain

United States of America
  reception of Mary Wollstonecraft's writings in, 8, 37, 49–52
  tricolor cockades in, 10, 134–45
  see also American Civil War; American Revolution
utopianism, 27, 38, 43, 48, 50, 106

violence, revolutionary, 36, 38, 44, 45, 57–8, 85, 89–90, 94, 97–103, 107, 110–11, 163–4, 174–5; *see also* pacifism/peaceful revolution
virtue, 102–4, 110, 112
Voltaire, *Candide*, 102–3

Wales and "revolution" in Welsh, 8, 56–72
Watson, Richard, Bishop of Llandaff, *A Charge Delivered to the Clergy of Llandaff, June 1791*, 64–5
Weissenborn, Friedrich Christian, 8, 36, 37–44, 47
Welsh Loyalists, 59, 66–8, 72
Wheeler, Ann, 50–1
White, Hayden, 116
William III of Great Britain and Ireland (William of Orange), 59
Wollstonecraft, Mary, 7–8, 36–53, 186n
  An Historical and Moral View of the French Revolution, 44–8
  Original Stories from Real Life, 38
  trans. of Salzmann's *Moralisches Elementarbuch*, 37, 38, 41, 44
  A Vindication of the Rights of Woman, 8, 36, 38–44, 50

women
  education for, 40–1, 43, 51, 52
  female warrior figure, 152
  feminist philosophy, 36–8, 40–3, 48–53
  rights for, 37, 41, 44, 49, 51

writing/written word, 169–70, 177

Yoeli-Rimmer, Nettah, 161

Zschokke, Heinrich, 117, 119

EU representative:
Easy Access System Europe
Mustamäe tee 50, 10621 Tallinn, Estonia
Gpsr.requests@easproject.com

www.ingramcontent.com/pod-product-compliance
Lightning Source LLC
Chambersburg PA
CBHW070355240426
43671CB00013BA/2511